I0762770

Also by Stephan Talty

NONFICTION

Koresh

The Good Assassin

Saving Bravo

The Black Hand

Agent Garbo

Escape from the Land of Snows

The Illustrious Dead

Empire of Blue Water

Mulatto America

FICTION

Hangman

Black Irish

THE AMERICAN SCHOOL OF SPIES

THE ARCHAEOLOGISTS WHO FOUGHT THE NAZIS AND SAVED THE TREASURES OF ANCIENT GREECE

STEPHAN TALTY

DUTTON
An imprint of Penguin Random House LLC
1745 Broadway, New York, NY 10019
penguinrandomhouse.com

Book design by Laura K. Corless

Title page art © National Archaeological Museum Archives

LIBRARY OF CONGRESS CATALOGING-IN-PUBLICATION DATA

Names: Talty, Stephan author
Title: The American school of spies : the archaeologists who fought the
Nazis and saved the treasures of ancient Greece / Stephen Talty.
Description: New York, NY : Dutton, [2026] | Includes biographical
information. | Includes bibliographical references and index.
Identifiers: LCCN 2025040599 | ISBN 9798217044719 hardcover |
ISBN 9798217044726 ebook
Subjects: LCSH: World War, 1939-1945—Military intelligence—
United States | United States. Office of Strategic Services. Operational
Group II | Intelligence officers—United States—History—20th
century | World War, 1939-1945—Greece—Antiquities | Cultural
property—Protection—Greece—History—20th century |
Archaeologists—United States
Classification: LCC D810.S7 T3567 2026 |
DDC 940.548673—dc23/eng/20260228
LC record available at https://lccn.loc.gov/2025040599

Printed in the United States of America
2nd Printing

The authorized representative in the EU for product safety and
compliance is Penguin Random House Ireland, Morrison Chambers,
32 Nassau Street, Dublin D02 YH68, Ireland,
https://eu-contact.penguin.ie.

For Brendan Talty

CONTENTS

PART III

PROLOGUE

The Sacred Rock

Helias Doundoulakis walked up the hill toward the Sacred Rock of the Acropolis. It was the summer of 1971. Days before, he and his family had left their house in Baldwin, New York, and boarded a plane for Athens. For years, he'd raved and lectured about the Parthenon and the glory of ancient Greece until his kids were tired of hearing about them. Now they were here back in the *patris*, and Helias, who'd marched the jet-lagged Doundoulakises out of the hotel just after dawn, trudged upward, the soil of his homeland crunching under the sandals he had bought specially for the trip.

Doundoulakis was a kind of super Greek American. The son of immigrants who'd settled in Canton, Ohio, he'd spied for the OSS, the predecessor to the CIA, on something called the "Greek Desk." After VE Day, he'd returned to America and gone on to a remarkable career as an engineer. He'd had a hand in the design of the Pan Am Building, the suspensions system for the world's largest telescope, and the oxygen tanks that helped rescue the three astronauts during the near-fatal Apollo 13 mission, in turn saving the United States from a mortifying Cold War fiasco. At that very moment, a pair of stainless steel plaques sat on the moon with the words "Helias Doundoulakis" stamped on them, an acknowledgment of his contributions to the Space Age.

As he headed upward, the engineer began to feel the heat. The ancient Greeks called the sun "he-who-smites-from-afar," and Helias, who'd been away for years, had forgotten how precise the term was. The sweat was beginning to dampen his shirt under the arms and along his neck as his feet chopped into the sandy soil on the surprisingly steep approach.

His children trailed after him. To them, this was almost excruciatingly boring: the Acropolis was the definition of ancient history. Helias was several things: a beloved father, a "complicated man," and something of a caricature when it came to the wonders of his ancestral homeland. When his sons were growing up, any subject remotely connected to this place would have caused Helias to cry, "It's Greek!"—whether it was an alarm clock (Ctesibius!), central heating (the Minoans, third century BC!), or a vending machine (Heron, or Hero of Alexandria, for dispensing holy water!). The phrase became a family joke. "It's Greek!" his kids would bellow to one another while holding a leather football or a Beatles album, then scream with laughter. But not Helias. He loved Greece without irony.

The temple was coming into view, muted gray against blue sky. The Doundoulakises crested the hill along with the other pilgrims and walked into the Parthenon. The scale of the thing impressed the kids despite their silent mockery; they braced themselves for a lecture on how the Greeks had built it. Sure enough, Helias, his voice thrumming with pride, had already launched into a speech, this time about the genius of the original Greek engineers. The soaring Doric columns, you see, despite how they appeared, were actually thicker in the middle, thus creating an optical illusion that from below made them seem straight. This led to a digression about how the Turks, during the Greek War of Independence, had begun destroying blocks of the Parthenon's marble columns to get at the metal clamps that held them together. They then melted the metal into bullets. In order to save the temple, the Greeks sent their enemy a supply of lead to use for bullets that could kill them. "The bas-reliefs that depict the Battle of Marathon, he showed us each one of them, what they represented," remembered his son James. "He knew the different soldiers and generals. It wasn't just a pile of rubble. Everything meant something."

Helias wasn't the only Greek Desk agent to return over the years. At around the same time, a young Ridley Sperling was brought to the Acropolis by her grandfather Jerome Sperling, an American classical archaeologist turned secret agent. Jerome guided his granddaughter through the space, explaining how the builders had carved the temple so that rainwater was funneled away from the stone. "He really wanted us to love it as much as he loved it," she remembered. And years before, a small figure had strolled among the ruins, most likely with her elderly mother, perhaps touching the bullet holes that remained from the German occupation. The daughter's name was Dorothy Cox and she'd escaped her hometown of Terre Haute, Indiana, to study ancient coins before becoming the Desk's tetchy, brilliant intelligence expert. (The OSS, which paid Dorothy less than male spies, later called her "the best man we have in Turkey.")

Helias and Jerome and Dorothy, along with the millions of tourists who came to the Acropolis after the war, read the placards dotting the temple that had been placed there by some of the other players in the story, the Greek archaeologists and curators who had lived under the Nazi occupation and fought and schemed and occasionally died to save the relics. Then there were the subagents and saboteurs, many of whom never met face-to-face and knew one another by code names such as Snapdragon and X-54 (Helias's cipher). They included the Boston Red Sox catcher turned spy, Moe Berg; an American film tycoon; the son of a prime minister; teenaged Greek American commandos; and a Nazi archaeologist who, in the last days of the occupation, weighed the wishes of the Führer against his own inconvenient love for the antiquities. Their visits were the closest thing to a reunion the Greek Desk and its friends ever had.

For the Doundoulakis kids, the Acropolis seemed like it had been sitting atop this hill since time began, waiting for young children to be dragged there and told about its virtues. It was there and it had always been there and it would always be there representing what it had always represented: Western civilization, democracy, or something.

But the spies, the numismatists, the curators, and the Greek American commandos who had fought near this hill knew another side of the Acropolis—of disaster narrowly averted. How close it had all been to disappearing! Not just symbolically, with the birthplace of democracy occupied by fascists and all that, but physically. Many of the statues and the relics and the frescoes that carried the ancient culture had come close to vanishing—twice. Once into Germany and a second time into nothingness.

In 1942, a man named Rodney Young had recruited these men and women to the Greek Desk. He'd come back, too, after the war; he had even dug in the nearby Agora, the ancient marketplace. It was this complex, larger-than-life man—an heir who fled from his homeland and his fortune—who'd assembled the classicists and helped turn them into spies and spymasters in order to save Greece and its ancient relics. The American part of the conspiracy began with him.

PART I

CHAPTER 1

The Sanctuary of Zeus

Just after dawn on October 28, 1940, Rodney Young set out along the streets of a slumbering Athens, followed by nine Greek workmen. It was still dark; the first rays of the sun wouldn't rise over the Aegean to the east for another hour or so. The ground began rising in front of Rodney as he reached the gentle slope of Mount Hymettus, his heavy black boots kicking up small sprays of dust. Bells hung around the necks of goats chimed faintly as the men ascended in silence.

Young, thirty-three and deeply tanned from hours spent under the Greek sun, had a powerful chest and strong hands. He was dressed in a brown work shirt with epaulets and sleeves rolled up in preparation for the day's heat, and he had darker jodhpurs tucked into sturdy leather work boots that came up nearly to the knee to protect him from rocks and thorns but also from the venemous nose-horned vipers native to Hymettus. Rodney had a long, broad, ruggedly handsome face, a strong nose flaring at the tip, and brown hair cut short at the sides, with a tuft over the hint of an incipient widow's peak. In this land of dark-haired men, he looked American or possibly British.

The archaeologist stomped over juniper bushes and myrtle, heading upward. His men followed behind, already damp with perspiration as they hustled to keep up with their leader, who was famous for "tramping the countryside at a pace that few could equal." Rodney was excited about the dig. Days before, he'd discovered pottery fragments from a thousand years before Christ's birth that were intricately worked and bore an inscription that he believed to be the ancient name of Zeus, god of sky and thunder. That single word, along with the other relics, would prove the ancient Greeks had had a high degree of literacy earlier than anyone thought. He wanted to get the artifacts down from the mountain.

Rodney and the other American archaeologists in Athens, many of whom came from rich families, formed a boisterous group. It seemed they'd all grown up in the same milieu, whether in Princeton or Manhattan or Cincinnati. They'd read the same classics, gone to the same prep schools, vacationed on the same lovely beaches, and gotten drunk at the same kinds of parties. The socializing continued in the Greek capital. Rodney and the others "organized tennis matches, barbecues at Cape Sounion, outings to Mt. Parnes and the beaches of Attica, junkets to Delphi and the islands, and dinners under the stars on their roof terrace overlooking Mt. Hymettus, Lycabettus hill, and the sea." Romance bloomed in the trenches; several of Rodney's colleagues met their wives and husbands in the middle of a dig.

Born in 1907, Rodney was an East Coast blue blood. His father was a prominent New Jersey attorney and head of the state's Red Cross chapter; his heiress mother was one of the Ballantines, Scottish rivals to the great German American beer dynasties of Pabst and Anheuser. Rodney's maternal great-grandfather, Peter, had come to

America in 1820 and saved enough to build in bustling Newark an enormous brewery and malthouse that together became "the most prominent objects in view" when people approached the city by rail or ship. Ballantine was an American institution. "I would rather have a bottle of Ballantine Ale," Ernest Hemingway wrote in an ad for the beer, "than any other drink after fighting a really big fish."

As a young boy, Rodney spent many hours shuttling between his family's country estate in Bernardsville, New Jersey, and the Newark mansion in the city proper. The Newark manse featured twenty-seven rooms, an elaborate mantelpiece inscribed with a "B" for Ballantine, and intricately carved wood panels that mimicked sixteenth-century Spanish leather hangings. Louis Comfort Tiffany's team had been called in to do something special for the library; they installed a stained glass window of a blond maiden basking in the rays of an opalescent sun.

Like the families of many self-made tycoons of the era, the Ballantines looked to ancient Greece to reframe their rough-and-tumble rise in America. The fireplaces, done in pale marble with a pink undertone, resembled Athenian tombs; Attic vases and frescoes adorned the interior. Even at the Young family's home in Bernardsville, Rodney's mother chose to follow the same style. "The gardens and neoclassical design of the house," read one account, "reflected Mrs. Young's passion for Latin and Greek culture."

The Greek Revival mansion in Newark, the vases and statuettes, the lessons on ancient Greece and Rome that the Young boys pored over in their private school had their roots in the reaction of elites to what they saw as the uglification of America, body and soul, after the Civil War. American classicists had a horror of the smokestacks, the belching furnaces, and the middle-class frippery in furniture and clothing that the Industrial Age had brought with it. Ancient Greece became a touchstone of a more beautiful, virtuous life. Rodney got his fair share of the idea. He learned Greek and Latin at the exclusive St. Paul's School in New Hampshire and read Homer and Thucydides in the original. Ironically, the hulking, ethanol-spewing breweries that catapulted the Ballantine–Youngs into the upper reaches of society were exhibits number one and number two of the new American vulgarity. But three generations of money had cleansed the family of their rough-hewn Scottish roots.

The men in Rodney's family—his grandfather, his father, and his older brother—had all attended Princeton, and when his time came, the young heir dutifully made his way south to the Gothic campus and enrolled; he rowed freshmen crew and earned a reputation as one of the class's "most companionable fellows." On weekends, he and the other swells took the train across the Hudson River to the Metropolitan Club on the Upper East Side, where he drank Mumm Cordon Rouge champagne and chatted up the daughters of Manhattan financiers. His New York reputation was different—more cosmopolitan and dashing—from his Princeton one; one author called him the "Cary Grantish darling of New York debutante balls."

Despite the parties, Rodney worked hard at his studies, graduating from Princeton in 1929 and moving on to Columbia for his PhD in classics and archaeology. Afterward, he announced his intention to join the American School of Classical Studies at Athens, a mecca for classicists, to dig in the Agora, the ancient marketplace that had only recently given scholars a view of Greek life in the sixth century AD. It meant that, while his classmates went off to the floor of the stock exchange or to junior associate slots on Madison Avenue, Rodney was choosing for his lifework hard manual labor. It was his first rebellion against a privileged boyhood. Rodney guarded his secrets well, rarely talking about his dreams or ambitions, but he clearly wanted something else out of life besides a standing reservation at the 21 Club and a place in the *Social Register*.

In 1933, the budding classicist left New Jersey behind and sailed for the Continent. After arriving at the port of Piraeus, he made his way to the American School, which lay in the central district of Athens at the foot of Lycabettus ("the hill that is walked by wolves"). The mountain was said to have been created when the goddess Athena dropped a heavy pile of limestone she was carrying for the building of the Acropolis. The suburbs of Newark had nothing to compare to this city and its buried relics. Here Young found a home.

CHAPTER 2

The Italian Planes

As the sun reached its zenith that October day, Rodney brushed away some of the clotted dirt the workmen had thrown up from the dig. He could just make out the outlines of a small bone. He picked it up, turned it in the light. There was a bit of flaking black on it; it had obviously been scorched by a flame. More than two thousand years ago, a male Athenian had made the same hour-and-a-half climb as he had that morning, most likely on a clear fine day like today, and sacrificed an animal to Zeus. Archaeologists had been digging up these votive offerings for years in the sacred temples called *temenos*, which in 500 BC would have featured "a monumental cult image of the deity, an outdoor altar, statues and votive offerings to the gods, and often features of landscape such as sacred trees or springs." The Athenians believed that when they burned offerings on the stone altars, the gods would descend and "eat" the fragrant smoke, nourishing them. This bone held in Rodney's hand was what was left of one such moment.

Half an hour went by. Rodney heard a faint buzz that died and then returned, slightly louder. He glanced up, saw nothing, then turned toward the northwest. There, picked out against the hot blue sky, were thin silver shapes. Planes. One tipped a wing hung with bombs as it dove toward the city and a bright red circle with a green dot inside popped into Rodney's vision. Italian planes.

The fighters went diving from the sea toward Mount Parnes, where King George II had his summer palace. As they dipped over the mountain and released their bombs, Rodney felt a slight wave of pressure in his chest. The slope's oak groves, dried out by a hot summer, caught fire, and soon after, Mount Parnes, the place where lightning strikes had alerted the ancient Athenians of the need to consult the oracle at Delphi, was burning.

The *crump* of bombs momentarily blotted out the wail of sirens warning civilians of the raid. Antiaircraft guns coughed. The planes turned west and vanished.

Mount Hymettus was in a military zone, and the dig team was exposed; the workmen must have been growing concerned. But Rodney Young wasn't going to be hurried. "He was absolutely gregarious and incredibly dominant," said one colleague, "an extraordinary human being." He was also bullheaded and obsessed with the relics. He told the men to keep working. For Rodney, retrieving "the Ancients"—what the Greeks called the relics, as if those stone and ceramic things lived and breathed—was worth risking one's life for. He must have thought, *When will I be able to return to this sanctuary and its hidden signs and symbols? When will anyone?*

At two in the afternoon, the planes reappeared. Rodney called to the men in the trench. They came scrambling out, grabbed their tools and the relics they'd found, and hurried down the mountain. Rodney wanted to get to the famed American School of Classical Studies at Athens, his home base, as quickly as possible.

They made it to a stand of cypresses and aromatic pines watered by a spring, the remnant of a lost river that once flowed through the capital centuries before. The then they headed down into the eastern suburbs, where passersby told them that the Greek prime minister Ioannis Metaxas had just declared martial law. Farther ahead, Rodney could see crowds surging through the narrow lanes and he heard a babble of shouting and the sound of marching. When the team entered the city proper, they were pulled into a fast-moving river of bodies. The men dodged and pushed their way toward Lycabettus hill, at the foot of which the American School stood. The Acropolis, warmed by the afternoon sun, was visible to their left.

The attack from the air had electrified the city. "An irrational euphoria took hold of the Greeks," wrote one author. Church bells competed to deafen the crowds, echoed by the bang of cannon from the summit of Lycabettus. Giddy schoolgirls watched the skies for the next wave of Italian planes; men who had been bakers and accountants and garbagemen two hours ago were now marching in step toward their mustering sites, the sound of their boots carried over the tops of houses; girls and young women thronged Red Cross offices, where they put down their names to volunteer as nurses; groups of wild-eyed men, some with fists raised in the air, streamed by, chanting, "We will throw them into the sea!"

The American walked on, pushing his way through. A voice boomed above his head. "*Attention, kyries ke kyrii, Attention*. We have been informed that we are now at war with Italy!" The crowds roared, ignoring the sirens, which were a signal to run to the local air raid shelters. Men held up their hands toward the sky, palms open, in the traditional obscene gesture known as the *moutza*, or used both hands in the double *moutza*. The people were "going wild, as if the news was a gift from heaven we had all been praying for."

When Rodney reached Vasilissis Sofias Avenue in the heart of Athens, he found it barricaded; the Greek leader, Metaxas, fearing saboteurs and spies, had blocked foreigners from entering the zone. But the cops recognized that Rodney was a Yank and waved him through, calling, *"Zito i Ameriki! Zito i Ameriki!"* ("Long live America!") America held a special place in the Athenian heart—it was the new Greece across the sea. Rodney, not given to public displays of emotion, was moved. He shouted back, *"Zito i Elláda"* ("Long live Greece!")

Still, there was a melancholy undertone. How long, after all, *would* Greece live? The country was small, poor, and outgunned, with little hope of holding off the Italians or the Germans, who waited behind them.

Earlier that morning, at two forty-five a.m., Prime Minister Metaxas had been asleep at his private residence, 10 Stratigou Dagli, in the northern suburb of Kifissia, when the bell rang. A guard opened the tall, deep-maroon doors and found Emanuele Grazzi, the corpulent Italian ambassador, standing rather awkwardly on the stoop.

Nonplussed, the guard walked to the main bedroom and knocked; after a few moments, the prime minister emerged, blinking as he put on his black-rimmed glasses. Grazzi handed him a note from Benito Mussolini: *Allow Italian troops to cross into Greece or face an immediate invasion.* Metaxas's hands shook slightly as he read; to Grazzi, it seemed as if his eyes watered slightly, too.

"Alors, c'est la guerre," Metaxas said, speaking in French so that Grazzi, who was fluent in that language, might understand. "So, it's war." To the ultimatum, he replied, *"Ochi."* No.

That morning, as Rodney was tracking the planes as they dove toward the king's palace, Metaxas was at his desk composing a message to the nation. "Greece is not fighting for victory," he wrote. "She is fighting for glory and for honor. . . . We shall now show whether we are really worthy of our ancestors."

There was no chance of winning the war outright, Metaxas said. But as the descendants of the people who'd invented Western civilization, the seven million Greeks had "to rise as one man" and face the invader. The speech expressed a common belief: centuries of slavery under the Persians, the Romans, and the Turks long after the fall of ancient Greece had diminished the people. They were no longer the men and women described by Thucydides or depicted in the old friezes. "[Greeks] were clear that these were works of 'the Hellenes,'" wrote one archaeologist, "people who were seen as distinctive and different from the contemporary ones, living in another time, the mythical time of the Hellenes. They often possessed supernatural properties; they were seen as giants." The heroic qualities had gone out of the people. The subtext of Metaxas's speech was: *the war gives us a way to retrieve those qualities.*

Five hours after leaving the Sanctuary of Zeus on foot, Rodney finally made it to the iron gates of the American School. He swatted the bolt left, pulled back on the heavy barrier, swung it on groaning hinges, and strode up to the front door. On it, he found a notice: "The American Legation has telephoned that Americans should not go into town until further notice." It was signed by the school's director.

Soon after, the exodus began. British and American classicists booked their berths on ocean liners headed for New York and Southampton, leaving a skeleton crew of Greeks and some holdouts, like the American archaeologist Eugene Vanderpool, Rodney's roommate at Princeton, who would ferry supplies to the front lines and maintain, along with his wife, a nursery for the children of soldiers, all under the eye of the Gestapo. "Archaeology was put aside," wrote the school's assistant director to the managing committee back in the States, "regretfully, but of necessity."

He was only partly right. The Germans, who had for decades been the most powerful of the foreign archaeological teams working in Greece, remained. In fact, classicists in Berlin and Munich soon began packing their rucksacks for trips to Athens to join their countrymen already there: prehistorians, classical archaeologists, the interpreters of inscriptions known as epigraphists. The Luftwaffe began fitting their planes with cameras to do an archaeological survey of Athens and Attica that would produce eleven thousand photographs.

For years, the Nazi regime had taught its followers that ancient Greece had, in fact, been built by their ancestors. Aryans were the creators of the world's first great civilization. The archaeologists packing for Athens were astir with the possibilities for what they, guided by the wishes of the Führer, might find in the Athenian ruins. And what they might bring back to Berlin.

Not all of the German scholars, however, felt the same way. One of them, a brilliant young classicist named Roland Hampe, would prove to be a problem.

CHAPTER 3

The Curators

In the opening scenes of *Olympia*, Leni Riefenstahl's documentary about the 1936 Olympics, the camera pans across a black-and-white cityscape—not Berlin, but Athens. For six minutes, over brooding orchestral music, the viewer is shown a hall of classical Greek statues. The camera eventually settles on one: a crouched, naked male athlete, the *Discobolus* (or "discus thrower"), a Roman copy of the masterpiece carved by Myron in the fifth century BC. In the film, its oiled surface fades to a shot of a real German athlete preparing to toss a real discus. "The chilling message is presented with stark, poetic efficiency," wrote one author: "the glories of Classical Greece are reborn in Nazi Germany."

Hitler and his lieutenants were fixated, in varying degrees, on ancient Greece and its artifacts. The Führer, "besotted" by the *Discobolus*, had actually bought the ancient copy in 1938 and had it brought to Munich, where he put it in a museum. He believed the Aryan race had given birth to ancient Athenian culture, especially at the pinnacle of the fifth century BC when Pericles built the Parthenon. In *Mein Kampf*, Hitler wrote that a racial kinship (*Rassenein-*

heit) connected the ancient Greeks, the Romans, and the Nazis in one straight line.

It wasn't just Hitler; Germans had pined for Greece for generations. The Royal Prussian Cadet Schools, which trained future military leaders, and the *Nationalpolitische Erziehungsanstalten*, which trained the country's political leaders, taught their students that the Spartans had come from the Teutonic hinterlands, and drilled them in the Spartan virtues: discipline, stoicism, courage. German writers recast the Peloponnesian War as a contest between the racially pure Spartans and the racially mixed Athenians. The Spartans won as the Germans would win against the Slavic hordes and the French baguette eaters.

Was this, though, really so different from what was happening in upper-crust British or American schools? Rodney had learned at the exclusive St. Paul's that America had been forged in a Greek mold, and the boys at Harrow and Eton thrilled to Lord Byron's mad exploits in service of his spiritual homeland. Elites in many countries loved Greece. But the Germans' adoration of the dark impulses of Sparta and their insistence that they were the actual genetic ancestors of Plato and Socrates were starkly different from the British reverence for the culture.

There was an obvious problem with the theory. Nobody could find any Greek relics in Germany or any German relics in Greece. This disturbed and mystified the Führer. To remedy the lack of actual evidence, the SS chief Heinrich Himmler created the *Deutsches Ahnenerbe—Studiengesellschaft für Geistesurgeschichte* (German Ancestral Heritage—Society for the Study of Ancient Intellectual History); he staffed it with scholars and archaeologists and ordered them to find the missing link between the two cultures—that is, artifacts. Archaeologists began dig after dig, but instead of stone icons and exquisite statues, crude timber fortifications and rather plain wooden drinking mugs kept turning up. Hitler was unimpressed. He required things as ravishing as the Parthenon and the Artemision Bronze, the masterwork that had been hauled up in a fisherman's net in 1926. Where was the glory of ancient Germany?

As the Wehrmacht swept across Europe, the *Ahnenerbe* followed behind. Its members were expected not only to make new finds, but to bring the Ancients back to their true homeland, Germany. "We, with our spades, fight for our country in the same way as soldiers with their weapon," wrote a German archaeologist. "Thanks to these proofs, we can scream to the world: 'This country should stay German, because no other nations settled it but our German ancestors.'"

At the top of the list of places to begin the quest was the National Archaeological Museum, housed in an austere neoclassical building in the heart of Athens's Exarcheia district. The marble palace, spanning nearly ninety thousand square feet, was divided into dozens of halls devoted to different eras and cultures: Mycenaean, Cycladic, Neolithic. Its storerooms held eleven thousand objects, the cream of the country's collection. Here were the Mask of Agamemnon, the Antikythera mechanism, and towering *kouroi* statues, meticulously arranged to tell the story of Greece's past.

And the Artemision Bronze. The exquisite six-and-a-half-foot statue that dated from 460 BC portrayed Zeus (or Poseidon, if you believed a rival theory), the "father of gods and men," drawing back to throw a thunderbolt (or a trident, in Poseidon's case). The Bronze was almost as famous as Tutankhamun's golden mask; Greece put it on a stamp and the thousand-drachma banknote; people from all over the world came to see it. On its buff-colored stone base in the center of an echoing hall, the piece was oddly transfixing; its equipoise seemed to charge the air around it.

The collection was the center of the archaeological world. But for Greeks, it was another thing entirely. There was a much-beloved story about General Ioannis Makriyannis, who led forces during the 1821 rebellion against the Turks and the subsequent Greek War of Independence. The general allegedly came across soldiers on the Poros Islands who'd stumbled on two magnificent statues. They were debating selling the pieces to collectors for a haul of cash. Makriyannis argued with them. "Even if you are offered ten thousand *talara*," he said. "do not allow for these statues to leave our country. These are what we fought for." The quote might have been a romantic confabulation, but it was true that what Americans felt for original copies of the Constitution is what Greeks felt for their statues. They were, in some sense, Greece itself.

Three years before, as war clouds gathered to the west, the Greek government had sent a letter to the archaeological department of the Ministry of Education and Religious Affairs. Create a national plan to protect the antiquities, it said, in case of air raids "and street fights"—that is, the chaos that would follow an invasion. The government ordered archaeologists to draw up a master list of relics and to rank them from most important to least, then to find a way to keep them safe. The Ancients at the top of the list would be preserved at all costs, while the ones at the bottom would be left exposed to destruction or theft. The curators had refused, insisting "that there was no way to make such a choice and that all antiquities (exhibited or stored) would have to be saved in the event of war." But how, when Hitler wanted them?

Someone floated the idea of putting the relics in "architectural towns," places located miles from the spots the Germans would occupy—or the opposite, sites so central and famous, so undeniably irreplaceable to world culture, that the Nazi regime wouldn't dare endanger them by opening them up to attacks from long-range Allied bombers. The thinking went that the Germans couldn't possibly place guns at the Acropolis, for example. The Greeks could get the international community to declare these sites "sacred and inviolable," then put the Ancients there. Oases amidst the carnage.

But the Wehrmacht's brutal advance across Europe dissolved any hopes about a gentle occupation. And who could have really said where the Germans would put their guns anyway? The plan was abandoned, and nothing happened.

Then came the Italian bombers. Fourteen days after the attack, on November 11, 1940, the Directorate of Archaeology issued an edict to all museums, curators, and employees across mainland Greece and the islands: preserve your relics at all costs. The time for ideas was over; get it done. The government created a secret group to oversee the task: the Committee of Hide and Secure. The outfit consisted of three Supreme Court judges, the secretary of the Archaeological Society at Athens, a famous professor, and several well-regarded curators. Civil engineers and architects were also brought on board, which hinted at which direction the committee was headed: burying the Ancients until the war was over.

The committee ordered its far-flung conspirators to use cover when discussing the plan: planes. When money was raised, it was earmarked "for aviation." The prefect of Attica and Boeotia agreed to support "the Hellenic Air Force" and the Archaeological Society responded with a donation of 691 drachmas, an "offer of the employees of National Aviation." Feuds among Greek archaeologists were put aside; one employee, a prefect of sculptors dismissed months before for "non-attendance at work," a perennial problem in Greece, was called back for his skill in handling delicate stone.

At the National Archaeological Museum, the curators pondered the task before them. The museum's holdings were enormous: pottery, thousands of vases, and statues, some of them life-size or bigger. One gigantic hall re-created the grave room of Agamemnon, king of Mycenae and a central character in Greek mythology: its "gold ornaments, cups, diadems, masks, bronze weapons, gaily painted vases, works of ivory, silver, and semiprecious stones" transported the visitor back to the time of *The Iliad*. To imagine these things crated up and shipped off to chilly Berlin gave the archaeologists pause.

The curators came up with two ideas: "cover the statues with sandbags after protecting [them] with wooden scaffolding," or bury them. The problem with burial was that Athens, like most Greek cities, was built on limestone, which, when heat and pressure were applied, gave the city its vast quantities of dense Pentelic marble. Limestone and marble required special equipment to tunnel through or dynamite to blast through, something the Greeks wanted to avoid. This meant there were limited places in the city where the statues could be secreted. Fortunately, the museum itself was built on earth, not stone; the curators decided to bury everything possible under its floors. This was the opposite of what archaeologists did, which was to bring history out of the dirt, but the committee approved the plan. Reburying the Ancients would accomplish two things: first, it would protect the treasures from bombing raids, and second, it would hide them from the German archaeologists, souvenir-hungry soldiers, and generals who might want to sell a two-thousand-year-old artifact and buy an Alpine villa with the money.

News of the plan percolated out at parties and digs; archaeologists and classicists began volunteering to help. Many Greek scholars, along with archaeology students, offered their expertise, as did a British archaeologist from Cambridge, a French expert on the site of Delphi, and American and even Austrian archaeologists. In fact, the director of the Austrian Archaeological Institute, Otto Walter, joined the burial team. He visited the museum and was sent to the basement to assemble a catalog of what was going under the ground. Rodney Young came, too.

The museum directors chose the north hall for the burial crypt. The civil engineers on loan to the project had studied the museum foundations, tested the firmness of the soil in various spots, and determined that this was the place to dig. Workmen carted the statues and sarcophagi out of the way, stored them in other areas of the museum, then returned with pickaxes and shovels. There were no backhoes or jackhammers available: the excavation would have to be done by hand.

The men cracked open the nineteenth-century mosaic floors, hauled away the debris, and began digging deep pits, piling the dirt up against the walls ten and twelve feet high. As they dug, other craftsmen hammered planks of wood into custom crates, then painted numbers and letter codes on the raw wood to indicate what was inside. Technicians molded splints around the more delicate pieces, then let them dry. Teachers copied out catalogs and records by hand. A chemistry professor from the local university came by to take a look at the *Ephebe of Marathon*, more commonly known as *Marathon Boy*, a bronze sculpture that had been hauled out of the Marathon gulf in 1925. It and the other large bronze statues were wrapped in tar paper to protect them from moisture and placed in wooden boxes. Ironically, during the excavations, a cache of broken pottery was discovered under the museum. In the act of hiding relics, the workers had found more. This was Greece.

As the hammering echoed through the exhibition halls, Rodney and the other volunteers built from scratch a series of wooden "cranes" large and strong enough to lift the heaviest pieces. The cranes were actually scaffolds with pulleys and ropes secured to the top beams. A statue was carried over to a crane, just below the pulley; ropes were let down and tied around the hips and armpits, wherever the shape allowed for purchase. Once the ropes were secure, Andreas Panagiotakis, the sculptor directing the burial, called out, "Fire up!" and the statue tilted into the air. Slowly, the men edged its base out over the pit. The pulley creaked as the statue sank slowly below their feet.

Rodney never spoke about his work there, but the first-year archaeological student Spyros Iakovides recalled the frenetic rush to get the relics under the earth. "We all worked against the clock, in fear of the German invasion," he said. The sculptor ordered Iakovides to the basement, where his job was to wrap the Tanagra figurines in old newspapers in preparation for burial. The figurines were terracotta figures of ordinary Greeks from the third century BC, clad in shawls and hats, often sitting or lounging in natural poses. After having been cast in molds, the elaborately costumed statuettes were often painted in watercolors, some of which remained on the stone. Iakovides studied the figures' lifelike faces as he wrapped them; they were so clearly rendered, he felt as if they might speak to him. Once they were finished and lowered into the ground, he thought the statues resembled "people in a demonstration," caught up in the flux of life.

Young and the others arrived day after day. "Really early in the morning, even before the moon had set," one volunteer wrote, "the people who had undertaken this job would gather at the museum and they would leave for home really late at night." Once the statues were lined up, sand was poured over them. Rodney watched as the dirt inched upward, covering the base, then the feet and thighs, until all that was left was an uneven length of ground. The workers came back, pounded the sand flat, then poured concrete slabs on top.

Volunteers filled sandbags, then packed them against the museum windows. Other valuables, such as the crates and crates of fragile clay vases as well as delicate bronze pieces, were packed into a new extension of the museum near Bouboulinas Street, which had a storage area that was partially underground. Once they were placed there, sand was shoveled in up to the concrete ceiling. The catalogs and books and records that documented where each piece came from and when and what it was found with were boxed up and stored in a vault at the Bank of Greece, followed by a number of crates filled with golden treasures from Mycenae, necklaces and daggers and gorgeous headdresses, along with the Mask of Agamemnon, which had been made from a single sheet of gold. Twenty-two crates were carried up Philopappos Hill and installed behind the iron gate of the Prison of Socrates, where the philosopher was said to have been jailed before his trial in 399 BC. Private citizens accepted deliveries and hid the icons in their attics or at the bottom of decorative vases. Bronzes, sculptures, and clay artworks were secreted in air raid shelters. Boxes of ancient coins, sixty-one of them, along with chisels and arrows, went to the bank vaults. Workers drilled four shafts on the Sacred Rock of the Acropolis, along the northern side of the Parthenon, and lowered statues into the holes.

It was a gargantuan effort. Rodney and the others returned for six months, though we don't know how many days the American spent there. The museum, along with every other gallery across the country, had to submit a "concealment protocol" signed by the directors and stating which pieces they'd buried and where. Finally, in the late spring of 1941, weeks before the Germans marched in, the last statue disappeared under its coat of sand and the last slab was laid and cured. The curators took a final walk through the halls, stopping by the few statues that had been left behind as too minor in importance to save. "The view of the museum in April 1941, stripped from all its content, was an image of abandonment," wrote one archaeologist. "Naked walls, dug-up floors in many halls, empty showcases."

The Ancients of the museum were safe for now.

CHAPTER 4

The Front

All around Athens, digs were canceled; the exhibits at the Agora museum were taken down and packed away. Workers went up on the roofs of the American School buildings and daubed twenty-foot "USAs" there to discourage Allied planes from releasing their bombs overhead. The staff swept out the bomb shelter near the school grounds and kept it open all day and night.

Unwilling to let go of Athens, Rodney put off buying his ticket home. Digging in Greece was unlike digging almost anywhere else in the world for reasons that went beyond the magnificence of the finds. The Greeks had a link to antiquity that was difficult to capture; it was one of the things that drew archaeologists to the country. "The ruins have a romantic or an impersonal, aesthetic appeal to all people," wrote one of Rodney's contemporaries, "but to the Greeks they are a living force." An American classicist had been working on a site near the Tomb of Clytemnestra one day when a priest passed by. "One of the laborers stopped him. 'Father,' he said, 'won't you bless the tomb of Clytemnestra, so it may bring more tourists to our village?'" The priest frowned. "I, to bless the tomb of that murderess?"

he said. "Certainly not." Clytemnestra was a figure from three thousand years before, but for the priest and the locals, it was as if she still breathed.

Many Greeks believed that the icons and monuments housed "benevolent spirits" or that the statues were bewitched persons trapped inside the stone by magicians and, if one listened closely, one could hear the entity within, often referred to as an "Arab," weeping. The workers who transferred the Parthenon marbles to the port of Piraeus on their way to England as part of Lord Elgin's collection gave up their work, claiming that they had heard ghosts in the marbles "crying and protesting." In Greece, you could stroll through the ruins of the court where Daedalus was said to have taken to the skies on a pair of wings he made from wax, feathers, and thread. Or you could sail to Crete and run your hands over the Gortyn Code, the oldest legal inscriptions in Greece, inscribed on a stone wall. You could sit in an ancient amphitheater where Sophocles's actors had rehearsed, and you could watch one of his paeans with the crowd around you bored or rapt.

After deciding to stay, Rodney jumped on his motorcycle and rode north to the coast, where he boarded a boat for the island of Lemnos. The Royal Alpine Club was having its annual hike there in the mountainside town of Thanos, and Rodney joined them. He found himself talking about the war situation with a Greek general over a spitting campfire.

The news was grim. Mussolini had sent a submarine to the harbor at Tinos, where Orthodox Christians were celebrating the Festival of the Dormition, marking the ascension of the Virgin Mary. The sub had sprayed the dock with gunfire, then torpedoed a Greek cruiser, the *Elli*, killing nine sailors. Meanwhile, the Wehrmacht by the fall of 1940 controlled most of Europe.

Rodney returned to a restive Athens. He took his things from his flat and moved into the American School, where he found a place in the penthouse apartment of the young American archaeologist Virginia Grace, an expert in amphoras (ancient Greek jars). Judging by their later correspondence, the two began a romantic relationship. Bucharest fell, and then Rome.

Finally, the archaeologist made up his mind on exactly how to join the war. Byron had fought for the Greeks, Orwell for the Republicans in Spain. Why shouldn't he follow suit? Rodney volunteered for the Greek Army, the first American to do so. But his application was rejected. He was a man without an army to join.

The assistant director of the American School in Athens was setting up a supply line for medicines to go to the front; his wife came up with the idea of also acquiring an ambulance, which Rodney saw as an opportunity. He telegraphed his father along with a Princeton professor, asking them to drum up money for the project by targeting alumni of the school. Young Sr., wanting to get the money to his son as quickly as possible, wired him fifty-five thousand dollars before the first donations came in. Rodney intended not only to raise funds for the vehicle, but to drive the thing, "a brazen decision for this coddled child of the gilded age."

Rodney had inherited much of his great-grandfather's thrusting energy. In photos from this time, he seems to lean toward the viewer, smiling, as if he just might spill out of the frame. There's a physical intensity to his presence, even in old black and whites. "His imposing physical bulk," wrote a fellow archaeologist, "combined with something imposing in his manner to produce an awe in many who encountered him. As was once aptly put in reference to his conduct of archaeological meetings, 'When he presides, he presides.'" He didn't coddle anyone, but he was gregarious, intensely so. "Any gathering was the livelier for his presence. . . . He had a talent for hospitality, for cheerful and witty conversation. His sense of humor was irrepressible, and if his sallies were at times disconcerting, they were always amusing." His gregariousness didn't extend to displays of physical affection, however; like many men of his generation, he seemed to dread them.

The trustees of the American School back in the States, far from the expanding war, disapproved of the ambulance idea; one called Rodney's plan "impetuous." There was no chance for the Greeks to hold off the Axis powers, and their "inevitable" defeat would make life difficult for American archaeologists. When the Germans won, they'd control every dig for years or decades to come. The trustees didn't want to make an enemy of the Third Reich. Instead, they counseled a wait-and-see approach. The Greek government, too, was dragging its heels. The American ambassador wrote Metaxas and King George II, imploring them to authorize the ambulance "as a precious witness to the love of the Greek people which is felt by Americans who habitually live and work among them." Rodney, "an ardent American Philhellene," would bring it to the front and help save Greek lives. Metaxas finally gave in. In his letter, he singled out Young, whose "gracious offer of his services I deeply appreciate."

A sturdy chassis was quickly found and Rodney hired a local motorcar company to retrofit it. By January 1941, the ambulance was ready: white, long, and tall, with a large scarlet cross painted on its roof to warn Axis pilots this was a Red Cross vehicle, decals of the Greek flag entwined with Old Glory along the side, and writing on the chassis denoting the sponsor as the American School in Athens. It had a capacity of eight plus a driver. Rodney stuffed the bay and the empty seats with medical equipment, warm winter clothes donated by expats in Athens, heavy wool socks, and footwear.

An American journalist caught up with him for a quick interview. "New Yorker Drives Greek Ambulance," the United Press reported on January 10, 1941. Why volunteer? "I have learned," Rodney replied, "to love both ancient and modern Greece." Then he filled the tank with gas and headed north as his "eyes blazed like the eyes of the dragon in Siegfried."

As he approached the front at Epirus, close to the Albanian border where the Italians had come across, the warm plain fell away and a grim, frozen warscape emerged through the broad ambulance window. He passed makeshift cemeteries with handmade wooden crosses, acres of mine-laid mud, and field hospitals that emitted the odor of amputated limbs. The Greeks had fought brilliantly here, pushing the Italian troops back in pitched mountain battles. But the battle had settled into a stalemate.

Rodney found shelter in a three-room wooden canteen whose roof leaked when it rained and whose walls were barely insulated against the freezing winds; still, he knew he was fortunate. Medics in the camp treated many cases of frostbite and dysentery as well as bullet wounds. Most mornings, he woke up, squeezed behind the wheel of the ambulance, and began ferrying coffee, jam, chocolate, and cigarettes up the mountains, then loaded the wounded into the bay before picking his way carefully down the twisting, muddy switchbacks that led down from the summits. He wrote out messages to Mussolini on shells loaded into artillery guns, helped fire the guns, joked with the soldiers, flirted with the nurses, and proved himself a "most companionable fellow" indeed. On one memorable rescue mission, he stuffed soldier after soldier into the ambulance until there were thirty-five soldiers in and on the vehicle.

The danger invigorated him. "Young thought he would never die," wrote one historian. He was at his most vital and large-hearted in this wasted scene; the danger, the freedom of movement, and the sense of serving others, something his father had impressed on a young Rodney, quickened his personality. One nurse remembered the strapping, clean-cut American appearing out of the din of the battlefield, cracking jokes, bestowing comic nicknames on people he'd met along the way, and recounting his exploits up in the mountains. "He was wonderful," she said. "It was like having a big brother."

Three months in, on a seasonable March afternoon, Rodney was standing outside the canteen chatting with some frontline soldiers and a female relief worker as they ate their meals. The ambulance was parked nearby. Rodney heard a sound from above. The whine grew louder and tighter as an Italian plane dove overhead and bombs tumbled away from its wings. The men and women fell face down, waiting for the impact. An explosive struck earth twenty feet away and "threw a shower of steel fragments over the ground." The ambulance rocked on its springs as the shrapnel sliced holes through its chassis, and a metallic sound close to Rodney rang for a moment in his ears. He looked down. Metal shards had punctured his canteen; a stream of water was leaking out of it as if in slow motion. They'd also torn through his lower back and thigh.

The adrenaline lifted Rodney to his feet. He gasped out, "How are you?" to the relief worker who'd been standing next to him.

"I'm all right. How are you?"

Rodney paused. "I'm wounded," he said, then slumped to the ground, unconscious.

Fighters gently turned him over, fetched a litter, and lifted him onto it. The litter went into the back of the ambulance, which headed for a hospital. The wounds were serious; the shrapnel had penetrated Rodney's stomach wall and intestines. Athens's newspapers ran with the story. "New American blood is now added to that shed in 1821 for Greek independence," wrote one. *The New York Times* ran four articles on the wounded aristocrat in two weeks.

After he was stabilized, Rodney was taken to the rear lines and then on to Evangelismos Hospital, close to the American School. His family dedicated a processional cross to him in the Episcopal cathedral in Newark. Crown Prince Paul, the king's son, paid a visit and pinned a medal in the name of the king on Rodney's shirt. The secretary of the archaeological society in Athens wrote that he prayed for Rodney's recovery and "we raise up the heroic and noble archaeologist among us as a living monument of American friendship, which his shed blood sanctifies as sacrifice to the great idea of freedom."

The Germans marched into Athens on April 27, 1941. Rodney, still in pain, watched the occupation take hold from his room at Evangelismos. Greeks across the city locked their doors and tuned to the main radio station, where an announcer tracked the progress of the troops neighborhood by neighborhood. "The capital is falling into the hands of the conquerors," he said finally. "This is free Athens calling. . . . Very shortly, the Radio Station of Athens will no longer be Greek. It will be German, and it will broadcast lies."

Through his friends in the city that first day, Rodney likely heard of the antics of Walther Wrede, the head of the German Archaeological Institute. At nine thirty a.m., Wrede was informed that German troops were marching toward the Acropolis. He ran to the upper-floor observatory and rejoiced to see the red of the Reich flag "shining in the sunlight." Wrede phoned his contacts and arranged for a welcoming party to meet the troops. As the soldiers arrived, he and his German friends showered them with flowers and pressed cigarettes into their hands. Many wept with happiness. To Rodney, there would have been something obscene about a fellow classicist "handing" the city to the conquerors as if it rightfully belonged to him. Dressed in his Nazi uniform, Wrede then met Field Marshal Walther von Brauchitsch and escorted him to the Parthenon, where he gave the commander a personal tour of the ruins. Another official sent Hitler a telegram: "We raised the German flag over the Acropolis. Heil mein Führer!"

The radio switched to the Greek national anthem, "Hymn to Liberty." Athenians wept at the music. "Now they understood well that the fatal end had arrived," wrote one. "The black night of slavery had fallen on the place that first gave birth to and first adored freedom."

The Germans gave every indication this was not an occupation but a homecoming. On June 28, the Wehrmacht held a "Marathon Sport-Fest" at the city where in 490 BC the Athenians had driven off the Persians. After speeches, German soldiers dressed in breastplates and *pteryges* (white strips of leather worn at the waist and shoulders) appeared and re-created the battle with swords and shields. They were acting out scenes from their boyhood books.

How were the Germans? an American journalist later asked Rodney. "Corrupt," he said. "They would accost Greek civilians on the street and tell them to hand over their money and jewelry." When Rodney spoke with a German officer about the occupation, the other man told him that "there were twice as many people in Greece as the new order wanted and by the time the war was over . . . the rich would be poor . . . [and] the poor would be dead." By July, he was well enough to ride a bicycle; he decided it was finally time to return home, but to do what, he wasn't sure. To leave, he had to receive permission from the Germans. The application was routed to Berlin and promptly rejected. The only people granted visas were a few war correspondents the regime was kicking out.

Rodney and others tried the Italian authorities. Back in the States, friends and family of stranded Americans pulled strings on their behalf. The Italians were informed that their consular officials in Washington would be unable to leave the country as long as Americans were held hostage in Greece. The officials gave in, and Rodney booked a trip to Italy, then to Lisbon, and finally passage on the ocean liner *Exeter* sailing for New York.

By August, he was installed at the family's Bernardsville mansion. A reporter called at the house for an interview. They talked war strategy. "If Russia can hold out this winter, Germany will be defeated," Rodney said. "German morale will crack."

"How does it feel to be home?" the reporter asked.

"Mighty swell!" Rodney said with his usual vigor.

He might have been lying. He'd reported to his local draft board, which declared him 4-F because of the lingering effects of his wounds. With nothing to do, Rodney walked around the Bernardsville mansion, which was filled with the sounds of clicking billiard balls and piano music and laughter from occasional garden parties that he was most likely required to at least look in on. Rodney was a superfluous man in a time of world war. He fell into a black mood.

There were plenty of reminders of what was happening across the Atlantic. The Greek victories on the Albanian front had captured America's imagination. Headlines and radio broadcasts marveled at the Greeks' raw courage. A poor rural nation was pushing back against the fascist onslaught that seemed ready to submerge the world, and it was winning. Cinemas, spurred by the mogul Samuel Goldwyn, collected money for the front, raising $1 million ($21 million today) in nine months. Grauman's Chinese Theatre hosted a massive telethon, "America Calling," broadcast live on CBS, NBC, and on European stations and featuring the patter of Clark Gable and the song stylings of Shirley Temple. On the East Coast, Radio City Music Hall hosted a "Greek Festival for Freedom." Judy Garland, Irving Berlin, and "practically every major New York–based star of the era" sang and danced in front of a sold-out audience. Bad weather shut down the live radio link to the Albanian front, but no matter. Greece was awake.

Senators rose in Congress to praise America's spiritual homeland and spurred their colleagues to support the effort. The president of the Juilliard School prefigured John F. Kennedy's *"Ich bin ein Berliner"* by remarking that "today every American is in some sense a child of the Acropolis." There was the feeling that Prime Minister Metaxas's challenge to his people to conduct themselves in ways that would make them worthy of their ancestors had been met. Despite the fact that he'd ruled as a dictator himself, Metaxas continued to toss thunderbolts at the Nazis. "Greece will fight to the end," he wrote. "The Greeks will fight the fascists wherever they meet them, in Albania, in Africa, even in hell." Americans, still neutral and yet increasingly disturbed by the Wehrmacht's success, thrilled to the words.

As a homegrown war hero, Rodney was eager to pitch in to the effort. He traveled to distant cities to give talks as his sponsors passed the hat; he even crossed the Peace Bridge into Canada to give a speech at the Classical Club of McMaster University, whose members were naturally sympathetic to the Greek cause. The event raised a thousand dollars, which would buy bandages and medicine for the soldiers. On the one-year anniversary of the Italian offensive, Rodney spoke at the Grand Central Palace in Manhattan, where thousands of young men were inducted into the armed forces. He told the ranks of soldiers that if he could only find a ship headed to Greece, he would be the first on board. It was something, speaking to the men, but they were going to leave for Europe and he would not. Back in his Newark mansion, he read papers filled with news of Nazi victories, which made him "want to play the ostrich and not think about it at all." Amateur fundraiser was hardly the role that Rodney Stuart Young had imagined for himself in the war, but he was stuck with it.

In early 1942, Rodney found himself back at Princeton, chair-bound in a little office as he pored through Greek and Greek American periodicals and wrote summaries of the contents for the Office of the Coordinator of Information in DC. It was a paper pusher's job, largely meaningless, and Rodney quickly grew to despise it.

He was in despair. "The sooner we all die," he told a colleague, "the better."

Two hundred miles south, in his Beaux Arts mansion in the heart of Georgetown, the former Wall Street lawyer General William Donovan was also thinking about Greece. Two years before, President Franklin Delano Roosevelt had asked Donovan to create an intelligence apparatus in Europe and the Balkans. Donovan took two long trips to the region to evaluate needs and possibilities; for the Mediterranean leg, he flew into Athens, met with Prime Minister Metaxas, and traveled north toward Salonika, talking to aid workers and American expats along the way before moving on to other theaters. He came away from the trip impressed by the high morale of the Greeks and sobered by the brutal conditions in which they fought. "He had inspected ordnance, shipping, signal corps, maintenance depots," wrote *Time* magazine on the general's trip. "He had slept in sleeping bags, on desert sands, on the jogging backs of mules. He had talked to kings, prime ministers, generals, admirals." He had also met Rodney Young. The American was driving his Red Cross ambulance, ferrying wounded Greek soldiers to field hospitals, when Donovan's entourage came across him. Young might even have driven Donovan to Albania to get a closer look at the front.

On his return to Washington, Donovan went to work on two related ideas, one traditional and one not. He confirmed the need for a classic spy network led by men and women with deep experience in the regions they'd be covering. And he was convinced that the Allies couldn't rely on conventional forces alone to defeat the Germans; to bolster the Army and the Navy, he proposed a series of small guerrilla units to be drawn from immigrant communities in America, trained in sabotage, and infiltrated into the homelands of their parents: Italians, Yugoslavs, Norwegians—and Greeks. The two groups—the spies and the commandos—would work in tandem to defeat the Germans.

Donovan went looking for men and women who knew Greece to work as secret agents and for a spymaster to run them. However much time he'd spent with Young, the general had apparently come away impressed. Young's name might have appeared in Donovan's search in other ways, too; the two men were both tied into the Washington elite, and Young certainly had the right pedigree for the OSS, which drew heavily from places like Yale and Princeton. The general wrote the archaeologist and asked if he was interested in putting a team together for Greece. Rodney, immediately revitalized, said yes.

CHAPTER 5

The Museum

On a sublime April day in Athens, German officers arrived at the neoclassical building that housed the National Archaeological Museum. They climbed the marble steps on Patission Street and walked into the cool dimness of the entrance hall. As they strolled through the first exhibition space, their footsteps paused. The men gazed around, turning slowly. The place was empty.

Not completely, actually. The stone bases were there, but without the sculptures that had sat on them. The walls had small placards pasted on them, but the frescoes and vases they described had vanished. The walls were bare, the display cases stripped, the statues the Germans knew by photographs and reputation—gone. All that remained were the museum director and his staff, who had lined up in one of the main halls and now stood there in silence.

The commanding officer went up to the director. "Where are the artifacts?" he said.

The director said nothing. The burial operation had taken six months. They'd finished only ten days before; the concrete laid over the trenches was still curing.

The officer repeated the question.

"Antiquities are where everybody knows they are," the director said. "Under the ground."

The German didn't seem to get the joke, which was not quite a joke. He turned and went slowly down the line, asking each curator and assistant in turn where they'd hidden the relics. The staff couldn't know what the penalty for silence would be—the Gestapo wasn't here, and no rules had been set. Could they really be shot for hiding a statue? They didn't know, but no one spoke a word.

The Germans toured the rest of the museum, then left. They were tolerant for the moment. The occupation had just begun; one had to give the Greeks time to accept their new position in the world. The Reich would go on for a thousand years, and many of the officers fully believed Greece would be theirs for all of them.

But they did need answers. Soon after, a group returned to the museum with a list of 103 pieces they wanted exhibited, including the Artemision Bronze. The curators debated what to do.

Another team of Nazi officers went to the Acropolis. They confronted the *evzone* guard, a soldier named Konstantinos Koukidis, and ordered him to bring down the Greek standard and hoist the Nazi banner. According to stories that raced through Athens that night, Koukidis refused, wrapped himself in the national flag, and jumped from the Parthenon's ledge to the rocks below.

The suicide was an urban legend; it didn't happen. It did express the Greek mood, however.

The Nazis did go to the monument and did winch down "the Blue and White." The swastika was hoisted in its place and whipped in the breeze on a tall pole so it could be seen "from all directions, from land, sea, and air." A photographer snapped a picture, and a movie crew rolled film. The photos went all over the world, and the newsreel delighted German cinema audiences when it played before the main feature. One of the oldest symbols of the free world now meant something different entirely. In Pittsburgh, a newspaper columnist wrote, "If that can happen, we say, anything can happen. Nothing that can come can be so grotesque."

Just over a month later, two eighteen-year-old university students, depressed by the news from Crete—the Nazis had just occupied the island—went for a stroll by the Parthenon. As they walked, they spotted the swastika waving in a light breeze high over the city. They decided it had to come down.

The site was crawling with German troops. The two debated how to reach the flagpole without getting shot. They headed over to Panepistimiou Street and climbed the steps into the Vallianeio Megaron, the National Library, where they asked at the reference desk for books on the structure and geography of the Parthenon. Poring over the books, they found a route that might hide them from the Nazi patrol that guarded the *Propylaea* (the monumental gateway). The two would find the Pandroseion cave on the north side of the monument and go in that way.

The students waited until full dark. They found a lantern and a knife, then set off for the flat-topped Acropolis Hill. After leaping over the barbed wire the Germans had installed around the base of the site, they listened for the guards. Judging by the voices that floated over the stone to them, the students could tell that the Germans were half drunk on beer. The two crept around to the northwest face of the hill and scaled its 111-foot rock wall, found the entrance to the cave, and, using some scaffolding left behind by archaeologists, climbed to the little landing where the flagpole stood. One of them gripped the pole and began climbing. He caught the heavy swastika banner, then took the knife and cut it down and tossed it to the waiting arms of his accomplice. The two slipped back into the darkness and disappeared into the city streets.

The next day, the flagpole was bare. In the newspapers that afternoon, the Germans announced the death penalty for the culprits in absentia. The news made international papers.

A new German flag went up, and the Acropolis became a tourist destination again. From May to December, 120,000 German troops toured the site, led by guides; each soldier was handed a pamphlet that glorified the secret roots of the place. "The huge number of German soldiers visiting the Acropolis and the intense demand for the pamphlets," one officer wrote to Berlin, "are two indications of the extent to which the times and serious events of the war have created fertile ground for the re-spreading of humanitarian thought." He meant Nazi thought. The Acropolis now meant something else.

A few weeks later, London suffered one of the worst nights of the Blitz. German bombers appeared over Bloomsbury and dropped incendiaries onto the buildings below. One of them was the British Museum; it was hit by dozens of bombs and caught fire. Around 250,000 books, some of them irreplaceable, burned. The Duveen Gallery—which had been built to house the Elgin Marbles—filled with acrid smoke. Luckily, like the Greeks, the Brits had removed the sculptures and icons; they were now lying in deep cellars of government buildings and unused tunnels of the London subway. The Ancients were safe. But London was free, and Athens was not.

CHAPTER 6

The Greek Desk

Rodney went looking for operatives, casting a wide net, though one knit with the silk strands of money and pedigree: the Greek Red Cross; sporting clubs; relief organizations; and American businesses such as John Monks & Sons, which had built the Marathon Dam outside Athens; the Near East Foundation; the American Express Company; and Standard Oil. Aid workers and doctors were near the top of the list, as they came with ready-made cover and were allowed to travel in occupied countries. Rodney's ex-professor Ben Meritt at Princeton (a noted Greek epigraphist) agreed to oversee a hundred volunteers spread across twenty universities who would subscribe to every Greek American newspaper and scan them for vital news and, less wholesomely, seditious opinions. Even General Donovan pitched in during his constant traveling. Whenever he met a likely candidate in Buffalo or Birmingham, he would launch into an impassioned pitch. "We need people like you with imagination and daring," he'd begin, then tell the recruits about the OSS's far-flung network of guerrillas. Donovan signed up more than a few operatives, sending them as far away as Burma.

Meanwhile, Rodney convinced the Greek Orthodox Church's powerful Archbishop Athenagoras, shepherd to about 150,000 souls, to run a census of "every Greek person in America, screening parishioners, with the name, age, skills, languages, and military experience for males of military age." Donovan was already thinking of inserting a guerrilla force in Greece, and he would need men. By now the country was fully occupied by German, Italian, and Bulgarian units. A "Great Famine" neared its height in Athens and other cities; by the summer, hundreds of thousands would be dead of starvation. Greek guerrillas were popping up here and there, staging ambushes and raids on Nazi units, but the Germans responded with ferocity, killing thousands in mass reprisals. Around 5 percent of the Greek population would die during the occupation, two and three times the rate in countries like France and the Netherlands.

On April 21, from his base in Astoria, Queens, the archbishop sent a letter to every Orthodox parish in the country. The cleric was "full of Pride and Happiness" at being asked to join in a secret project. "I did not think that the Government of the United States . . . would recognize the ability of the Greek youth of America." Now they had.

> *The Glory of America reaches the Heavens and looks to God for guidance, because our country is fighting for Right and Justice of Mankind, the Liberation of the Oppressed people, and for a better tomorrow for us all.*
>
> *It is important that all of us must do our Duty, and put our entire strength in our work. I am confident that all of you will do your bit without hesitating.*
>
> *Athenagoras*

If the war was a chance for native Greeks to wring centuries of slavery and occupation out of their bloodstreams, it was for Greek Americans a chance to show they measured up. The OSS wanted mechanics, radio operators, safecrackers, pigeon trainers (for delivering messages), medics, and commandos. Each had to volunteer for "extra hazardous duty behind enemy lines." Thousands of applications poured in.

As OSS members pored through the forms, Rodney began filling out his core team, all of whom would be archaeologists of one sort or another. One of his first letters went out to the spirited, tough Dorothy Hannah Cox, an excavation architect and numismatist (a specialist in ancient coins) who had worked at the American School. If Rodney's family was "in brewing" in Newark, Dorothy's was "in boxcars" in Terre Haute. Her father had made a fortune buying and then renting out the train cars that went trundling across the heartland, carrying iron ore and radios and leather couches.

From the beginning, she was different, almost scandalously so for 1910s Indiana. "Dorothy was small (for a Cox) and dark, very strong-willed and intelligent," said a family historian. "Dad always said she should never marry, and she didn't." D, as her family often called her, was a defiant child; her father had a rule that she and her siblings should be washed, dressed, and seated for breakfast at a particular time every morning. The other three always made their way to the table promptly, but tiny D would often come traipsing down the stairs of their Terre Haute mansion a few minutes late, either because she was lost in her own thoughts or, more likely, resented the schedule.

After graduating from Bryn Mawr, Dorothy decided she wanted to be an architect and set off for Columbia University, where she was often the only woman in her classes. She graduated in 1917 in the midst of World War I. For Indiana, her choice of career was strange; when Dorothy came home on a break, the local newspaper sent a female reporter over to the Cox mansion to get the details. "Terre Haute Will Soon Boast a Girl Architect," the headline read, and the journalist reported that she had found her subject a little bewildered at all the attention: "Miss Dorothy Cox, just in from the Country Club, her brown hair windblown, her gray eyes gay and laughing, dropped down on the window seat in the library of her home. She unbuttoned a heavy, cadet blue coat and swung ever so slightly a pair of very trim, gray silk-clad ankles. About every movement was a statement—charmingly girlish." When the journalist asked Dorothy what was causing the excitement, Dorothy exclaimed: "Why I don't know—I'm surprised—surprised that it should seem so unusual!"

If Terre Haute's goggling at her chosen profession was a warning, Dorothy blithely ignored it. "'I intend to go to New York next week and shall begin architectural work,'" she told the reporter. "'Mother always believed that we should do something, and I was always fond of drawing and mathematics, so—well, I just took this up!' And again came that delightful, rippling laugh." Dorothy was looking forward to making her own way in Manhattan. "With so many young men leaving [for World War I], there will be a great many openings for girls in that field. I think that the only reason that this profession seems unusual for a woman is that women just do not think of taking up such work."

That wasn't the reason. When Dorothy arrived in New York, she was invited to join the all-women Cosmopolitan Club, whose members included Eleanor Roosevelt and a sprinkling of Rockefellers.

Dorothy dined out, making her career wishes known to the ladies who lunched (to be, she hoped, communicated to their pliant husbands), and she dropped by the offices of the better architectural firms, dressed to the nines. But she couldn't get a job. Her reception wasn't that surprising. In 1917, women couldn't vote (not for another three years), enlist in the armed forces, or work in certain professions. Dorothy, twenty-five, had always done what she wanted the way she wanted; now she'd hit a hard barrier.

She finally found employment in a firm that was turning out blueprints for tract houses, but she wasn't allowed to do anything creative and soon quit. Abandoning the idea of getting a splashy offer in New York, Dorothy signed up for the Red Cross, a more traditional female organization, and shipped off to France, where her talents were put to use. Dorothy was given the job of running an entire hospital for displaced children, her first encounter with war refugees. When the U.S. Army took over the hospital for their wounded, however, they relieved her of her duties and put a man in the job.

With the war over, she returned to New York. There, her career path took a turn when she accepted a scholarship at the American School in Athens. The aim was to become an excavation architect, the person who examined a site's historical clues, made a plan for the excavation, and documented the finds as they turned up. She sailed for Greece and, after completing her studies, found work on a dig. Most women in the excavations were unpaid volunteers, but that would not do for Miss Cox. She insisted on receiving equal pay with the men and got it.

But a typical Greek dig lasted about three months, and when that dig was done, no other jobs were offered. Dorothy returned to New York just as F. Scott Fitzgerald's *This Side of Paradise* appeared in the windows of Scribner's Bookstore, unofficially kicking off the

Roaring Twenties, but her prospects quickly sank to a new low. The Bryn Mawr alumni bulletin of 1921 reported that their classmate had taken a job "as a substitute housekeeper in Pembroke Hall!" The exclamation point was warranted: a devilishly smart, rich, well-connected student returning to her own college to work in such a menial position was disturbing news for her fellow Mawters. After applying for museum jobs in the Midwest and not getting a single response, Dorothy sailed again for Greece, where she opened a school to teach women how to make embroidered goods for the American market.

She got onto a new excavation. "Living was rough," a family member remembered, "poor housing . . . always the problem of dysentery." The start time was five a.m., a typical hour for Greek excavations in order to beat the heat; the work, done bent over in ditches or wielding a shovel or pickaxe to break up ground, was often grueling and monotonous, and each item and change of soil color found during the day had to be recorded after dinner. One afternoon, while Dorothy and three male archaeologists were driving to the site, local bandits ambushed their car. The crew pushed the doors open and ran from the vehicle, dashing for a nearby stand of trees. Dorothy heard shots behind her; one of the male archaeologists made it to the trees, bleeding from a bullet wound.

But Greece wouldn't release her from its spell; the finds were incomparable. Years later, Dorothy would vacation in Mexico, where friends took her to some Aztec ruins. She was unimpressed. In her eyes, very little compared to the Greek antiquities for beauty or meaning. By 1925, she was adrift again. "Future plans unknown," said the *Bryn Mawr Alumnae Bulletin* at the end of the rather disturbing update on their '14 classmate.

A decade and a half later, Dorothy opened an envelope postmarked Washington and addressed to her middle name.

Dear Hannah:

It had occurred to me that with your experience in traveling and working in the Near East, you would be a good person to pump for information. I just called up Lucy Talcott to ask her whether I could still find you in Princeton and she said that you would not only be a good source for pumping but might be available for work of various kinds.

If you could come down here some day early next week to be pumped, this office would pay your expenses and perhaps you could tell us whether you are available and for what.

Sincerely,
Rodney S. Young

By now Dorothy had rebounded from her faltering start and built a career in archaeology. She'd stayed in Athens, worked digs when she could find them, and begun to branch out into coins; she would eventually become "one of the three most eminent authorities in the United States" in the discipline. Rodney had probably run into her at the American School or on an excavation and been impressed. As a confirmed man's man, his relations with women were often contentious—they would occasionally be contentious with Dorothy—so his respect for her work must have been substantial.

Dorothy had the right credentials. She spoke fluent Turkish, Greek, and French; in Lyon, she'd worked with traumatized war refugees, which would be part of her brief with the OSS, and she had proved her mettle there. The OSS offered her an agent's role at secretarial wages at the same time her male peers were being promised Army commissions and officers' salaries. Dorothy was disgusted but hardly surprised. Years before, she'd protested the unequal pay between men and women on a Greek dig; now, older and more care-worn, she accepted the lower wages.

Dorothy was fifty, older than the other recruits, single, graying, and somewhat frail in health. Excavating over many years in high heat had worn her down; many "dirt archaeologists," who worked in the field as opposed to the classroom, suffered from arthritis in the knees and back, among other ailments. Her future hadn't worked out the way Dorothy had painted it to the reporter in Terre Haute. She'd known more hardship and failure than she could have foreseen, but if anywhere had earned her devotion, it was Greece. She took up Young's offer.

Rodney also had his eye on Jerome Sperling, an archaeology professor at Yale who'd worked excavations in Turkey. On May 27, 1942, he wrote Sperling to ask "whether you would consider going out to the Near East in the near future." The letter came out of the blue; Sperling hadn't applied for a position and was probably unaware that Young was even assembling a team. It reached the classicist on vacation with his wife and two sons. Days later, he replied.

> *Dear Rodney,*
>
> *Thanks for your letter and for all of your troubles. I have now had enough time to consider the proposition and I wish to accept. . . .*
>
> *My mind is in a somewhat effervescent state, but I am trying to jot down some ideas for discussion. This business looks like a great thing to me, Rodney, and I hope that everything will come out for the best.*

The sandy-haired Sperling had spent years excavating ancient Troy, overlooking the Turkish coast, which he knew well. He could read Ottoman Turkish in the Arabic script. He was open-minded, abstemious, and physically tough. As a teenager in Sheboygan, Wisconsin, he'd taken a job that involved loading hundred-pound sacks of potatoes onto a truck bed; the labor had built his upper-body strength and propelled him into the bow seat of the University of Wisconsin eight-man crew. And, intriguingly, he was strongly anti-Communist, a contrast to Dorothy Cox and other members of the Greek Desk who leaned left.

The spies couldn't go into Greece yet; it was simply too dangerous for operatives who couldn't pass for natives. They'd be headquartered in Turkey and Egypt instead. Rodney penciled Sperling in for the Istanbul desk, provided he could pass the training course. For the seaside town of Izmir, he found the erudite, modest Jack Caskey, who'd spent time as a boy in Athens and spoken Greek "from the cradle"; his archaeologist father had worked for the American School before moving on to the Museum of Fine Arts in Boston. Rodney filled out the rest of the team with friends and academic stars, including one who was one of the last men at Harvard to write his dissertation in Latin. Virginia "Tiggie" Grace, the beautiful, accomplished amphora expert with whom Rodney shared an apartment in Athens, came aboard later; she would work with Sperling on ciphering and translations, among other things. It was hardly an ecumenical group: overwhelmingly male, all WASPs, most from monied families, not a Greek American in the bunch. But they were friends who shared a vocation; it would matter.

When he wrote to his choices, Rodney insisted they keep the offers to themselves and to close family members. Invitations to join the Greek Desk were "so exceedingly secret and hush-hush," more than one archaeologist deduced that could mean only one thing: espionage.

In all, about two dozen classicists accepted, many out of a sense of patriotism and noblesse oblige. Rodney's father had been the president of a Red Cross chapter and, in the old WASP manner, taught his son that the price of great wealth was service. A majority of the others had been raised in the same way. American archaeology was a small, exclusive club. To refuse to fight for Greece would have been not only to let down one's country and one's vocation but one's class somehow. The recruits rarely if ever discussed the fear and apprehension they must have been experiencing; the tone of their letters during this time was brisk, interrupted only occasionally by low notes of anxiety. "I have not been worried about events in Washington or abroad," Sperling wrote Rodney at one point, "since I know the work has to be done anyway." Studiously avoiding worrying about something often means one is worried about it. And during training, instructors would find that some of the agents, especially Caskey and Sperling, seemed unusually troubled about making small mistakes. Their nerves pinged with tension for obvious reasons.

It was clear to the classicists that the Greek ruins and the artifacts were in danger every moment the Germans occupied the country. Their desecration mattered to the classicists; this was their lifework. And there was the symbolism. The image of the swastika flying over the Acropolis was distressing, even more so than the swastika flying over Rome or Warsaw. Greece was not only beauty; it was democracy in chrysalis.

Still, the assignment wasn't to be accepted lightly. Using archaeology as a cover for espionage was controversial within the community; after World War I, the anthropologist Franz Boas had accused scholar–secret agents of "prostituting science." And the spy game had made archaeologists targets in the new war; the Nazis had grown suspicious. In World War II, the rules would be different. "Membership in . . . an expedition," wrote one expert, "entitled one to a firing squad without the delay of a trial." Young and the others found other covers: Dorothy would go in as a Greek War Relief worker, Sperling as a bureaucrat with the Office of War Information, and Caskey as a lend-lease specialist.

Already, one American archaeologist, Eugene Vanderpool, Rodney's Princeton roommate, had been arrested in Athens and sent to an internment camp on the grounds of a German castle. Vanderpool made the best of his time, giving lectures on classical Greece to his fellow POWs; the day he'd been arrested, he'd happened to be carrying a copy of Thucydides in his back pocket. Luckily, the Gestapo couldn't connect him with the *andartes*, the Greek guerrillas, so he wasn't taken out and shot. Others associated with the Greek Desk wouldn't escape so lightly.

Unlike in many other OSS outfits, the archaeologists came with a preexisting bond to one another and to the places where they would serve. They wanted to defeat Nazism, to save the Greeks they knew and didn't know, to rescue the Ancients, and even perhaps bring the fresh air of democracy back to the country in whatever way they could. "Greece gave us the tools of liberty," Rodney later said to a fellow classicist. "We owed it to her to fight for her soil."

CHAPTER 7

The Farm

In July 1942, the archaeologists began their training. The operatives had a full medical exam and got shots against typhus and other diseases, then were ordered to RTU-11, known as "the Farm," a former horse estate twenty miles outside Washington. They were told to keep their identities secret and not to mention their last names under any circumstances, which must have been amusing for the archaeologists, as many of them had known one another for years. On arrival, they were shown into the stately manor house, whose upper floors had been converted to dorm-style living quarters where the archaeologists would sleep and socialize. At dawn, the trainees trooped downstairs for breakfast and their first class. It was a setting fit for tweedy, upper-crust men and women who might have roughed it on excavations but were used to the better things in life off the job.

The team learned cryptography, codes, subversive warfare, agent recruiting, and a smattering of German. Instructors showed them how to conduct an interrogation, how to draw a map, and how to write a letter that contained military intel in cipher. They were instructed on how to create a cover identity, shoot a gun, knife a sentry, and lie. The pop of gunshots ringing out over the woods and the sparsely populated countryside became the background noise to their days. The classicists who'd be stationed in Washington—mostly women, who formed a third of the OSS workforce—learned how to speak Japanese, break codes, and track German battleships. After a long day of classes, they were brought to parties where undercover OSS agents plied them with alcohol and tried to get them to spill their secrets. None did.

The agents were quizzed on German and American equipment and ordnance: What kind of heavy transport vehicles did the Nazis use? What did they *look* like? Was this bomber a Luftwaffe asset or an Allied one? As the agents trained, psychologists kept watch, analyzing their reactions to stress. Confidence was mentioned again and again in their evaluations. The shrinks were there to weed out the inept and the insufficiently brave. Could the scholars withstand a basic Gestapo interrogation? Would they give in to blackmail?

The training lasted only four weeks, in contrast to that for other OSS outfits; recruits to the Communications Branch, for instance, went through a full ten-week program. There was a lot for these academics to cover, especially considering that none of them had ever coded a message or run an agent. Nor were they going abroad to be plugged into an existing spy infrastructure with protocols and mentors to get them up to speed. The archaeologists would be expected to create one from scratch in foreign cities under the watch of local intelligence services. America had little experience in foreign espionage, and General Donovan and his lieutenants were in many ways making it up as they went along; this certainly showed at the Farm. Presumably, the OSS hoped that the archaeologists' language skills and their familiarity with the region would go some way to making up for the fact that they were being thrown into a new arena with only a month to learn how it worked. Some felt the course was inadequate. "In general, nobody in the Greek Section was trained for his job," wrote one recruit with some bitterness. "The lack of OSS instruction in the techniques of observation and reporting was particularly scandalous."

Among the recruits, Dorothy shone. She was quiet and "nondescript" but quick to learn and devoted to the mission. "Dorothy can be recommended to you without qualification," read her evaluation. "She has done an excellent job in training and has shown traits of personality which should stand her in good stead in the field. . . . She is intelligent, agreeable, easily teachable, and should be very useful. Contrary to the case of some of the other women we have had, I think you will find that men will work very nicely with Dorothy." But the OSS was realistic; there would be some men, Americans and Turks and Brits, who would see a woman in the field as a secretary. She was instructed to use the code name Hiram in internal memos so her peers outside the Greek Desk would think she was a man.

Rodney received raves as well: a "star . . . too good to miss." Keeping his semilegendary temper under wraps, he let his natural sense of command shine through. Another analyst wrote that he was "definitely grade-A . . . a good man with a splendid background for this work." Jack Caskey, on the other hand, was above average but a touch passive. The evaluators didn't doubt his bravery but worried about his habit of waiting for every box to be checked before he took action; in espionage, very few missions would allow time to do that. Sperling, too, got mixed reviews, with negative attention focused on the extreme pains he took with even minor details. "It is difficult to predict how useful Jerome will be in the field," wrote one evaluator. His performance was "hindered by the fact that he was overly tense and serious in an effort to be profound and cautious." Sperling seemed strangely enchanted by "the aura of mystery which appears to surround everything he does." At one point, an instructor pulled

Jerome aside and told him that he always seemed to be keeping a secret. "You know," Sperling replied, "that is exactly what my wife says!" It wasn't the answer the instructor was looking for.

The classicists were given their brief: develop a network of spies; gather intelligence; insert operatives and agents in-country to guide the Greek American commandos who would follow them; arrange for the sabotage of Nazi infrastructure; and prepare for D-Day. This would allow them to establish a far-flung network of bases: Istanbul, Izmir, Athens, and Cyprus.

The team finalized their code names, all bird based. Rodney was Pigeon, Dorothy Thrush, Sperling Sparrow. Before the men and women left—separately or in pairs to avoid detection—on blacked-out ships that would dodge submarines on their way across the Atlantic, their superior at the OSS gave them a final piece of advice. They'd grown up in comfortable homes where the unspoken WASP ideals of fair play and gentlemanly dealing were taken for granted. They were to forget all that and wage war in the old, savage way. "We must . . . use stratagem, and be frugal in civilized scruple," he said. "We are in a nasty business, facing a nastier enemy."

CHAPTER 8

The Sanctuary of Artemis

The looting began innocently enough. Young men in a foreign country, their enemy largely defeated, spent their off-hours blowing off steam. On a moonlit fall night in 1942, near the time the Greek Desk members were setting off for their posts, German soldiers, perhaps a few sheets to the wind, snuck into the Temple of Athena Nike and began climbing the pillars pocked with bullet holes. Gripping the stone between their legs, they took the bayonets from their rifles and carved their names in it.

Argolis was home to the Tomb of Clytemnestra, wife of the mythical ruler Agamemnon, who in Greek mythology led the Greeks in the Trojan War. An archaeologist who'd been touring sites reported to Athens that he'd visited the site. "I was able to see for a moment the name of a German . . . to the right of the entrance, and the name of an Italian written in lead," he reported. The soldiers had even competed to see who could climb highest on the stonework and carve their names with the edges of their bayonets. "I also saw the slabs of the circle of the royal tombs, which were broken by Italian soldiers, and they broke one and thus threw the upper half of a new fragment into one of the tombs."

The graffiti was upsetting, but soldiers and tourists had cut inscriptions into Greek stone for millennia. What was more disturbing were the reports of large-scale destruction and theft that began to trickle into Athens. In Sounion, at the southernmost tip of mainland Greece, German soldiers turned the famous Temple of Poseidon into a fortress and installed eight machine guns. Short of building materials, they demolished two-thousand-year-old sculptures and used the crushed stone to build a gunpowder storehouse and a telephone booth. The Germans then killed two Arab prisoners "for an insignificant reason," dug their graves, and piled temple marbles on top of them.

Monuments were being used as stables, garbage dumps, and garages; museums became drab storerooms and cinemas. The Greek Desk most likely knew little of this, as Rodney's instructions to his agents prioritized all things military. The grinding damage being done to the Ancients did surface occasionally in the West; later in the war, a British MP rose to ask the under-secretary of state for air to issue instructions that bombers exercise "the utmost care" to avoid damaging the Parthenon and other sites.

Soldiers planted dynamite and blew apart ancient fortifications; they collapsed walls and bulldozed sections of ancient gates to make way for German trucks. The city of Asini in the Peloponnese had been occupied since Neolithic times and boasted a well-preserved acropolis built by the ancient Mycenaeans. In the eighth century BC, the local king unwisely sided with the invading Spartans against their powerful rivals, the city-state of Argos (which most likely gave its name to the ship helmed by the mythical Jason and the Argonauts), leading to the city's destruction and the scattering of its people. "Underground shelters, munitions stores underground and in houses," wrote one archaeologist from the site, "nests of heavy tele-guns and machine guns and various other buildings of the Italians and Germans destroyed the buildings and made the area ugly."

At one site where "ancient fragments" had been unearthed, a line of cars queued up as if in an early drive-through. German officers got out of their vehicles, browsed among the most appealing relics, and loaded a few into their trucks, then drove off. A guard watched the line of idling vehicles, craning his neck to see what was being stolen: clay horns mostly, plus fragments from a "healing temple" named after Asclepius, the doctor-demigod of Greek mythology.

The Greeks reported these thefts and others to the Germans, who promised to look into them. When the response came back, it often stated that the items had been taken by locals. This was occasionally true: there was at least one case of Greek bandits dressing in enemy uniforms and storming a museum. Occasionally the locals, too, seeing an opportunity to increase their grazing land during the famine, damaged monuments or fouled excavations. But it's clear the thieves were mostly Italian and German soldiers.

"In the event that German troops are suspected of the crime," the Germans wrote the Ministry of Education, which oversaw the ruins, "precise information must be provided on all characteristics that are relevant for the identification of the troops' members. (Uniform, color, license plates of the cars, etc.)" Many times, the soldiers escaped before that information could be gathered. Ordinary Greeks shouted at them for stealing. "We are called Huns and barbarians," complained one Nazi officer. But the Wehrmacht did nothing.

A museum keeper in Tanagra sent a memo to Athens. Two officers and a private had asked to see the collection. He opened the doors and the men began to act as if they were shopping in a boutique or rather shoplifting, as they had brought along a suitcase into which they placed the head of a statue and a marble hand. "They offered to pay me," the keeper said, but he told them he would contact the ministry. The men kicked him out of the museum, finished their browsing, and left with the suitcase. Another keeper found his museum door broken open with an ax, the collection of bronze headdresses and clay figurines looted, and his library and scientific notes "scattered and destroyed."

The ministry sent out investigators. Along the coast, they found a spray of shells from long-ago funeral pyres littered on the ground, the display to which they had once belonged now vanished. Judging by their location, the investigators deduced that the rest of the figurines had been thrown into the sea. But the criminals had long since fled and there was no one to ask about what had happened. "The inhabitants of the city," an investigator wrote, "are not in a position to give any information about the looting because they always live in confinement." He didn't elaborate. Either the residents were afraid of the Germans, were under a curfew, or were too hungry and weak to venture out.

The Germans sited antiaircraft batteries and other military hardware in and near some ancient temples, inviting aerial attacks from the Allies. One tower was used as a cannon target. When the ministry protested a machine-gun nest near a sensitive site in Mykonos, the Germans replied that the guns "are not intended for antiaircraft defense, but for protection against guerrilla attacks. Consequently, these serve for the safety of the public, the Museum and those inside it." They would stay.

When Italian troops placed antiaircraft guns inside the Acropolis, the officials at the ministry, rather movingly, dropped their usual businesslike tone and asked the German archaeologists in charge of the Art Protection Service if they would please honor the "spirit of the eternal civilization" that was embedded in the marble of the place. They, the Germans and Greeks and the Italians, were "transitory generations of people" that would soon disappear. Could they not save what was most beautiful and meaningful to all of them and would be to their children's children?

To the Germans' credit, the guns were removed. The Art Protection Service also agreed to put up posters warning their soldiers not to harm or steal the relics. "Whoever destroys the artistic decoration of the marbles of the great places of archaeological sites," read one, "damages the public opinion of the German army and will be punished accordingly." But the punishments never came.

Soon after the occupation began, the Germans were widening a dirt road to a quarry on Evia, the second-largest island in Greece. The bulldozers growled and mounds of dirt grew on each side of the road. The blades made a grinding sound and the foreman called a halt. The workers had struck stone, or stones, aligned in straight lines; they were flat and long and bore signs of human shaping. There were also circular stones set on bases of rectangular ones.

If any of the soldiers had known their Greek mythology, they would have been awestruck. This was the Sanctuary of Artemis at Aulis, where Agamemnon had been stranded with his men, unable to sail to the battlefield in Troy because of the lack of wind. The breathless air was a punishment: Agamemnon had stalked and killed a golden-horned deer sacred to Artemis, the virgin goddess of the hunt. Furious, Artemis demanded that the hunter sacrifice his own daughter, Iphigenia ("strong born"), princess of Mycenae. The Greek playwright Euripides wrote:

> *We brought your child to the place where the Greek army had gathered, all together and all at once. When King Agamemnon saw his daughter proceeding to the altar to her death, he heaved a deep sigh and turned his head to one side and wept. He covered his eyes with his robe. But the young girl stood beside her father who had given her life and said: "Fathers, as you bid me, I am here. I give my body, freely on behalf of my country, for all the land of Greece. Lead me to the altar."*

In one version of the myth, just before her throat is to be cut, the princess turns into a deer and flees with Artemis; the winds return and Agamemnon sails for Troy. Plays, novels, operettas, and epic poems told and retold the story over the centuries; it would be retold in films and plays after the war. And the Germans had accidentally stumbled on the physical place where the myth sprang from, a place mentioned in the annals of ancient geographers and Arab travelers.

But the Wehrmacht needed cement to build an airport. There were no archaeologists on-site to study the stones or plumb their meaning. "We do not know what antiquities were found," wrote one archaeologist sent out to observe the site. By the time he'd arrived, the relics had been ground into gravel.

Some German archaeologists did respect the sites. One came across the remains of an ancient village and scrupulously recorded the "horizon topography" of the sites, taking three thousand measurements. "The main result was the discovery of a very well-preserved and very large mansion with an antechamber. . . . And the equipment of the house with stoves, oven, storage vessels, was well preserved, so that many new conclusions emerged not only about the external form of the building, but also about its internal equipment. The finds were rich." He invited the Ministry of Education to visit and turned the dig over to the Greeks.

Such gestures were rare, however. Many other new finds were simply pillaged. "Today Mr. K. Kourouniotis told me that German soldiers digging in Skaramangas found Mycenaean tombs and he saw tin vessels," wrote one source from the port town in western Greece. The source wanted to beg the German commander "to take care so they don't get lost," but he was afraid. Apparently, the Germans had become tired of archaeologists interfering in their plans. The man said nothing.

The curators grieved, and the common people worried. Especially in rural parts of the country, it was believed that by destroying the ancient temples and monuments, the Germans were calling down disaster on Greek heads. In 1759, the Ottoman *voivode* (governor) of Athens, Mustafa Agha Tzistarakis, had ordered a column from the Temple of Olympian Zeus demolished in order to make way for a grand mosque. When, months later, the plague arrived, Athenians marched angrily in the streets, condemning the governor for releasing the pathogen. Now the Germans were releasing death into the countryside once again.

The Greek archaeologists personally knew many of their German counterparts; before the war, they'd worked together on getting permits for digs or excavated side by side. Even the committed Nazis felt a deep love for the heirlooms, in many cases far beyond anything they felt for living Greeks. The Greeks wanted to believe that at least some of the German archaeologists were brothers under the uniform. They might turn away from atrocities and starvation and public executions, but they would not intentionally harm the Ancients.

Within a year of the invasion, the Greeks realized they were wrong. Their protests were "based on the understanding that the occupying state, created by the Germans, was an Authority that the occupying authorities had to respect." But that wasn't true. Each soldier, however low in rank, took what he wanted, confident that the Greek curators had no power worth mentioning. Nor did the Greek classicists feel that their German colleagues were doing enough to stop the destruction. After the war, the Greek minister of education summed up the view: "German archaeologists treated the Greek archaeologists as enemies . . . and this behavior was justified by the law of the stronger."

CHAPTER 9

The Apartment in Izmir

Just before New Year's Day 1943, Dorothy Cox arrived in Cairo, the first of the Greek Desk to make it to the war theater. Her brief was to supply Allied military strategists and policymakers with Greek intel, but she was also expected to help the Desk's spies get up to speed. The Egyptian capital offered lush hunting ground for the spy, but Dorothy wanted to talk to newly arrived Greek refugees in particular. They would have the freshest intel on what was happening inside the country; she wanted to get to them as soon as they stepped off the boats they'd escaped on. The agent soon traveled to Izmir, a seaside port on the Turkish coast that was swarming with recent exiles. She was ostensibly working for Greek War Relief, a cover that gave her access to the soldiers, policemen, civil servants, and ordinary citizens escaping Athens and other cities. An early memo from the Greek Desk informed operatives to be on their guard, as "informers have infested this part of the world since the memory of man." That was good news, actually; it would mean that Dorothy would have plenty of sources to tap.

Still, the headstrong, "absolutely fearless" numismatist was a difficult fit for a Muslim country. She was not deferential by nature, and she tended to dress in mannish clothes: long skirts, blouses buttoned to the neck (sometimes accompanied by a man's tie), military-style jackets with epaulets, a wide-brimmed black hat with a black silk bow band. She was an oddity in conservative Izmir; she hoped the more emancipated Greek men would respond to her.

The archaeologist found an apartment on the quay near the Greek consulate and got to work. "There was at hand in the transient refugees, an inexhaustible and ever-changing supply of sources," she wrote. "The difficulty was in choosing the best, it was impossible to see them all." Her flat became a one-stop armory, spy shop, and nautical resupply store. Scattered around the house were Americans "who ought not to be seen," agents waiting to be infiltrated, "almost ripe" radio operators, caïque captains looking for jobs, propeller shafts waiting to be repaired, piles of army rations, and "a choice of .38s, .45s and a Beretta." Had Turkish secret intelligence raided the place, Dorothy would have been arrested, but the agents and radiomen were presumed to be loyal to the cause, and the Greek captains earned part of their living by shuttling refugees out and spies in, so they had little incentive to turn her in.

To help sort through the men and women, Dorothy searched Izmir for an assistant. What she wanted were "three special qualities: he should be able to mingle easily with his fellow-countrymen of all types, scraping acquaintance with them in cafés and restaurants and at the same time inspiring confidence in them; he should be able to size them up as to reliability and intelligence; and he should himself be avid for information." She found a young Greek "of no particular social standing" and hired him. The "scraper" brought refugees to her apartment, which Dorothy found was more congenial than her office.

She quickly developed her own procedures. A single subject often went quiet—"he needed another to spur him on, to prompt him with a 'And don't you remember?' or to turn to another and say 'You know more about that than I do.'" Groups of three men worked best. If she talked to more than three at once, it was impossible to keep track of the stories. Dorothy warmed up her nurturing side, giving the refugees a quick bite, brewing them tea, and listening. "Under the influence of Turkish coffee and cigarettes, especially American, they told what they knew and drew maps, diagrams, etc." The flapper-esque persona she'd maintained in Terre Haute had been flattened by time. She was tougher now; the disappointments of her life showed in her gray eyes. They drew out confidences.

Despite her critical role in the rapidly expanding operation, OSS bureaucrats treated Dorothy like a glorified secretary. They ignored her messages and failed to provide her with supplies or even send her a single communication for the first five months. But Dorothy was resilient; she began smuggling gold, food, clothes, and medicine to the *andartes*, receiving excellent intel in return. Slowly, she earned the respect of the brass.

But how much of what she was being told was actually true? Dorothy had a personal library of Greek reference books in which she could double-check some of what she was hearing but little else. She couldn't cable Athens to vet an informer's politics or friends. "I find reliability very hard to estimate," she confessed to a colleague. "I think I know when a man is interested and sincere; if his calling or habitat make it seem probable that he knows what he is talking about I trust him." But this was not infallible. "He is sometimes wrong. They like to think they know more than they do, and the really cautious ones are rare." She often relied on feel. Not all of the refugees were victims or who they said they were or particularly honest.

One escapee from the southern town of Gythion came in and

spoke for hours. He wanted to be trained as an operative and sent back in; he knew the country. "He seems to have covered the whole of Greece," Dorothy wrote. "He left Macedonia sometime in '42, stopped in Mitylene, Lemnos and elsewhere." As the session went on, Dorothy, cross-referencing what she was hearing with the many hours of testimonials in her head, realized everything the man said was at least eight months old. And he was pushing a narrative of one group in particular—Armenians—being persecuted. Dorothy wrapped up her report: "I wouldn't employ him under any circumstances. I can't say why." The Greek Desk declined to take him on.

The refugees responded to Dorothy's softer style. "My house is sort of a boarding house for men in our service," she wrote the Desk's accounting office back in DC. "I give them bed and breakfast or, if they are rundown or ill or something, other meals." She began to build her files.

After months of interviews, Dorothy was ready to reveal her rules for spies working inside Greece. She typed up a dense sixteen-page primer, a kind of agent's bible.

In Athens, she wrote, agents should look for apartments or houses in the central city; the suburbs "are combed every day by the Security Battalions [looking] for Communists." Houses should have a minimum of two exits, and agents were to be inside by seven p.m. But they shouldn't remain inside all day; that would arouse suspicion. Hotels were out; security would check agents' papers if they tried to get a room, and all visitors were carefully scrutinized. If they were in their rooms and saw the dial on their rotary phones turning, Dorothy wrote, they knew the line was being listened to from the Athens central exchange.

Choosing the right residence was high on her list of musts: "99% of all arrests are made by the Gestapo at people's homes, almost never in the streets." If you rented in the wrong area, you exposed yourself to suspicion. Once the operatives had a place to live, they had to go to the local gendarmerie and get a new ID card—the old one would list a random address chosen by Dorothy in Izmir. It wouldn't work for long.

The men were to avoid going to the same coffee shops and restaurants over and over again. If in Athens, they were to avoid the following places: Giannakis coffeehouse; Loubier snack bar; Adams bar; Orphanidis bar; Jimmy's tavern; all the taverns in Kolonaki. They should occasionally conduct business under their cover; if they were supposed to be a black-market dealer in food, they should buy and sell food at the going rate. If they were suspected of working for the Allies, the Gestapo wouldn't bother conducting an investigation or following them on the street. "The suspect is arrested and made to confess by various methods."

They shouldn't talk with two or three people without first agreeing on a "cover conversation." If they were going to carry guns or incriminating papers after sunset, which was advised against, they should carry enough money to bribe a Greek policeman. Dorothy instructed the agents on how to spot different security officials: "Gendarmerie officers' uniforms are similar to those of the Greek Army, except that they have dark blue collar-patches, and silver epaulettes in the higher ranks. The rank stripes on their caps are also silver." She detailed their salaries so that one could get a sense of how much to offer them.

Transporting matériel had to be done on foot or by car. Most horses, mules, and donkeys had been requisitioned by the Germans; those that were left had been eaten by starving Greeks. This part of her report mirrored the diaries of ordinary Greeks. "There is nothing," wrote one journalist. "No meat, no fish, no pasta, no vegetables, no cheese, eggs, onions, olives . . . There are many, many who do not eat. They start their day with a sage without sugar, at noon some grass, some wild radish picked by the grandmother. At night, nothing." As Rodney had predicted, the Germans were starving the Greeks into submission.

Dorothy was also very much of the left. It was her belief that only "supermen or super morons" could be neutral in the war, which was another problem. The British distrusted the anti-royalist rebels she was helping; one Greek Desk operative described the English mindset as "that of a jealous elder husband when another younger man pays attention to his younger wife." Long established in the Balkans, the Brits were the masters of the region, and boasted an infrastructure the Greek Desk couldn't begin to match. The two sides were competing for the same intelligence, which the Brits often declined to share with Dorothy. "The Brits are still clamping down on us and I have no information worth reporting," she reported two months after arriving in Izmir. "Something will have to break soon." The British felt the Americans were naive amateurs, bumbling idealists unfit for hard regions like the Balkans. And the Brits "held too many rungs" on the information ladder to just ignore them.

She wrote Washington: "I am worried about the idea of sort of working against the British, but some of it was coming to them not only for their general attitude, but because they have employed some very indiscreet men." In the first few months of her stay, at least three agents had been killed because of the "high-handed carelessness" of the English spymasters. Dorothy didn't trust them.

CHAPTER 10

The Caïques

Rodney arrived in Cairo in May 1943 and moved into a handsome three-story stone villa near the Greek legation. A staffer showed the spymaster to his room, which he found to be completely empty, not a stick of furniture in sight. He set down his bags and, the next morning, began to create an intelligence network out of thin air.

The city was less frenetic than it had been the year before when Erwin Rommel's advance sparked the embassies and spy agencies to burn their files, sending a rain of smoldering confetti on the city; back then, one could hold out one's hand and collect a handful of smoking fragments. The panic had passed, but the febrile mood remained; at the Cairo Royal Military Academy, Captain Gamal Abdel Nasser was plotting his revolt against the British, and the spy agencies were turning their attention from the desert war to Europe. "Cairo was a halfway house, a place to catch your breath before the next plunge," wrote the spy and writer Patrick Leigh Fermor, who'd worked as an operative in Greece, "but you never forgot the war was watching."

The OSS was arriving in force; the Greek Desk was only a small cog in the agency's sprawling mission, and its operatives were joined by those specializing in Egypt, Turkey, Yugoslavia, and elsewhere. They joined Abwehr agents trawling Cairo's bars, listening for snippets of gossip about D-Day or FDR's health, as did the Russians and the Brits and the French. The Americans frequented the cafés and dance clubs; it was later said the OSS's initials stood for "Oh So Social." The best place was on the banks of the Nile at Shepheard's Hotel, the "Grand Old Lady of Cairo," where generals dressed in khaki ordered gin slings at the Long Bar and shouted over the sound of the orchestra, which played big-band swing late into the night. Intelligence officers made the nightly rounds from dinner at Fleurant's, the St. James, or Le Petit Coin de France, followed by dancing at the Scarabée Club or the Kit Kat Club, both of which were housed in barges moored by the riverbank. The Kit Kat Club was notorious; "officers were warned to be particularly discreet in front of the Hungarian dancing girls," and eventually the OSS had to ban its spies, including Rodney Young, from going there, causing a drought in available intel. So it was back to the Shepheard, whose Swiss manager, Charles Baehler, maintained a policy of strict neutrality in the competition between nations. "A man can learn more in an hour [there]," said one American operative, "than a week in the field—provided he keeps his mouth shut."

The Greek Desk utilized the city's wares and hiding places. Virginia Grace, the amphora expert turned operative, snuck into a Giza tomb and buried some incriminating papers there, along with the records of the Harvard Pyramids Expedition. Jack Caskey, the somewhat timid agent who'd grown up speaking Greek, hunted for gold; agents would need it to buy food and weapons inside Greece. He located 225 pounds of the stuff on the black market and snapped it up.

As for Rodney, there were a hundred things on his to-do list. He scoured the city for "theatricals": clothes and battered suitcases that agents could take into Greece and not stand out from the locals. He had on hand a large stock of used shirts, pants, and suits, whether shipped from Washington or gathered by his local contacts he never revealed. Rodney discovered they were "of the Sears Roebuck variety and recognizable as such two blocks away." His operatives would look like suburban Americans on the way to the bowling alley or drive-in movie. What were his suppliers thinking? The wrong shirt or an overwide lapel could get an agent arrested. Rodney brainstormed and came up with a solution: the refugees coming out of Greece would be given the Sears, Roebuck styles in exchange for their own outfits, which would be fumigated and mended, then worn by agents going back into Greece.

Cables had to be translated, refugees interviewed, agents recruited. Rodney demanded his people speak Greek and preferred men who'd served as soldiers or operatives, sometimes nicking them from the British. The diplomatic pouch from Izmir brought daily reports from Dorothy and Caskey. Rodney analyzed them and drew up plans for action. In a secluded upper-class suburb of Cairo, he founded a spy school in a ridiculously opulent palace called Ras el Kanayas that was owned by the brother-in-law of Egypt's King Farouk. (It was actually the brother-in-law's third-best palace.) There he scrounged together a training staff; without much support from the OSS, he had to find his own instructors. His radio expert was a Greek American he'd befriended on the journey to Cairo; his cryptography teacher was James Oliver, an American epigraphist. Young finalized his first batch of agents, had them vetted for their politics, and assigned them to a specific mission inside Greece. The first, Settler, consisted of two Greek operatives who would head to Athens, secure a boat, acquire materials to be used in fake documents, and provide Young with intel on police activity and no-go areas in Athens.

At the same time, Rodney began the arduous process of putting together an amateur merchant marine. He would need vessels of some sort to get men and matériel into the country; he would need bases in North Africa and Turkey and Cyprus to stage, load, and service the vessels; he would need stamps and papers to get them in and out of Greek ports with arms, agents, and contraband under the noses of the Germans.

Originally, Rodney had been promised submarines to smuggle in his operatives, but the Navy had other priorities; they would have only a few spots open for his men. After researching the ports, Rodney arrived at a solution: caïques. The traditional fishing vessels of the Aegean, they were made of pine, painted white, and usually had sails. Rodney began buying as many as he could lay his hands on and hunting up outboard engines to put on the sterns; he couldn't have operatives stranded a few hundred yards from the coast because of an offshore wind. He added "dealer in nautical spare parts" to his list of side jobs. "Pete, on a rumor that there is a vast junk heap at Camp Huckstep, is going out there to pick over the junk for boat engine parts," he wrote in a memo.

"If we can get an adequate supply of old parts to use as spares . . . we can go on." Rodney even inquired into the possibility of turning old tank engines into outboards in order to get engines quicker.

Even with these new power plants, the boats were vulnerable. The fastest caïques could manage eight knots, the slowest German patrol boats twelve knots. They weren't going to outrun anyone; the agents had to rely on deception and wit.

Stamps proved to be surprisingly tricky. Greek Desk vessels going in or out of the ports were required to carry the official documents a real fishing boat would possess. Seemingly everything required a stamp, a pass, a paper, or a permit; to get caught without one or with a fake one meant the caïque would be confiscated and the agents either shot or sent to a concentration camp. Rodney patched together a library of German official documents—seamen's passes, meteorological bulletins, a German Admiralty chart of the North Aegean, a fishing boat's logbook—some of them taken off refugees interviewed by Dorothy. Rodney recruited a team of counterfeiters and gave the documents to them for copying. But the stamp collection remained woefully inadequate and often outdated. Greek and German officials were changing all the time because of transfers or promotions; the signatures on the papers had to change along with them. The Brits were ahead on documents: they'd instituted a system whereby all refugees coming out of Greece surrendered their identity cards on arrival at a foreign port. The ID cards were then sent to a central office, cataloged, and studied: the officials' names, their signatures, and the stamps were painstakingly recorded and copied. It was an ingenious system, and Rodney used every ounce of his considerable force of personality to get access to it.

His days stretched past the hot Cairo dusks. It was a jerry-built force he was assembling. Some of the Greek agents carried ancient blunderbusses, not modern rifles; they wanted to know if Rodney could find ammunition. "Look, we are running a five-ring circus here," he wrote to his colleagues on July 20. "Next week I have to go to Beirut to pack people into a submarine, examining previously their underwear for laundry marks." He hadn't been trained for this; he was making it up as he went along.

The OSS bureaucracy was often a disappointment. When Rodney asked his superiors for help with the stamps, he was met with excuses and delays. "Damn it all to hell," he raged to Caskey after many weeks of waiting for results, "WHY did I even believe that

Washington could do or would do what they promised?" This would become a major theme in the Greek Desk correspondence.

The Brits bedeviled Rodney, too. Rodney's resentment toward them eventually coalesced around one figure: Noël "Hadzis" Rees, who was the head of MI6 in Izmir, Turkey. Described as "an impeccable Englishman in gray flannels and Royal Harwich Yacht Club blazer," he came from a long line of British aristocrats who'd lived in Turkey for generations, "racing yachts in the bay and horses at the hippodrome." Rees rubbed elbows with the Greek crown prince and supported his claim to rule Greece; he drove a Rolls-Royce to the British consulate. Rodney didn't resent the display of wealth, nor was he impressed by it. It was Rees's subterfuges and power grabs that he and the other Americans found insufferable. And Rees's sheer rudeness. "I would not take these rages of [Rees's] too seriously," Rodney counseled Jack Caskey, who ran the OSS base in Izmir. "The more often and the more violently he has them, the more likely he is to burst a blood vessel and die." What began as an intelligence rivalry would soon bloom into something more.

Rodney finally persuaded the British to share their library of stamps, but what to put them on? "The stock of the proper kind of paper are almost unobtainable in many cases here in the Middle East," he wrote a Navy lieutenant in a top secret letter.

> *We have requests from Greece for harbor master stamps, health stamps and German control stamps. We also have a log and control book for a caique which worked under German requisition. It would be most useful if we could have facsimile books made up on this model and a collection of the stamps which would have been used in it. Brand new books would not be too useful and would be conspicuous, so if we had our books with say*

> *half a year of imaginary voyages filled . . . with paper stamps and signatures.*

Dorothy was doing yeoman's work in Izmir, but she could speak to only so many refugees a day. A potential informant might be walking through another port on another day and his information lost. The Desk sent out a wide blast for intel on "safe routes, police regulations, forbidden zones, curfew hours etc. This information should be available from majors, doctors and naval officers coming through your parts." And when "local cloak and dagger people" advised the Greek Desk that their boats should fly their own banner so neither the Germans nor the *andartes* fired on them, Rodney's team drew up a rakish pirate banner—a black pennant relieved by a single red five-pointed star—to flutter on the prows of the vessels. Rodney's amateur navy now had its own flag.

Rodney gave instructions to his agents for the men who would be going in. He wanted a grading system to evaluate their intel:

> Alpha: *I saw this with my own eyes.*
> Beta: *A trusted source saw this with his own eyes.*
> Gamma: *My sources and I didn't see it, but believe it to be true.*
> Delta: *Doubtful but worth mentioning.*

"Do not only give the numbers of units," he told his agents. "Give descriptions of insignia on collars, shoulders, sleeves, etc.—also numbers and badges painted on transport, tanks." By collating the information from agents across the country, he would get a holistic picture of German troop movements and strength. From that, war policy and future maneuvers could be deduced. Over the months, Greek Desk lingo rose up organically. Agents and operatives were "bodies," as in "the caique arrived today with 3 bodies." Radios were "stations." A German believer was "a hot Nazi," to be avoided at all costs. An unusable banknote was a "dingo," a scheduled transmission a "listening date." A successful communication was "worked"; an unsuccessful one was "not worked."

Sperling was next in. The train taking him to Istanbul was engulfed by sandstorms between Cairo and Haifa, and food vanished from the galley car. When he reached Beirut, the only room he could find was in "a Syrian imitation of a third-class French pension. . . . My room was that belonging to the proprietor's daughter, but the young lady, thank heavens, was not thrown into the bargain." He finally made it to the Turkish capital, Ankara, and found the rooms the OSS had rented for him. The next day, he showed up for his first day on the job and his office mate informed him that he'd just arrested a foreign man at gunpoint for trying to bribe a staff member for intel. It was an omen of things to come. "The atmosphere here is entirely different from Cairo," he wrote Rodney, "and I have already seen many of the things that are supposed to be fictitious." Sperling set up a covert radio station for comms and began introducing himself to the heads of the Turkish secret police.

The archaeologist was tasked with getting permission for the forward bases where the caïques could be stored, provisioned, repaired, and manned. At first, he found his contacts to be pleasant and helpful. "The Turks urged that we have men and equipment and boats ready as soon as possible," he wrote Rodney. He quickly got an advance base, Dublin, approved and proposed several others.

He enjoyed the skulduggery. Despite the advice of his instructors at the Farm, who'd told him to live his cover instead of playing it, Sperling quickly went native in the espionage sense. He bought a trench coat and a signet ring, began to speak in ciphers, and jokingly referred to himself as "the inscrutable mystic, the Russo-Chinese Sperling H.H. Hush Hush Stinkovich." Urbane and quick on his feet, he was a hit at diplomatic parties, especially in Ankara, where local wags suggested the embassy's emblem should be crossed cocktail glasses, and in the Istanbul consulate, which he found to be "a madhouse of intrigue and counter-intrigue." He also let his superiors know that Yale had offered him a job in its archaeology department, a position that could justify "prowling about Elis and Achaia and Arcadia . . . under the benign 'cover' of archaeology." Once the archaeologists went into Greece, they could use their classicist background to snoop where others couldn't.

Then politics intervened; the government had turned against the Allies' war policies, and as a result, Sperling found himself frozen out. Later that month, he called a meeting with the director and assistant director of Turkish intelligence. They told him permission for the bases was withdrawn. "It's time to get out," he wrote Rodney. "The Turks don't want us or our project."

Rodney was growing annoyed at Sperling's worrywart tendencies and his sad missives (one was signed "Yours in pain and confusion"). He wanted plain, clear, factual messages and he wanted Sperling to buck himself up.

> *We had in Washington hopes that we would not be trammeled by bureaucracy and ignorant and ambitious people. We all wanted to get ahead and do a job. . . . It is impossible to shake yourself free into an ideal, sensible world and you may as well make up your mind to [accept Istanbul] as it is now.*

After many weeks of negotiating the Turkish labyrinth, Sperling wrangled permission to open two other bases, code-named Key West (just south of Kuşadasi, Turkey) and Boston (in Chandarli). This was not a minor accomplishment; it took politesse, a talent for intrigue, and a steel spine to keep up with the Turks. Few could have managed it. The OSS rated Sperling's performance highly: "In all other ways—in willingness to work long hours and Sundays, in patient and intelligent performance of varied duties during months when the staff was small, in unfailing courtesy and in his quiet, dignified, respect-compelling bearing—Sperling has excelled." His letters remained opaque at times, and Rodney groused to the other archaeologists about them, but he'd chosen the right man for the job.

In the space of a few months, the Greek Desk increased its payroll from eight operatives to eighty, with men outnumbering the women by a large margin. The first caïques sailed for Greece to supply the *andartes*. A typical load included machine guns, maritime equipment, "B rations" for fifteen men for thirty days, sleeping bags, cots, gun-cleaning kits, clothing, mackinaws, socks, gloves, coveralls, shelter tents, Primus stoves, seventy rifles, nine cases of .30-caliber ammunition, fuses, crystals, and heavy wire. The guns and ammo had to be taken out of their original boxes and repacked in unmarked ones, and the crews disguised themselves as merchants, which meant Rodney not only had to procure guns, explosives, clothes, and radios, but he also had to find faux-black-market products like sugar, soap, wheat, and cheese. The goods were out in the open, the guns hidden below. Live goats were brought on board to be butchered for dinner on the long journeys, which sometimes stretched to fifty hours or more.

After months of hard work, the ships were ready to take agents in; the stamps were up to snuff, and the operatives were champing at the bit. In August 1943, the Settler mission, which would provide military intel from Athens, boarded an MI6 submarine with a radio concealed in the false bottom of an oil drum. They were carrying

.42-caliber handguns, glass "Q" pills filled with cyanide, and clinking gold sovereigns secreted in their lightweight belts. They were headed for the shoreline in Attica, about ten miles from the capital.

After they left, Rodney paced his room, anxiously waiting for their first scheduled transmission and leaving his desk at regular intervals to check with the code room for updates. "They DID NOT come up on the air last night," he wrote after a few weeks. "I haven't vomited yet." The silence went on for days, then weeks. On November 10, Rodney's operators stopped transmitting their requests at the specified times. It seemed the Greek Desk's first operation had gone astray.

But in December, Settler popped up on the air. They'd experienced one foul-up after another: the oil drum had leaked, their radio had been destroyed, and one of their sources had been executed as a potential saboteur. Still, Rodney was practically weak with happiness. "You cannot imagine how much we worried about you during all that time," he wrote the lead agent. The Greek Desk was underway.

PART II

CHAPTER 11

Helias

Helias Doundoulakis stepped into a white caïque in Alexandria Harbor. With its swooping lines and single mast, it was exactly like the others bobbing on the filthy tide around him, except for the two outboard engines that had been fitted to the stern. It would be very fast, Helias thought, but also very noticeable. What poor Greek fisherman had money for two outboard motors?

Helias was Agent X-54, bound for Salonika in northern Greece, where he would set up his network of spies and operatives. His cover would be that of a businessman originally from Crete looking to make big money in the capital as a wholesale dealer in wood, coal, and oil; his brief would be to supply the Allies with intel and analysis on German troop positions and activity. He'd originally been scheduled to go to Cairo and then onto a plane that would drop him by parachute near the Greek city; the flight had been canceled due to heavy concentrations of German troops near the landing zone. The caïque was plan B: Alexandria, then Cyprus, then Izmir, then Greece.

There were two other passengers in the small cabin: Spyros, a former Greek naval intelligence officer, and an American soldier bound for Dorothy's posting in Izmir. The captain of the caïque, a Greek, was talkative. He recounted how he and the crew had come to work for the OSS. While the ship was dawdling in a Greek port one afternoon, German soldiers had boarded and commandeered the vessel, shanghaiing the men into working for the Reich. They would not be paid, they were told, only fed. The Greeks obeyed, ferrying men and matériel for the Nazis for weeks. Then one night the sailors leapt on the Germans, knifing them in the darkness and tossing their bodies into the Aegean. Whether the attack had been about money or politics, Helias didn't know.

The agent noticed one of the sailors was staring at him. Helias's clothes were new, and the nylon belt he wore around his waist (filled with gold sovereigns) was intriguing. The seaman called to the captain. "The Americans must have a lot of money," he said in Greek, not realizing Helias was fluent in the language. "If we killed them, we would be rich."

Helias was carrying a .32-caliber Colt pistol in the right-side pocket of his belt as well as a smaller gun disguised as a writing pen. He said nothing. He glanced at the fretting of sunlight on the water, wondering if he had time to reach for the Colt. The boat rocked gently on the tide.

The captain turned on the sailor and told him to be quiet. "You don't know who the real enemy is!" he cried. "If I hear you say such stupid things again, I'll throw you into the sea."

Helias acted as if he hadn't understood but whispered to the two other men that the captain was right. They didn't know who the real enemy was either; it might have been a Greek sailor or a Turkish harbormaster as easily as a Gestapo officer. "Stick together," he told them.

Two years before, eighteen-year-old Helias had ambled through the rows of the family's hardscrabble vineyard in Crete. His father walked beside him, spraying the vines with insecticide. The Doundoulakises had spent several pleasant years in Canton, Ohio, where they'd emigrated in search of brighter horizons and where Helias had been born. When his grandmother had fallen ill, the family made the return journey to the island to care for her. Helias was just two and his older brother, George, four when they returned; the boys couldn't remember Canton. But through family stories of their brief stay among the wonders of Ohio, they felt themselves to be American. They often talked of returning.

The vines were heavy with grapes, fattened in the warm spring. Four thousand years ago, the Minoans had produced wine here on terraced farms. Archaeologists regularly found huge ancient grape presses and fragments of *pithoi* (storage vessels made of fired ceramic) on the island. Near the Doundoulakis place was the palace of Knossos, where the British archaeologist Sir Arthur Evans found the first remains of the Minoans and the stone tablets covered with their still undeciphered ideogram alphabet, Linear A.

Bees buzzed in the rows; the air was drowsy and thick with heat. Helias and his father finished a row and turned down the next. As they walked, Helias heard a droning sound, low and distant at first. But the volume spiked until it was almost painful in his ears. He looked up to see two German planes shooting toward him and his father at treetop level.

The German pilots fired from their mounted machine guns. Bullets cut the leaves on the vines but missed the two men as they ran for a nearby ditch. After another strafing, Helias and his father made it to their farmhouse, where the radio announcer reported that German parachutes fluttering to earth had been seen across the island. Crete had remained free during the initial invasion, but now the Wehrmacht had arrived.

In the months afterward, the Germans destroyed the family vineyard and Helias fled for the mountains, where he made contact with the British Special Operations Executive, or SOE. He'd trained with the Brits for two years—it was there that he met the British writer and grecophile Patrick Leigh Fermor, who would become a lifelong friend. Because Helias was an American by birth, he'd eventually been transferred to the OSS, which felt they could use his language skills—he'd learned some German by then—and turn him into a spy before infiltrating him back into Greece.

Helias became a recruit at Rodney's spy school in Egypt. His weeks there were fantastical, an experience not describable to his parents back in Crete. When he arrived, he found the palace splendid beyond his experience of the world. Before the war, he'd lived in a three-room Cretan farmhouse without electricity or an indoor toilet, but on his first day at the school, an OSS major slid back a sculptured pocket door on the first floor and revealed a "colossal spiral staircase in the style of Hollywood movies." There were billiard and Ping-Pong rooms, exercise rooms, and lecture rooms, along with magical buttons on the wall that would whisk away the wooden partitions hiding a ballroom that fit three hundred guests. The palace was done up in various hues of marble; Helias was installed in the pink apartment. The trainees also had the use of a hundred-fifty-foot yacht on which meals were brought to one's own private cabin. At dinnertime, the meals were prepared by an Egyptian chef and served by American soldiers; many of them in their crisply ironed uniforms were the sons and daughters of Congressmen or other luminaries who'd secured their children postings far away from the battlefield. Those young aristocrats asked him, Helias Doundoulakis, if he preferred the red or the white.

The experience had the feeling of a hallucination. "When the major spoke, I stood there as if I were hypnotized, and I asked myself, 'Did they really call me? Had I actually been chosen to be part of this?'" His fellow Yanks were rich by local standards and generous. One even gifted him with a military-style watch: expensive and German made. He loved to wear it out on the town.

His instructors were less genteel. On his first day of class in one of the palace's high-vaulted rooms, the instructor looked over the faces turned upward at him, some young and eager, some dead-eyed with long experience. "The training that you will receive will transform you into thieves, cheaters, and liars," he said, "for the sole purpose of accomplishing your goal as spies: to 'steal' information and documents in enemy territory, in order to thwart the Germans from carrying out their plans." An OSS officer taught each man how to crack a German's skull with the butt of his gun and how to snap open safes with a thin metal wire he was to keep in his wallet or belt at all times. Helias and the other recruits were set loose in rooms made up to look like ordinary apartments or offices that had desks and locked drawers, each with a different mechanism or tumbler. Once Helias mastered picking those locks, he proceeded to combination-lock safes. He took a photography course in which he learned to use a ridiculously expensive Nikon camera adapted to shoot in low light.

Then the men moved on to infiltration. The source of the information on how to get into Greece and how to elude arrest once there was never disclosed, but some of it must have come from Dorothy Cox. Helias learned he would be given a fake address for his journey in; it would be chosen randomly from a telephone book for his destination. "You will be invisible," said the instructor, "mingling unnoticed with other civilians." When Helias went to a Cairo tailor for two suits to wear into Greece, he had the labels removed so no one could trace the clothes to Egypt. He settled on the radio code name "Cando" for his transmissions. Cando for Canton, Ohio.

Helias made it to Izmir on the caïque. The OSS knew the Germans were watching the port, photographing any suspicious arrivals. After waiting for hours, Helias was smuggled ashore and brought to an out-of-the-way office in the port town where someone—most likely Dorothy or her assistant—handed him an envelope containing thousands of dollars' worth of Greek drachmas. He chose Nikolaou as a last name for his cover (Dorothy wanted all the agents to use their real first names so they'd respond to them naturally), and a photographer snapped his picture for his fake ID card. The OSS officer handed him a large can of olive oil. "Here is a present," he announced. Helias's radio transmitter was hidden in a secret compartment at the bottom of the can. He also met his radio operator, Cosmas, a Greek naval intelligence officer originally from Salonika. "I know hundreds of friends from all walks of life," Cosmas told him. The hope was that the friends would become the team's first sources.

After a rough night crossing, the caïque approached the tip of the Halkidiki peninsula in northern Greece. The captain covered the exhaust pipes of the outboard engines with mufflers and told the passengers not to talk, as the sound would easily travel to shore. The engines fell into a soft rhythm as the crew scanned the horizon for German patrol boats.

It was four a.m., just before sunrise. One of the men spotted a light. It blinked on, then off. The captain turned the caïque toward a small pier whose slots were crowded with boats. The captain told Helias to jump on an old cargo boat tossing gently on the waves a small way off. Helias and his team headed that way; as the first light of day spread over the water, the outlines of houses perched near the waterline emerged from the dark. One of the doors opened and a man came running out soundlessly. The captain sheared away from the cargo ship, and the man, their OSS contact, found Helias and his men on the shoreline where the captain had dropped them.

"Where did you dock?" the contact said. Helias told him there were no open berths, so they were going to hop aboard the cargo boat before spotting him. "What?" the man said. "There are four German soldiers sleeping on that boat!" It was a wonder, he said, their muffled engines hadn't woken the Nazis.

After fortifying the men with mugs of strong black coffee, the OSS agent told Helias that getting to Salonika would be difficult. The *andartes* were blockading the roads to the city, pulling men out of cars, and forcing them to join the guerrillas. Horses through the mountain passes were a possibility, but they, too, were being waylaid by the *andartes*. The only other way in was by ship, and since the occupiers had requisitioned all the local vessels, the only ones available were run by Germans. "You're lucky today," the contact said. "I know of a German boat that arrived on Sunday loaded with barrels of retsina [Greek wine]. . . . Go and ask them if they can take you." Cosmas, appalled, refused to go. He would risk the roads.

After accepting a loaf of bread and cheese from their contact, Helias and an agent named Spyros set off. As they neared the water, they spotted a young German sergeant standing by the boat, counting barrels of retsina as they were rolled up. Helias spoke to him in German. "For the last two weeks, I have collected olive oil," he said, hoisting the can with the radio hidden inside. "I'm afraid the partisans will take it. Would you be so kind as to take me wherever you're going?"

The sergeant studied the two men. "Yes, you can come along," he said. The two boarded the ship and dropped to the deck near the mast, on which a German flag flapped.

Spyros was coming apart. His face was twisted as if he were in pain, and he was sweating profusely. "Relax," Helias whispered. "Nothing's going to happen. Stop showing them your fear."

After setting off, the boat hugged the rough coastline. The day grew monotonous. Near noon, the German brought out lunch for his crew, and Helias dug out the bread and cheese. As he cut the loaf in half, he caught the eye of one of the Greek sailors. The man was talking to the German sergeant, glancing over at Helias and Spyros. To Helias's horror, the man was plainly gesturing toward the can.

Helias bit into the bread. "What is happening?" he said quietly to Spyros. "Why is he pointing to our can?"

Spyros said the Greeks knew there was something hidden in the container. His voice was unsteady.

Helias told Spyros to calm down. He stood up and walked over to the group. As he approached, one of the Greeks held out a plate, on which Helias could see sliced tomatoes. *He just wants oil,* Helias thought, *for salad dressing.* The German sergeant looked on.

Helias nodded, turned, and grabbed his can; then he walked back while unscrewing the cap. After bathing the tomatoes in oil, he returned to ashen-faced Spyros. Helias felt wonderful; he marveled at his newfound ability to lie. "I had learned, through calculated . . . deception to create a shield around myself and my friends." It was almost as if, without him quite realizing it, the OSS had created inside him a doppelgänger, one who differed slightly in terms of confidence (more) and ethics (less). He found this intoxicating.

Early in the afternoon, the boat pulled into a harbor near Salonika. Helias and Spyros found the café where they'd arranged to meet Cosmas. After eating a good lunch, they approached the cashier. "Seven," the man said. Helias froze. Seven—meaning what? Seven drachmas, seven hundred, seven thousand? He knew that after the German invasion, the Greek government had begun printing money to keep up with the costs of the Nazi occupation. Inflation had reached 13,800 percent before he'd escaped from Crete. What was it now?

Helias tried to do some math in his head but couldn't. His instructors had told him never to ask a question whose answer a Greek would find obvious, so he fumbled for the notes as he slowly surveyed the café. Behind him, another customer had his drachmas ready to pay. Helias scanned the notes as he turned; it looked like there were several hundred at least, but he couldn't be sure.

He looked down and counted off seven hundred in his hand. The room seemed to grow hotter. He handed the notes to the cashier. The man said nothing. Helias and Spyros left the restaurant.

They caught a ride on a horse-drawn cart going to Salonika. As they trundled along, the driver turned to them. "I forgot to mention," he said, "the road we will be traveling will take us close to Salonika's airfield." There was a German checkpoint there where soldiers conducted searches of travelers. "Sometimes they even order people to strip off their clothes," the man said. He was worried that his passengers were carrying contraband and he could get in trouble.

Helias was in disbelief. It was only the first day and there were snares at every turn. Was this what his life as a spy was going to be like?

He decided to act as if he were angry. "Of course not," Helias told the driver. "Who do you think we are?"

When the driver turned back to the road, Helias whispered to the others. They had guns and gold sovereigns, plus a radio hidden in an oil can. Helias's first instinct was to toss their possessions to the side of the road bit by bit as surreptitiously as they could. Cosmas disagreed. "Let's wait," he said. They would see if the Germans were conducting strip searches.

Before he could finish the thought, however, the cart turned in to a courtyard. Helias could see two German soldiers ahead, one older, one younger, standing at a checkpoint at the opposite end. They were carrying automatic weapons.

The cart was the only one in sight. There was nowhere to go.

The driver pulled up to the guards, climbed off his seat, and pulled the olive oil can out, grunting as he carried it over to the guardhouse. Helias jumped down and, as the older guard began questioning him, bent over and unscrewed the cap on the metal can. The guard paused for a moment and dipped his finger in the can. It was olive oil.

"Take off your jacket," the guard said.

"At that moment, I thought my heart was about to burst from my chest," Helias later said. He took off his jacket and the guard placed his hands on Helias's shoulders, then began moving them down. Helias felt it difficult to breathe.

The guard's hands stopped. Helias raised his eyes to meet the man's gaze and saw the German was staring at him.

"How old are you?" the man asked.

"Twenty," Helias said.

"I have an eighteen-year-old son serving in the German Army," the man said. "I haven't heard from him in six months. . . . You look just like him." The man's gaze seemed to turn inward. "The same hair," he continued, "the same eyes, the same expression . . ."

His hands moved again, toward Helias's waist now. The edge of his left hand brushed the gun in Helias's belt pocket. Helias waited for the German to step back and point his automatic. Before the man could react, Helias touched his shoulder. "The war will end soon and your son will return safely," he said.

The man's hand moved away. Perhaps he thought he'd touched the hard nylon belt.

"Let us hope so," he said.

The Germans waved the men through and the horse's hooves clopped along the road to Salonika. Helias had come through three close moments in the space of a few hours. An older man might have thought, *I'm lucky*. Helias thought, *I'm good*.

CHAPTER 12

The Commandos

Andrew Mousalimas stood in the choir loft of the Greek Orthodox Church of the Assumption, listening to the priest below, the sound of his voice different up here in the wide Beaux Arts space on Oakland's west side. It was Sunday, December 7, 1941. The priest was in the middle of the Small Entrance, a prayer borrowed from the Byzantines that Andrew knew by heart. The Greek Orthodox liturgy—with its chants, communal singing, and handling of precious icons—was subtly different from those of the Baptist and Lutheran services taking place around the Bay Area that morning.

As the priest droned on, Andrew, who'd just turned seventeen, noticed the boys in the rows beneath him beginning to bow their heads and drop into whispered conversation. The whispering moved back and eventually reached his row, and he learned that the Japanese had bombed something called Pearl Harbor hours before. The parishioners below began to stir, too; the news was moving quickly through the congregation.

The priest gave his final blessing and Andrew and his friends raced down the loft stairs, through the doors, and out into the street. After church, Oakland's Greek Americans gathered in front of the church for an "unofficial social hour"; freshly washed Chevrolets and Buicks were parked two and three deep as the men dressed in dark suits and the women in tight-waisted dresses gossiped and laughed. Andrew threaded his way through the crowd until he heard the sound of a radio turned up loud. It belonged to one of his classmates lucky enough to have a car; he'd tuned to a news station. A circle of young men with slicked-back hair gathered around the car. It was true; they were at war with Japan.

The neon signs on the storefronts of Seventh Street, along with the streetlights in front of Andrew's house, soon went dark in the soft Oakland nights as reports of Japanese subs prowling the Pacific coastline sparked a blackout. Air raid sirens rang out during the school day, sending Andrew and his classmates home. With his buddies, he debated which service they would join and when.

In the '30s, when Andrew was growing up, Greek immigrants and their sons and daughters had grown fairly accustomed to the discrimination that permeated the culture. They had little choice. Newspapers referred to the newcomers from Athens and the islands as "ignorant, depraved and brutal" and lobbied for their deportation because they were "a vicious element unfit for citizenship." In the 1917 riots in Salt Lake City, men had prowled the city streets looking for dark-haired foreigners to lynch. In the South and the Midwest, the Ku Klux Klan had picketed Hellene businesses, attacked customers, and forced owners to sell out to "whites" at steep losses. Indiana Greeks woke early one morning to find crosses burning on their lawns. A Klansman passed a note to a Florida restaurateur:

> *You are an undesirable citizen. You violate the Federal Prohibition Laws and laws of decency and are a running sore on society. Several trains are leaving Pensacola daily. Take your choice but do not take too much time.*

John "Yannis" Giannaris, whose parents had emigrated from the village of Aris in the southern part of the Peloponnese, felt different from his "American" classmates. He was from Chicago, the son of a barber. When Giannaris was little during the Depression, he and his mother would go looking for an apartment for their family; he remembered knocking on doors of the wood-frame cottages in the Ravenswood neighborhood. They would speak to the owners, and after a few minutes of promising negotiation, the owners would ask his mother's name. When they heard "Giannaris," the answer was always the same. "Oh, you're Greek. We don't rent to Greeks." His mother would thank them and move to the next listing, but Giannaris seethed. He had been taught to love America and his fellow Americans, but in his early years, he often found doing so difficult. He was an idealist by nature, an idealist with anger issues. "Diogenes, walking around in daylight with a lighted lamp, searching for an honest man, became my ideal." When he came across dishonest or unjust people, he became enraged.

Mousalimas had similar experiences. "This was the era when we were called dirty Greeks," he said. When he went to Oakland High School, he was told that Greek kids couldn't join fraternities or the more exclusive clubs, that they were forbidden from dating the "right" girls or playing sports. "We were the outcasts," he remembered.

Then the war came. In church the week after Pearl Harbor, Mousalimas listened to a letter from the archbishop in Astoria being read out from the pulpit. "I submit to our great President, Franklin D. Roosevelt, my sentiments of unreserved devotion to his glorious leadership," the priest read, "assuring him that all my clergy, church membership, and myself, are at his side. Our countrymen: We are already in the war and we must win it. GOD BLESS AMERICA!"

The heroics on the Albanian front became front-page news. In a matter of weeks, immigrants who'd been turned away from jobs or called "greaseball" or "wop" (Greeks were often mistaken for Italians) now found other Americans buying drinks for them in bars. "During the years of the Albanian war, it was an honor to say that you were Greek," one said. "I remember when the Americans would hear us speak, they would ask us what our language was. Whenever we said it was Greek, they would embrace us and kiss us. You cannot imagine the kind of things that happened."

Soon after that morning in the choir loft, Andrew and his friends went in ones or twos to the recruiting stations, signed up, and received their orders for basic training. Across the country, Greek boys were sent off to war; clusters of aunts, uncles, parents, sisters, and *koumbaros* (an elastic word meaning anything from best man to close family friends) embraced them at train and bus stations. Wrapped packages of pastitsio (a baked pasta casserole) and moussaka were stuffed into their bags. These were the sons of grocers, restaurant owners, laborers, professors. They went to Greek-language school three times a week, worked in Greek businesses, dated Greek girls. They shared a remarkably common upbringing.

In Chicago, eighteen-year-old Giannaris visited the local Navy recruiting station. He wanted to fly fighters; the image of a Grumman F4F Wildcat lifting off an aircraft carrier was his beau ideal of what his war would and should be like. But the doctors found astigmatism in his eyes. Dejected, he joined the Army instead.

When the Greek boys reported to basic training, they were given uniforms, GI haircuts, inoculations, and IQ tests. They had to complete their induction forms, duly filling in their names, serial numbers, and blood types. When they came to "religion," there were three choices: Protestant, Roman Catholic, or Jewish. For a Greek Orthodox boy to check any of those would have felt like a small mutilation.

Mousalimas stood up and took the form up to the sergeant. I'm not filling this out, he told the man, until I can put my faith down correctly. The Army, remarkably, relented; his dog tags read "GO" for Greek Orthodox. But it was something of a one-off; most other boys weren't so lucky and went to war as reluctant Protestants or Catholics or nothing at all. For his part, Andrew was elated at his success but only briefly. "Hell, it made no difference," he realized. If he were shot, there were no Greek Orthodox chaplains to give him last rites anyway.

William Donovan had plans for Mousalimas and his friends. The OSS commander had pursued the idea of recruiting young Greek American commandos who spoke the native language and were intimately familiar with the culture—men who were also, presumably, ready and willing to kill the occupiers of their ancestral homelands. He'd told FDR the units might help the president become the "great liberator" of Nazi-controlled Greece and its Balkan neighbors. In January 1943, FDR signed an executive order creating the 122nd Infantry Battalion, one of a handful of battalions made up of second-generation Americans who would fight in the places their parents had left.

At the time, there were Japanese Americans being held in internment camps in California. The FBI kept lists of foreign-born "subversives," and the New York tabloids regularly theorized about various fifth column cells burrowing their way into the heartland. Donovan believed that the ethnic enclaves scattered across America were being imagined in the wrong way. "We had often been told . . . that this mixture of nationalities in America was a weakness and could be penetrated and exploited by our enemies," he wrote later. "But we did convert that so-called liability into a great asset." The 122nd was named for the 122 years that had passed since Greece had freed itself from the Ottoman Turks. More than twelve hundred men volunteered for the battalion.

With Rodney Young overseeing the project from Cairo and with Helias and his fellow operatives in place, the spy apparatus, as rickety as it was, was producing reams of intel. The caïques were fully provisioned and ready. The men of the 122nd would be the last puzzle piece of the mission. They would be the point of the *doru*, the Greek spear.

The twelve hundred were ordered to Camp Carson in Colorado for training. Before departing for Greece, Giannaris returned home to Chicago for a last visit. One of his father's friends spotted him on the street and called him over. "When you get to Greece," the man said, "I want you to give my brother, in the village, twenty dollars. And when you come back, I'll pay you." Another "uncle" next to him chimed in, telling Giannaris to give his brother twenty dollars, too.

Greece? Giannaris played dumb; he told the men he had no idea what they were talking about. "Look," the first man said, "the FBI was through this whole neighborhood. . . . They asked about you, how well you spoke Greek. Now what the hell is that for?"

Everyone knew they were going to the *patris*.

Mousalimas, Giannaris, and the other recruits boarded troop trains headed for Camp Carson. As Mousalimas rode eastward, he was annoyed by his fellow Army privates, mostly sons of Okies who'd gone to California from the Dust Bowl. He found them ill-mannered. Lonely, he walked through the rattling troop train and came across a Black soldier in his thirties. The two struck up a quick friendship. The Black soldier "had a fabulous wit, but was very depressed," Mousalimas remembered. When the Oakland boy told the man he was headed to Camp Carson, the Black soldier remarked how lucky he was; for his part, he was headed to Camp Shelby in Mississippi, "the other side of the sun." Mousalimas had no idea what the man was talking about. He knew only certain parts of what being an American was like.

The train pulled into Colorado Springs and glided to a stop with a whoosh of steam. Mousalimas hoisted his pack and stepped off the metal stairs. He looked down the long platform; he was the only soldier disembarking. When he made it to the barracks, he met his fellow soldiers, a mix of Greek American boys like himself and a smattering of older Greek nationals—refugees and escapees and sailors whose ships had been torpedoed. The average age of the Americans was just under nineteen years old. The American boys taught the Greeks English, and in exchange, they learned Greek swear words and songs, sometimes on the marches through the Colorado firs. Mousalimas was intrigued to learn that if the natives served honorably, they would earn their American papers; if not, they'd be sent back to the homeland. That was their reward for risking their lives: citizenship.

The recruits hiked, ran obstacle courses, shot out targets on the rifle range, read maps and compasses, threw live grenades at imaginary foxholes, and ducked live machine-gun fire. They hiked and hiked and hiked. War games were played for keeps; captives were placed, hands tied, in mountain creeks cold with ice melt. The troops were given ten seconds to "kill" a man, without a gun, in any manner they saw fit. And they hiked and hiked some more; the OSS wouldn't be supplying them with jeeps, so they had to build up endurance to cross the rugged Greek mountains on their own feet.

The recruits all knew only a small percentage of the twelve hundred would be selected for the mission. The hikes and target shooting were actually a competition. At mealtimes, the soldiers banged their hands rhythmically on the edge of the mess hall's wooden tables to toughen them for knife fights. "We were men of extraordinary will and trained to kill," Giannaris said. For them, "it was a war of deep roots." They were returning to liberate their parents' homeland. "We had this feeling of great passion for *'pisti'* [faith] and *'patria'* [our ancestry]."

The commandos were cocky and wild. After one brawl with regular troops in Colorado, a number of Giannaris's men were arrested and threatened with court-martial. The OSS's Donovan sent a telegram to Camp Carson: "Hands off. These are my fighting men."

The twelve hundred were cut down to 212, who were divided into eight units. Mousalimas made the cut and went into Group IV; the smart, ferociously disciplined Giannaris was named captain of Group II. After Colorado, the chosen troops were shipped to just outside Washington, DC, to the Congressional Country Club, which had been taken over by the OSS for the duration of the war and renamed "Area F." The trainers were American OSS officers, British commandos, and one hard-edged member of the French Resistance, who clearly considered these well-fed American boys to be soft. "If you don't like it here," he sneered, "you can go back to your mommy." Giannaris and the others absorbed a compressed curriculum of fieldcraft, map and compass reading, tactics, formations, knife fighting, tactical exercises, weapons training, and night maneuvers. All of this in two weeks. As had happened with the archaeologists, the OSS's inexperience showed.

Maryland had been chosen for its wooded terrain, which bore some resemblance to the mountainous Greek landscape the recruits would be working in. On pitch-black nights, they would roam the hills, learning to use a compass or, when the compass was taken away, to navigate by the stars and moss on the trees. One night, the route took the men through the hills around Chevy Chase. Mousalimas was crawling on his belly when he glanced up. "In front of me was one of those beautiful colonial homes that Chevy Chase is famous for," he said. "The home had a big bay window; the living room was lit up, and I could see its elegance vividly. There were adults and children in the room, appearing to be enjoying a family gathering." He felt like a homesick alien.

The commandos were told they had an expected casualty rate of 90 percent: "There will be no withdrawal route, no replacements, no supply lines." They would remain in Greece until the Germans surrendered or left.

Wherever the men went to train, the Greek community embraced them, sometimes in a smothering grip. Besides the dinners and masses and galas, there were invitations to local homes where souvla (barbecue) and mageritsa (lamb soup) awaited them, along with one or two marriageable daughters. More than one commando found himself trapped in a strange living room, being asked pointed questions about his family, while a young woman sat prettily in a freshly starched dress, looking at him significantly. The practice of *proxenies* (arranged marriage) was far more common in the East than in the Midwest or in California; many Greek American parents in New York or Boston found themselves with multiple girls squeezed into shotgun apartments; in such cases, the handsome commandos were a godsend. One soldier in New York, not wanting to insult his hosts, excused himself, went into the bathroom, turned and locked the door, then opened the window and shinnied down a pipe two stories to the ground. Not everyone escaped; another "found himself engaged"—how he wasn't quite sure—on his first date with a dark-haired girl in Manhattan.

The scenes would be repeated in places like Athens if a soldier was stationed near his parents' families. One recruit "suffered from a malignant plague of relatives," complained his commanding officer. The commandos were part of a long-dreamed-of project, the coming of age of the Greeks in America. Before they had even fired a shot, the young soldiers were heroes to the Pappases and the Constantinous from coast to coast. They could have gotten just about any girl they wanted.

By the time the commandos were getting ready to leave, they were ludicrously fit. They looked good, too. The Army had provided them with one of the first batches of the Eisenhower jackets (officially, "Jacket, Field, Wool, Olive Drab"), which were much smarter than the longer four-pocket tunics they replaced. The men were issued the new leather jump boots, an honor they shared only with airborne paratroopers. In towns the commandos passed through, other soldiers would often come up to them and ask, "Who *are* you guys?" One Greek American remembered a dull afternoon in Virginia when different companies were marching across a parade field as they prepared to embark for Italy. "I could see these poor soldiers in these infantry outfits, scared and ill-prepared for combat duty," he said. "Our group was marching with joy. We were hyped up and ready for combat. We wanted to go into battle. We were not forced to go into battle."

The Army was delighted with the men's high morale; still, it led to tensions. Some commandos, feeling the weight of failing their fathers and grandfathers, became near maniacal. This group included Giannaris. He told the commandos that they were going to be "harder, tougher, more enduring" than the other units, harder than the Marines or the British SAS or the German squads they'd be facing. Every single task, no matter how minor, had to be completed with exacting precision. No obstacle on the course could be half-assed, no unauthorized water break could be taken on hikes, and no shot could go astray on the rifle range without Giannaris finding out about it and making the offender wish his parents had never come to America. His men grumbled about how "unbelievably tough" the captain was on them; they considered him a rigid, by-the-book son of a bitch. When the unit mingled after hours with men from other squads one evening and compared notes over rounds of drinks in town, the topic eventually turned to the habits of their commanders. After a few more drinks, the soldiers took a vote on the "Officer Most Likely to Be Shot in the Back in Combat."

Giannaris won.

On November 17, 1943, the commandos arrived in Charleston to board the ship for Europe. When they arrived in Italy, which had recently surrendered to the Allies, they were trucked to Bari, a port city under the control of the British. It was the last stepping stone before Greece. There the men waited for their orders with great impatience.

As the weeks went on, their embarkation date was pushed back because of foul weather or Nazi incursions into the region they would be headed to. The mood in the barracks tightened. When they were given leave to go into town, the commandos drank wine as they eyed the Italian troops parading in ones or twos in Bari's town square. The Americans took to stopping the soldiers; they pointed to the medals and ribbons the young men wore on their blouses. "And what campaign is this one from?" they'd asked. If an Italian soldier answered, "*Grecia*," a commando would take out his switchblade, slowly open the blade, and snip the ribbon off the man's uniform.

CHAPTER 13

Bodies

By early 1944, the radio room at Greek Desk headquarters in Cairo, manned by an operator during the scheduled transmission times, hummed with incoming messages. Rodney had spent months placing agents in strategic points to prepare the way for the commandos, and they started coming up on the air from points north, south, east, and west. A typical early transmission:

Telegram F1
Georgiades, Adrianople
NO. 02
8.29.43

Trouble past, I hope. Old organization in Evro collapsed, I'll start new one even if I have to go in myself. Not much help from old hands here professional jealousy maybe. Give me little time promise do good job fertile field.

For John Giannaris's Group II, now preparing to set off for the homeland, Rodney had come across one candidate who seemed promising:

> *About 23 years old. Born an American citizen, but has lived most of his life in Crete. Worked for British intelligence, for which he organized a successful network in his part of the island. . . . Young but very experienced in undercover work, and thoroughly understands* organization *of intelligence network. In appearance rather stupid; but extremely subtle and ingenious.*

The man whom Rodney code-named X-53 was George Doundoulakis, Helias's older brother. Photos reveal George's hangdog expression and slightly vacant eyes, but in reality, he was perhaps slightly more ingenious than his very ingenious brother. After the war, the elder Doundoulakis became a renowned physicist and was awarded twenty-six patents in radar and narrowband television.

The reason he was available at all was blackmail: a Cretan villager had learned Doundoulakis was working for British intelligence and demanded a million drachmas to keep the secret from the Gestapo. George sent two high-school friends to kill the man, but the informant tipped off the Germans before the assassins arrived. George fled to the mountains and hid in a dripping cave for months until the Brits sent a torpedo boat to retrieve him. He then went over to the Americans.

Once inserted into eastern Thessaly, George sent his first letter to Rodney. "We are all well," he said. He'd already begun building his web of *andartes* and subagents to distribute leaflets to weaken German morale and to collect quantities of sand to pour into the grease boxes of German trains. "Already one third of the rolling stock is in the repair shops," George wrote, and the Greek workers who maintained the cars promised him they would add emery dust to every engine that came through the shop. His men were following guards at a nearby harbor: when "even the smallest caique" entered or left the port, they had eyes on them. "They operate two caiques of 15 to 20 tons to guard the coast. These caiques are manned by Greeks and by 3 to 5 Germans each having their own arms. There are also 3 *Maschinenpistolen* [machine pistols] and 1 machine gun."

George thought like a scientist. To show the extent of his network and their connections, he composed complex Venn diagrams, with each circle representing a subgroup of operatives. Rodney was pleased; George was a bright spark. If anything, he was too aggressive.

Once the agents began arriving inside Greece, Dorothy's intel on operating under the Nazi regime inside Greece was tested. The agents were indeed able to turn greedy or patriotic cops to the cause, as she had predicted. "Many of the police were employed by us as operators," reported an agent from Crete, "and the bulk were used for checks, cutouts and special runners. In the . . . town of Ano Archanes, for instance, a policeman was our chief local operator and the chief of police was our check-up man." Another unexpected resource was priests: "The clergy on the whole took pride in being patriots and even fighters, and did good service as checks and cutouts." Doctors, who made house calls and were often exempt from curfews, returned with intel.

But not all Dorothy's techniques worked. The bribes she had recommended were often "useless and dangerous," reported one agent. What the archaeologist hadn't factored in correctly was the extreme poverty inside Greece. Who had extra money to pay off policemen in a starving city? Only black marketers and agents working for foreign intelligence services. What informers and cutouts wanted instead of money was security. "A round-about bribe was our assurance that inside men would be pulled out in time if seriously threatened," wrote one operative, "and that all men in our service would enjoy special privileges and status when they were shipped out to Egypt."

The Desk learned as it went along. When meeting "targets" in the countryside, agents began placing lookouts at nearby roundabouts and instructing them to watch especially for the armored cars used by the Germans. If one was spotted, the lookout would fire two quick pistol shots in succession. The Germans had learned to ignore random gunshots, as the *andartes* often took potshots at birds or rabbits, hoping for fresh meat for the dinner pot. The technique worked "tolerably well." The archaeologists passed it on to other operatives.

When Helias arrived in Salonika, it was thick with men in uniform. *There are more German soldiers here than civilians,* he thought as he and his team scouted the city. Their first order of business was a place to stay. Other agents in other parts of the country were struggling with finding places to live. "At the time finding houses in Athens is very difficult," wrote one to Rodney. "Many patriots agreed to lend their houses for the operation of the wireless [radio set], but lately terrorism on the part of the Germans . . . has intensified so much that even the most courageous patriots are afraid to offer their houses." If Greeks were found renting to Allied spies, they were "destroyed."

Helias found a temporary place to crash for a few days, then went searching for a safe place to hide the radio. He would be transmitting to Cairo accounts of German ships in Salonika's harbor, departures and arrivals of troop trains, unit insignias and movements, and Greek political sentiments, so he needed a place to meet his team and transmit the intel securely. A Greek contact stumbled across an abandoned textile factory in Agia Triada on Salonika's east side. Helias walked over for a look. Peering through the blown-out windows, he could see the building featured a tall A-frame roof with beams running the length of the ceiling, fifteen feet off the floor. Antenna wire could be laid across the tops of the beams. The former owner was a Greek Jew who, after being forced to wear a yellow star and seeing the gravestones at Jewish cemeteries demolished, had taken his family to the mountains to save them from the coming roundups. An enormous gate shielded the view of the factory from the street, which would help with concealment; in the small guardhouse next to the building, Helias found an old woman, Mrs. Eleni, had set up house. He would have to deal with her.

The team rented the factory. Nearby, they found an apartment in Serron Street occupied by a lovely, black-haired, twenty-eight-year-old widow and her three small children. The father was a Greek military officer who'd been killed on the Albanian front. In exchange for food money, the widow, whom the agents nicknamed Sultanitsa, would allow Helias to stay in her living room, which he would convert to a bedroom. He could also eat his breakfast and dinner with the family.

The next day, Helias went to the factory with his two operatives, Cosmas and Spyros. He ordered a load of firewood to be dumped just inside the gate; the pile of lumber would show that his business was a going concern and it would obscure the activities inside the factory. His partners hired two guards, one of whom would make a show of cutting the wood into smaller, more salable sizes while also keeping an eye on the street. The other would patrol the block, pretending to watch for thieves while surreptitiously making notes of pedestrians who strolled along the street once too often.

Helias grabbed the antenna wire and climbed up to the first beam. He strung the wire over the wood, then moved on to the next one. While perched on a beam, he glanced through the window to look in the next-door neighbor's yard; in it, four German officers were sitting in the sunshine at a card table playing backgammon. Clearly, they lived in the place. It was unfortunate, but Salonika was full of Nazis, and Helias was eager to get on with the mission. The factory was ideal, and the confidence he'd gained by fooling multiple Germans on the way to Salonika had stayed with him. They would set up here.

After removing the radio from its secret compartment at the bottom of the oil drum, he placed it on a small table. Helias plugged in the headphones, adjusted them to fit his rather large head, then laid them back down on the table. He took out a cigarette and smoked it as he waited for the call from Cairo. They'd arranged for a three p.m. transmission every afternoon. There was always a moment of tension for both sides: Cairo wondering if their agents would come up on the air and the agents wondering if the quartz crystals inside the radio—which had been cut and ground to resonate at a particular frequency—had been correctly made. On the table next to the radio and his headphones, Helias laid out his .32, another .45 pistol he'd picked up on the way to Greece, and two grenades placed in a small box. If he was discovered during transmission, he planned on tossing the grenades out the window as a diversion and escaping with his men the other way.

As Helias waited, the sounds of the street, the muffled conversations of the neighbors, and the tramping of donkeys pulling carts down the road filtered into the sun-filled space. He wondered if German triangulation units were circling the streets nearby. To pick up unauthorized signals, they were known to prowl Salonika with their vehicles disguised as laundry trucks. Radios were banned in Greece, so any signal really was unauthorized.

Helias took out another cigarette and lit it. At two fifty-five p.m., he put on his headphones while Cosmas and Spyros looked on.

There wasn't silence, only a faint droning hum. He waited, taking pulls from the cigarette and tapping the ash onto the floor. When the beeps came, they were clear. A long, a short, a long, a short. It was a "C." Then a short and a long: "A." The operator in Cairo spelled out "Cando," Helias's code name. Helias had made contact with the Greek Desk. He began to broadcast.

The intel coming from Helias and the other agents spread from Lesbos to Athens was rich and varied. An aerodrome was being built in the district of Evzoni. A submarine base was under construction in the Bexinar quarter. Offers came in from possible double agents:

> *A high-ranking officer of our network, a high-ranking, anti-Hitler German officer, whose identity will be revealed after the war, and who holds an excellent position, wishes to cooperate with us by transmitting to us his own valuable information. His only stipulation is that we pay him 30 pounds monthly, tentatively. He will also be in a position to help one of our agents who is in trouble. Please wire your orders as soon as possible.*

Agents sent blueprints of railway infrastructure by caïques returning to their bases; the commandos could use them to choose the right places for their high explosives to go. "Bridge situated at the railway station," radioed one operative.

Its height above the surface of the water is 4 metres and its length 26 metres. On the bridge there is only the railway line, and it is guarded by the outpost of the railway station which is 150–200 metres off the bridge. The foundations of the bridge are of stone. It is metallic and the suspension arcs are one metre wide and 3 centimetres thick.

Black-and-white photos accompanied the report, along with the assurance that certain Greek guards could be bribed to look the other way when the teams arrived.

Much of what their agents had to report was gruesome. The Desk kept a list of war crimes organized by village name, and they went on for pages each month:

VOUTYRO:
70 year old woman denuded and burned alive.
One man machine gunned.

KLAVSION:
An old woman attempting to carry belongings from her home which the Huns had set afire was forced, under threat of shooting, to remain in the house until its burning walls collapsed on her.

KRIKELLON:
One woman was beaten to death with the butt-ends of rifles.
One young girl was kidnapped as a hostage and has not been heard from since.

One report out of Kalavryta, an *andarte* stronghold, was particularly sickening. During an encirclement campaign designed to trap the partisans in the village in the winter of 1943, seventy-eight German soldiers were captured and later executed. Days later, German troops left their bases and headed toward the village, killing civilians and burning homes and monasteries on the way. When they reached Kalavryta, they ordered all the residents into the village school, where soldiers separated out men from twelve years old to ninety-five and marched them to a nearby hilltop field. The Germans looted the homes, burned what they could, then ascended the hill and machine-gunned the men standing there. A total of 438 Greeks was slaughtered. Their mothers and sisters were ushered into the school's other side, and the lock was snapped shut.

The soldiers set the school on fire. "The flames, the smoke," read one account, "the screaming of the women and children, created a scene which the writer is incapable of describing." One Austrian officer couldn't bear the sight and opened the door, saving the women and children. His fellow soldiers shot him dead.

> *The tortured frenzy of the women as they emerged from the school caused hilarious laughter on the part of the Germans, who told the women that their men were up the hill. The poor creatures ran to the place and found a pile of dead bodies and literally a stream of blood running down the hill. The Germans had killed all the animals and destroyed all the [farming] implements, [so] the women had to drag their men down to the cemetery . . . and dig graves with their hands.*

Nazi commanders had instituted a hundred-to-one reprisal system. If one German was killed, a hundred Greeks would be murdered. But the agents reported back that the populace was so far uncowed: "Every terror act sent fresh recruits to the guerrilla bands, increased popular hostility, and weakened the position of the collaborating elements."

By early 1944, Dorothy, who was coaxing stories like this out of her interviewees, was under growing pressure. For some reason, it was getting harder and harder to meet with the refugees. "The Greeks brought in . . . are being much more closely watched by the Turks," Dorothy reported. "Officers are put up in a pension and allowed to go about freely, but others are put in an [inn] with a Turkish soldier on guard and not allowed to leave except under the escort of an official of the Greek Consulate on official business." Why were the Turks blocking her from talking to refugees? Dorothy was feeling a bit paranoid. "Is this the Turks or, as I fear, British influence?" Winston Churchill and his lieutenants considered the Americans to be interlopers in the Balkans and were concerned they would support more liberal elements against the British favorite, King George II. Dorothy and the others believed the Brits were leaning on the Turks to freeze them out.

She suspected the hand of the MI6 commander, Noël Rees. "He talks about cooperation and common aims, but that is hooey," wrote one of Dorothy's colleagues. In some ways, Dorothy was simply too good at her job. She worked her British contacts for information while her scraper found Greeks off the street to feed her intel. Her reports were generally regarded as better than MI6's. "I suppose we have it coming to us," the colleague sighed. "Hiram really has been putting one over on our gallant allies in no small way."

British resistance wasn't just operational; Dorothy was increasingly disturbed by what she was hearing about Churchill's plans for Greece. Fearing a Communist government and a loss of influence in the Balkans, the British, led by Churchill, were intent on holding on to Greece postwar and forbidding elections. Once the Germans were defeated, they wanted to reinstall the king to power. How could the

Allies, with the help of the archaeologists, drive out the Nazis and their fascist lackeys only to prop up forces who opposed democracy in the birthplace of democracy?

That feeling was made more distressing by the reaction to the Americans, both commandos and agents, inside Greece. Locals who met the commandos or Greek Desk agents were in the habit of handing over letters addressed to FDR (the women handed them ones addressed to Mrs. Roosevelt) and asking the agents to please deliver them. The letters were mostly pleas to save Greece. One agent toured a remote region in uniform with an American flag on his sleeve. "Believe me, the people of the three villages where I stopped went mad with joy," he messaged Rodney. Another in the field met a Greek general who talked excitedly of America and its institutions. He was a big fan of Lincoln, had read Upton Sinclair's exposés of American life, and still loved the country. The operative wrote Rodney:

> *I didn't feel it was up to me to disillusion him as to our domestic situation and this approach which I've found very common always baffles me. At first, I thought it was put on for my benefit, but damn it I'm beginning to believe they really do picture America as a large edition of the Greece of 2500 years ago. That's why the "people" can't understand why the U.S. isn't giving them the guns to fight for what they think is their 1776.*

It was sometimes mortifying to be so well thought of.

The anti-colonialist feeling percolated through the Greek Desk. Rodney was certainly susceptible. "Royalist pests go on here," he wrote from Cairo. "The damn fools seem to insist on making a civil war." Dorothy felt the same way. When a Greek source begged her to open an American mission in his town, as the Brits were doing nothing, she was white with anger. "This week stands out as the most seriously anti-British week I have spent," she wrote Rodney. "I find these conversations difficult as I feel I must discourage anti-British feeling. But what is one to say?"

The Greek Desk trod a fine line. They wanted to topple the old system dominated by England, but they didn't want to push so hard that the Communists took over. It was a dilemma that would bedevil the West in the Cold War for decades to come. "People are apt to take the attitude that we are backing a band of wild communists who spend all their time oppressing the local peasantry," Rodney grumbled. He had a team embedded with the leadership of the leftist guerrillas, and their reports painted a different picture from the one the British publicized: there was a core of committed Communists, but most of the *andartes* were not radicals in any meaningful sense.

The Greek Desk's official brief was to oust the Nazis from Greece. Their private desires focused on saving the Greeks and the Ancients while ushering in something resembling democracy. They were banned officially from interfering in the internal politics of the country, but it was almost impossible to do any of the former things without at least dabbling in the latter.

CHAPTER 14

The Memos War

By the third year of the war, the National Archaeological Museum in Athens was no longer a museum. The building had been divided up and new tenants had moved in. The Mycenaean Room had become a concert hall for the state orchestra; the west wing was now the central post office. Farther in on the first floor, the welfare office had set up shop, and in the basement was a bomb shelter. A health clinic took over the oldest part of the museum off Tositsa Street; prostitutes and streetwalkers could be seen strolling through the halls on their way to get shots for the clap. The Germans had even commandeered some rooms and turned them into a prison for leftists.

The basement workshops would usually have been humming with conservationists in the middle of multi-month projects laid out on their tables like disassembled automatons. But now when a conscientious German archaeologist brought in fragments recovered from a work site or excavation, the pieces sat around. The museums couldn't afford shellac or other materials to bind them together. And besides, according to one archaeologist, "There is no point in gluing together antiquities, because they can be broken up again due to so many displacements and adventures."

The archaeologists and curators were now crammed into a small office in the new building. Every week, they received new reports of looting and destruction of Greek relics, reports they could do little or nothing about. Meanwhile, the culture ministers were trying to keep their people alive, sometimes quite literally. For years, the museums had been practically without funds. On June 20, 1941, a cleaner wrote the president of the Athens Archaeological Society:

> *Mr. President, I accept the honor of begging the Council . . . as it takes into account the tragic conditions under which we live, to increase my minimum wage, which monthly amounts to net drachmas 966. My child, who helped me last year, today, after frostbite and his forehead injury, is not able to work sufficiently. Suffering, exhausted, hungry, believe me, I beg you, take care of us poor people, otherwise we will die a bitter death from exhaustion and hunger.*

The Archaeological Society's archives are replete with such letters. In response, the officers contacted the Ministry of the National Economy, asking that sultana raisins and sugar be distributed to the staff and ushers to keep up their strength for tours. Even the higher-ups suffered. Months after the occupation began, the society's treasurer wrote its president that he was "in danger of being naked and barefoot." Could the society supply him with a pair of shoes? Knowing the "exorbitant cost" of footwear, the treasurer apologized for the request.

At the same time, the Wehrmacht was increasing the pressure on the ministers to display the relics. They were proud of their conquest of Greece; many of the German officers sincerely believed Himmler's claim that the Germans had shaped Attic culture centuries ago, that the true Grecian gift had its roots in their own people's DNA. They'd heard about Athens's treasure house of marvels since their boyhoods. Now they wanted to see them.

Hans von Schoenebeck, the head of the Art Protection Service, requested that the National Museum be reopened for the entertainment of the troops. He listed the pieces he wanted displayed, including the *Ephebe of Antikythera*, a bronze statue of a languorous young man. "In a time of war," the Germans told one archaeologist, "it was all the more necessary for people to seek refuge in art."

Those statues currently stood five feet under the museum's concrete floor, and the curators wanted to keep them there. To bring them up would not only expose them to damage from bombing runs; doing so could also give the Germans ideas about where the statues rightfully belonged. What if a high-ranking general toured the museum and took a fancy to a certain piece? The Germans couldn't covet what they couldn't see.

The Ministry of Education had archaeologists, custodians, and keepers spread across the country, but it had no troops or artillery pieces to fight for the relics. What it had was soft power. When it came to culture, the Germans wished to cover their demands with a veil of respectability or at least appear to be civil. Some of them had sincere reverence for what the Greeks had created, and few of them wanted to be seen as barbarians. The Greeks sensed an opening and exploited it ruthlessly. A war of memos began.

In one letter, a Greek official responded to a German request to shuffle the museum's collections by pointing out the obvious. "We have the honor to say that the Greek Government, which is very busy with other major problems that threaten our nation with extermination, is not concerned in the present to reorganize the Museums." The first death by starvation in Athens—that of Eleni Vlachou, aged fifty-something—had been registered on July 23, 1941. Athenians collapsed on the streets; their fellow citizens placed handkerchiefs over their faces. Who had time to think about statuary?

Of course, the ministry thought about little else but statuary, but that wasn't the point. When one German minister asked about gaining access to a collection in Salonika, the ministry responded that the relics were in disarray and "we intend to build a special museum building" for them in the future and "it would be pointless to reorganize what is inadequate and bad." In other words, no.

Misdirection sometimes worked, as did flattery. "The Office of the Prime Minister," read an early letter from the government to the German Art Protection Service, "as well as the whole of Hellenism, are well aware of the great appreciation of the German People, and above all of their esteemed Leader, for the relics of ancient Greek culture and are convinced that the collection of works of art from Athens were brought back to light in large part by German direction and after so much effort of endurance and love."

The Germans also wanted records of what the Greeks had in storage; archaeological catalogs and sketches placed the objects in space and time—a bull from the second century BC meant something very different from one carved during the first century. Hitler and his lieutenants weren't simply greedy for the physical objects; they also wanted the stories behind them, because the stories could be reworked. But the records couldn't be found. Request after request to the archaeological bureaucracy resulted in nothing more than bland apologies and mystification over where the things had gone. The curators knew where the records were, of course; they were sitting less than a mile away at 21 Panepistimiou Street in the vault of the Bank of Greece, where the curators had put them. And there they stayed.

Even if the records could be found, somehow they couldn't be found. When a frustrated Nazi officer ordered the entire staff of the Delphi Museum to appear before his staff one afternoon, the man asked their leader if he had a list of the Ancients in his possession. "I replied to him that there is a detailed and accurate list of the Museum's objects," the man said. "Then they asked me if it was possible to make a copy of the catalog, to which I replied that this is very difficult and I am unable to make a copy of the catalog." The museum director didn't report any threats from the Germans on this occasion, but many others would.

The director of antiquities in Athens admitted that the state had hidden the antiquities in the ground, as "there was no better possibility." Very well, responded von Schoenebeck, when could they be unhidden and displayed? "Retrieving part of the hidden antiquities is difficult," due to the fact that the pieces had been buried with the antiquities of other museums, was the answer from the minister of education. "It is not possible to do so without damaging these antiquities as well as without a large expense." Besides, the halls in which the relics would be exhibited were now "in many ways tilted or half-damaged." Were the curators supposed to allow the statues to topple over on uneven floors? Besides, the pedestals and pediments that the relics had stood on had all been destroyed (certainly true in a few cases, but there were plenty of stone blocks that could have served as temporary bases). Or the halls were filled with furniture, as parts of museums were being used for welfare offices or bomb shelters. Or the halls were on upper floors and the museum lacked lifts to get the antiquities up there. Even if the museums did have lifts, the staffs couldn't afford the movers to do the work; one official mentioned that this profession was populated by "mostly Jews," and no one had to mention what was happening to the Jews at that moment. And should the staffs by some miracle find strong-backed Gentile workers, those men were often malnourished and unable to work long days. If food was found for those workers, then the museums were short of "jacks, crowbars, ratchets, etc.," all of which the museums had possessed for years and used to bury their relics, but apparently, they had now disappeared. Then there was again the question of money. "Insurmountable difficulties" became a favorite phrase in the ministry's correspondence with the Art Protection Service.

As for choosing a selection of pieces to show the troops, there was more involved than you would have first imagined. "Because most of the ancient ones have been encased and placed in trenches and caves, choosing the best among them becomes almost impossible," the ministry said, as if curators had to see the sculptures in order to select relics they knew by heart. And even if the Ancients could be dug up, which they couldn't, they had often been "dismembered," and putting them together would take a long time.

These particular memos held a small grain of truth. People thought that vases and statues were pulled out of the ground intact; Hollywood movies always showed it happening that way. But this was often untrue. The marble statuettes, the bronze figures, and the terra-cotta relics were often found broken into dozens or hundreds of pieces scattered across a wide area. The pieces were documented, often photographed, then brought into museum workshops to be dry-fitted, with conservators moving the pieces around without using adhesives. It was like working a jigsaw puzzle, with conservators bent over long tables trying to match an edge to an edge, staring at the surface colorations, tool marks, even traces of original paint to find what went where. With marble pieces like the *kouroi* from the Archaic period, the workers looked for continuity in the natural veins of the stone or looked for patterns in the chisel strokes of the original sculptor. Bronze specialists looked at the patina, the alloy consistency, or the near-invisible seams that showed where the original sculptor had used the lost-wax technique. This all happened before a single piece was joined to another.

When the pieces were ready to be fit together, technicians often used natural substances like shellac, which was made by female *Kerria lacca*, tiny insects native to India and Southeast Asia. The insects sat on branches of host trees, like the palas or kusum, and probed along the bark with flexible, needlelike mouthparts known as stylets. When the insects sensed sap-rich sections, they pierced the bark and sucked up a quantity of sap through their stylets, then metabolized the sap and excreted a resinous substance through their bodies. The resin hardened when it hit the air and formed a strong coating over the insects and their eggs. Farmers scraped the substance off the tree branches and exported it along the old colonial trade networks. In hot, humid countries like Greece, shellac, which was strong and near invisible, held, and if a curator slipped up, it could be easily dissolved.

But during World War II, resin was in short supply, and the Greeks couldn't afford it.

The dialogue between the two sides felt farcical. There was a war on. Greek farmers were being barricaded in their homes and burned to death, along with their sons and daughters; Athenians woke each morning to fresh bodies on the street, handkerchiefs placed over their faces by early risers. The bureaucrats passed those bodies on their way to work, where they drafted polite letters about which second-century BC statues were available for viewing on guided tours. The Greeks knew what was happening, as did the Germans, but except in rare instances, each side proceeded with the business of antiquities as if they didn't.

The ministry's tone did sometimes turn frosty. In one letter, the director pointed out that, at the same time the Germans wanted to unearth some relics in Salonika, he'd received news from central Macedonia that a group of pieces recently removed from an eleventh-century Byzantine church had been dropped and "crashed badly." The statuary had contained "ancient inscriptions, many of which were unpublished texts that dispelled the darkness in Macedonian history." Now that darkness had returned, thanks to some cack-handed Nazis. Request denied.

Von Schoenebeck demanded a visit to the "hiding places"; perhaps at that point he just wanted to confirm that the statues were still there. After negotiations, the Greeks agreed and took him to the burial sites that could be accessed without breaking open museum floors. He confirmed the pieces were where they should have been and left. But in the weeks and months afterward, no statues came out of the ground. It would almost be possible to feel sympathy for the German archaeologist. The Greeks had protected their treasures from everyone from the Caesars to Napoleon, whose plunder was displayed at the Louvre. They had a real talent for it.

The Nazi bureaucracy had its own tricks. When a German soldier, perhaps digging a trench, came across a beautifully preserved fourth-century AD statue of a woman in Salonika, the Art Protection Service made a show of handing it over to the local authorities. The Greeks accepted the find and installed it near the Arch of Galerius and the Rotunda, the latter a circular monument dating from the same century as the newly unearthed piece. It was exactly how the administration of new discoveries should have been handled all along, and it was celebrated as a model operation. "There was a lot of noise about it in the press," one observer wrote.

But soon after, Hitler's office in Berlin announced that the statue was being transferred to Germany. Even Hans von Schoenebeck was shocked. He "raised an objection, as the arranged transport was completely contrary to the rules and principles of the Art Protection Service." He was angry enough to bring the matter to his superior; he pleaded his case before the Wehrmacht "with as much emphasis as possible." He lost. The Führer's office demanded delivery of the statue.

One morning, von Schoenebeck was arguing with a Greek official in his office. He said that in World War I, the French had "dug everywhere in Macedonia without permission." The official replied that the French had been constructing trenches at the front line, and this was different from excavating in Athens.

"No," von Schoenebeck replied, "they dug everywhere, and far from the front."

"Let's accept that this is how it happened then. You find the thing right and worthy of imitation?"

"No," von Schoenebeck admitted, "but I remind you that it is war and that the military's fighting spirit is courageous and bad-tempered when it thinks that it is doing a commendable work of civilization, as is the case here." The generals believed they had a right to dig, and they got angry when it was countermanded. There was little else to be said.

Ordinary museum employees who tried to protect the artifacts walked a fine line. When a series of brightly colored statuettes attracted the admiration of German soldiers in one museum, leading to the statuettes slowly disappearing one by one, the curator moved the collection into a dark corner of the room, "where, lying dormant, there is hope of them being saved." Germans often responded to such gestures with threats; they complained that "the Ancients are their own" and that they were "blood-heirs to the antiquities." The Greeks, in effect, had stolen the pieces from *them*.

Late one night, a guard in Corinth witnessed two Nazis absconding with a key to his museum. He ran to tell his boss, the "keeper of the antiquities," who went to the mayor and the police. They said they couldn't help. He reached out to the American School and to the German authorities, who opened an investigation. Soon after, German soldiers came to arrest the night watchman and questioned him for ten days. It turned out the two soldiers had claimed they were innocent victims of "enemy propaganda" and hadn't stolen a thing.

Custodians and janitors and directors fought the thieves, sometimes physically. "Many times, my head was found under the fists of German and Italian soldiers," wrote one worker, "in order to prevent them from taking various materials of the Museum." More than one low-level employee felt that protecting the Ancients was worth their life; they could be tenacious. "Most of the times I succeeded," the worker reported with evident satisfaction.

The Nazi classicists who'd come to Greece set to work, digging their pickaxes into the Greek soil in order to finally prove that ancient Greece had been founded by Aryan people. Hitler's chief theorist, Alfred Rosenberg—who'd originated many of the foundational Nazi creeds, including its racial theories and hatred for the Jews—ordered his team to Thessaly in central Greece, where previous digs had uncovered major finds from Neolithic and Bronze Age times. Rosenberg was hopeful that his men, led by the famous Nazi archaeologist Hans Reinerth, would pull from the ground "pre- and protohistoric Germanic and Slavic finds" that would at long last prove the connection between ancient Greece and the early Germans.

In June 1941, archaeologists arrived on Thessaly's hot plains in military trucks; they traced out trench lines and ordered their Greek prisoners or workers to begin digging. They hadn't asked the Greeks for permission to excavate, and the normal techniques were abandoned; no classicist measured the soil depths or recorded where each object came from or its relation to other artifacts. This was closer to archaeological strip-mining than traditional excavating. But it did produce results. Artifacts began appearing almost immediately: gorgeous fragments of pottery patterned in brown and taupe, axes, obsidian and flint blades, clay ovens, bone tools, ornaments, beads. The Rosenberg dig was a massive undertaking; under a piercing sun, dozens and dozens of workers bent over the trenches, plumbing the soil with their trowels and shovels, sifting the dirt in shaker screens, and hunting for small relics. The team found and stored away scores of artifacts each day. By December, six months into the dig, they'd pulled from the soil more than ten thousand relics completely denuded of their history and meaning.

In the middle of the excavation, Reinerth sent a message to Berlin. The mission was a success. In one part of Thessaly, his workers had uncovered a megaron, a rectangular great hall common to ancient Greek palace construction, that dated to the late Neolithic Arapi period. Reinerth was called in to study the foundations of the building; he concluded that they bore a striking resemblance to early Nordic designs. The early Germans had been there thousands of years before Christ, making their way into Thessaly from the north. The team packed up their tools, boxed up the antiquities for shipment to Germany, and left the trenches.

It was a crowning achievement for Rosenberg and his audacious theories. The missing link had been found.

CHAPTER 15

Giannaris

John Giannaris's landing craft bobbed on the sea off the coast of Greece near the island of Paxos. One of the officers alongside him clicked his flashlight on and off; in the darkness, a small light blinked in response. A motor coughed to life and a white line of surf traced in the blackness. It was a boat; Giannaris climbed down a rope ladder onto it. Within minutes, he and his commandos were standing on the shore.

The guerrillas that met them wore bandoliers of bullets crisscrossing their chests and the traditional *kaltsodetes*, the strips of black cloth wrapped around their calves over stockings; these men were reminiscent of the ancient Trojans Giannaris had seen in picture books as a boy. "At last, I was in the land of my progenitors," he said later. Giannaris found himself too moved to speak. In the dark, he reached down to the sand and picked up a handful of dirt, then squeezed it tightly in his hand.

The commandos were not, by and large, concerned with antiquities. Most of these Greek Americans probably did see the Acropolis or the *Discobolus* in their mind's eye when thinking about the country, but they weren't classically minded. Still, with thousands of stolen artifacts leaving Greece in the rucksacks of ordinary soldiers or in the vehicles or trunks of officers, they would serve a second function that most of them were unaware of: stopping the theft of relics by killing the Nazis stealing them.

The Americans packed their loads and began walking. When a Greek partisan asked Giannaris's name, he said, "Yannis" (John). He didn't want to mention his last name; he had aunts and uncles and cousins living in Greece, and if news of his arrival traveled, he didn't want them on a list. His father's home was already occupied by a Nazi officer, though the commando didn't learn this until later.

With their supplies loaded on mules, the Americans marched fourteen days to their base, avoiding main roads as they hiked. Even with their training in the Colorado mountains, the commandos found the terrain to be treacherous, and filled with ambush points. Giannaris's fellow commando Andrew Mousalimas parachuted into northeastern Greece with his Group IV soon after Giannaris went in. On the trek toward their base, Mousalimas found himself at the end of the column, responsible for watching for ambushes from the rear. The unit medic handed him "bennies"—Benzedrine tablets—to keep him alert but had to cut him off when the drug made Mousalimas "obnoxious."

Giannaris passed through towns he remembered from his Greek school; later, his unit would skirt the edges of Thermopylae on a mission, the place where the Three Hundred had sacrificed themselves against the Persian army. As a good Greek boy, he knew that if he ever lost his compass or his guides, he could lead his men by the monasteries that dotted the landscape. In Orthodox churches, the altar was always placed to the east.

The commandos—along with the other units and agents who had landed at about the same time—were given a pocket history of the war by the *andartes*. One operative remembered being accompanied by a particularly knowledgeable guide.

> *On his insistence, I had to see every burnt and pillaged house in every village and it was a pretty harrowing experience. It's horrible enough to have to look at pile after pile of rubble or a seemingly intact house with the few sticks of furniture remaining smashed beyond repair—but with the whole village following at my heels, men groveling in the burnt wheat they'd just harvested, women stoically showing me a charred family relic, and a few getting hysterical, it was really hard to take. They all looked to me for help and I knew that there was nothing that I—or anyone else—could do for them for the time being. I started off by trying a few hollow words of sympathy but they seemed so stupidly inadequate, I quit.*

When they came to a dried-out lake called Limni Xinias that had hosted several Wehrmacht camps, an *andarte* told Giannaris that months earlier the Germans had taken the 103 villagers and machine-gunned them there. The men passed a mound of loose earth, the mass grave. Giannaris called a halt and announced to his unit that they would be taking no prisoners. They were going to kill every Nazi soldier they came across.

Giannaris was astonished at how sparsely the country was settled. The men marched for hours without seeing a single farmhouse, the only sign of human habitation being the *kandylakia*, or tiny shrines in the shape of chapels, that dotted the path. To keep their spirits up, the men broke into the Greek songs the native commandos had taught them, including "*Koroydo Mussolin*," or "Mussolini, You Fool." When they did come across a tiny village, the Greeks were terrified. These tall, strapping Greek Americans, whose faces were familiar yet not familiar and who dressed in strange uniforms with a strange flag on the shoulder, appeared like aliens out of the brush. One courageous man approached Giannaris.

"Who are you?" he asked in Greek.

"I come from America," Giannaris said.

"How far is America?" the man said. "How long have you been walking? A month?"

"Longer."

"Oh, my God. Is America that far?"

The rural areas seemed as if they'd been untouched for centuries. That one had to cross an ocean to reach Greece from America was unknown to many of the people Giannaris met; many of the children had never seen or tasted chocolate until the commandos shared theirs. The amount of equipment the Americans carried was almost embarrassing. The *andartes* improvised; they didn't have mine detectors, for example; in fact, they'd never heard of mine detectors. Instead, they captured turtles and sent them crawling toward German positions. When they heard an explosion, they knew the path was clear.

Sometimes the men came across leaflets or handbills dropped by the Greek Desk, part of a psyop campaign to get Germans to surrender:

GERMAN OFFICERS!

For you and your soldiers the war is lost. Think about your situation: when the German army marched into Greece, Yugoslavia was overrun. Italy, Bulgaria and Rumania were your allies. The still powerful Luftwaffe protected you from heaven, and U-Boats stood watch along the coast.

But now: rearmed Yugoslavians and Greeks seek revenge, and your lines of communications are cut off. Italy is lost. The long retreat to the Brenner is nearly to end. Rumania and Bulgaria are turning against you. The Russians built the connection with the National Liberation Army of Yugoslavia, and your last overland route is gone.

Once settled near Papas, Giannaris began preparing for the commandos' first missions. The men each carried a comb that contained a file that could be used for sawing through a fuse or, if they were captured, for cutting a rope around their hands. In their packs were handkerchiefs that, when dipped in water, revealed a map of Greece printed in invisible ink. Their wool pants had one fly button that, when the cover was popped, revealed itself to be a compass. Secreted in the heel of one of their boots was an "escape kit": gold sovereigns that could be used to buy food or to bribe Greek policemen while the men were hiding. The final item was the most ambitious: a ballpoint pen that didn't write but instead shot a single .22-caliber bullet. The kit expressed the OSS's concern that a fair number of commandos would be captured in action.

When their radioman checked in with Cairo, the unit received its first target: the Athens–Salonika line near the station called Kaitsa, where the tracks ran across a low-lying valley before rising through the mountain passes. Giannaris ordered the men to take a handful of ashes from their cooled fires, mix it with a bit of water, and cover their hands and faces with it. He did the same. He took an empty pack of American cigarettes—Camels or Lucky Strikes, most likely—and placed it in his pocket. After their mission was over, he would drop it on the ground to show the Germans that the sabotage had been carried out by Yanks. Villagers he met on the march had begged him not to stage attacks near their homes, as the Nazis would come and exact retribution. This was his way of protecting them.

The men marched for three hours, followed by mules toting three hundred pounds of explosive. When they arrived at the station, Giannaris scouted the terrain and pointed to where he wanted his squads to go. At eleven p.m., they moved out of their hiding places and began laying the charges along the joints of the track, where one length of rail met the next. They worked steadily, placing C-1 and C-2 plastic explosives along a full mile of track and at the bases of telegraph poles they encountered on the way. A German pillbox squatted nearby, with a long horizontal slit that ran nearly from side to side. It remained dark. Other sentries watched the rail line for signs of the Panzer-Zug, an enormous, heavily armored train car that sped up and down the line, launching flares into the air and firing at the enemy with 88mm mortars and 20mm antiaircraft guns. It was the thing Giannaris feared the most.

The men pulled back and ignited the detonator chain. At the first package, a gout of orange fire spilled out into the blackness, followed immediately by a sharp, flat cracking noise. The lines of explosives blew. Flares went up and searchlights swept the hills; the pillbox slit erupted with tracers from an MG-42 machine gun, long dashes of flame lacing the dark. The Americans returned fire, then melted back into the dark hills, the tracks curled and broken behind them.

When they were back in Papas, one of the soldiers took Giannaris aside. He told him about the talk the commandos had had with other units back at Camp Carson, about how he'd been voted most likely to be fragged. The commando said that after seeing the power of the German forces and the care the *andartes* took to avoid them, the men felt differently. There was danger here; his severity was appreciated.

Giannaris and his men kept to the hills while the Germans held the cities, towns, ports, and rivers. The unit slept on the ground, which occasionally rumbled with earthquakes. A few of the commandos shivered with malaria; the others found water from cold springs to cool their fevers.

They became amateur ambassadors. "In the eyes of these people," Giannaris said, "I was America." The *andartes* would come around just to marvel over their Colt pistols and to trade intel. The conversation often turned to what Greece would be like after the war. "How often do you have elections?" the insurgents asked. "Do you have a king?" Giannaris said no. The Greeks were amazed by this. They wanted the same: to vote for elected representatives, to get rid of their dictators and their royals, who by the way weren't even Greek.

Giannaris was diplomatic. He said that, once the Nazis were gone, he was sure the birthplace of Western civilization would take care of its citizens; what the country had given the world would be returned to it tenfold. But in his heart, he felt differently. Before he'd arrived, he'd read newspapers and listened to the BBC. He knew what these Greeks—so cut off from the modern world that they'd never been taught that America lay across the ocean, so poor that they collected the tin cans that his soldiers threw away—had been kept ignorant of. When the Germans left, the British would work to install a rightist government and bring back the king. Nothing in the lives of these villagers would change; their children would grow up as hungry and misgoverned as they were. Or if the Russians reached the Balkans first, they'd live under a tyrant. Democracy was far away. "I said all these things," Giannaris remembered, "but deep down I could see the handwriting on the wall."

It pained him to think about it. Even the commandos were compromised in a way. One of the soldiers who'd joined his unit at Camp Carson, John Tsouderos, was the son of the Greek prime minister in exile and friendly with King George II, the man those *andartes* despised. When they arrived, Giannaris had to leave Tsouderos behind in northern Greece, as the unit was headed toward a pro-leftist region. But word still got out. "When they discovered who my father was," Tsouderos remembered, "it got a little touchy." A guerrilla walked up to him one morning and put a gun to his head. Only after the Americans pleaded with him was the *andarte* convinced to let Tsouderos live. Giannaris revered justice-seeking Diogenes; he wanted to be a righteous man. But if he helped free the birthplace of democracy from the Nazis only for it to revert to darkness, what was he really?

Once, while traversing the hills with his men, Giannaris entered a village where a British major was waiting impatiently for a local to saddle his horse. The major shouted orders at the Greek, who gestured in confusion at the unfamiliar English. The major's frustration mounted. He grabbed his swagger stick and lashed the man across the shoulders.

Giannaris was passing by. He turned and walked to the British officer and told him not to mistreat the locals. As he spoke, he grabbed the man's blouse and drew him closer.

The officer took great offense. He told Giannaris he would be court-martialed.

"Where are your witnesses?" the American answered.

The major pointed to the commandos. Giannaris turned and asked his men if they'd seen anything. They shook their heads.

Giannaris left the major with a threat: if he touched another Greek, Giannaris would come back and whip him. It was a moment of intense frustration and impotence; he'd done nothing really. As soon as the Americans were out of sight, the major would treat the Greek however he wanted. Like Rodney and Dorothy, Giannaris knew who had the power here, and it wasn't him and it wasn't the Greeks.

Giannaris was a single kinetic piece in the Greek Desk's map.

Andrew Mousalimas's unit blew up bridges, ambushed SS patrols, and aided in the rescue of British and American aviators. When a pilot shot down over Greece needed exfiltration, Mousalimas and the others created landing strips in the midst of olive groves and bare plains. With Cairo, the men would arrange a spot for the rescue planes to land at night when the Germans were less active. When they heard the soft drone of engines in the dark, they lined up in two parallel lines wide and long enough for a plane to land between. They created lamps by pooling kerosene in old cans and positioned them every thirty feet on both sides of the "runway." As the throb grew louder, an officer called out and the men stooped and lit the kerosene with their lighters. The dots would erupt in flame, and the pilots would nose their aircraft down, scoop up the aviators, turn and taxi, then vanish again into the blackness.

CHAPTER 16

Operation Honeymoon

By mid-1944, Rodney was overseeing a daunting array of missions: Emerald concentrated on the German occupation and organized stay-behind agents on the island of Samos; Helios funneled nautical intel to MI6; Dago (the Greek Desk was not always wholesome with its mission names) watched over ship movements in the Dodecanese; Lucian surveilled the ports and the Gestapo; Oracle studied road transport and connected Rodney with *andartes* on Mount Parnassus. OSS agents built four airfields, brokered agreements between the leftist factions, ran hospitals, and published an underground newspaper. One team even spied on the *andarte* leadership and reported bits of political gossip back to Rodney.

Early in 1944, Washington cabled a new request: to track down rumors about a new German rocket bomb, the V-2, that could reach London. It was rumored to be housed in airfields in Greece. Could Rodney help? He could.

To supervise the mission, he turned to George Skouras, a millionaire Greek American film executive who'd volunteered to play a part in the war. Skouras and his two brothers had gone to St. Louis around 1908, worked as busboys and bartenders, saved their money, and bought nickelodeons; they made a fortune, moved on to movie theaters, and made another. George eventually took charge of United Artists Theatres, and his brother Spyros took over 20th Century Fox. The brothers were rich, important, and supremely well-connected, and George wanted a job commensurate with his position. "Subject desires above all else to go into Greece," wrote an OSS officer who met with George in 1943. "He is confident that he can talk the warring factions out of their strife." The OSS turned George's peacemaking mission down. He'd now become something of an agent without a portfolio.

"Phalanx has informed us that the secret radio-controlled bomb is at the Mikra airfield," Rodney wrote to Jack Caskey. "We are planning to send a special mission of two specially-trained persons to try to get hold of this." Skouras sent the agents to check the airfields where the V-2 was supposedly hidden. One of them, X-6, reported that he had made it to the airstrip after "being pursued by the Gestapo, from which he escaped last week by drawing his pistol and threatening to shoot them." There was no flying bomb there. The V-2, if it had ever been in Greece, had been moved.

Skouras tried to find out what the mystery weapon actually was. The OSS tapped the spy Moe Berg, ex-catcher for the Boston Red Sox and "the brainiest guy in baseball," who spoke twelve languages and boasted a photographic memory. Under the cover of attending a lecture by the German physicist Werner Heisenberg, Berg traveled to Switzerland, met with an Italian scientist who'd worked on the V-2 project, obtained technical papers from him, and translated them. "These torpedoes, to be launched at very high speeds (about 500 to 600 Km/h) by fighter planes, were being made at Fiume, Naples and Spezia," he wrote his handler. "[The scientist] has offered to prepare blueprints on the wing designs resulting from experiments in the field of velocity 9.92 to 2.25 velocity of sound, but this would necessitate concentrated effort and the aid of a draughtsman for the period of a month."

Skouras collected the intel from Berg and his own sources and created a portrait of the superweapon. Rodney forwarded the information to London.

> *The weight of the bomb is estimated to be 1700 pounds. It has a wing span of approximately 10 feet and is about 10 feet long. This bomb consists of three parts: the nose of the flying body, the body itself, and a cylinder.*
>
> *Around it is a spun netting of fine copper wire which collects and forms into a cable, connected with remote control steering arrangements. Its forward part resembles an automobile cooler or radiator. Its after end is compressed and has conical shape.*
>
> *It is logical to assume that this very important missile is strongly guarded. . . . The receiving unit inside the bomb may be detonated if detached by amateurs.*

The Brits now knew what they were facing.

More and more of Rodney's important missions revolved around a single theme: protecting the coming invasion of France and the hundreds of thousands of American and Allied soldiers who would execute it. One risk to the invasion was close to the Greek Desk's area of responsibility, and it had been looming over the operation for months. It was now too pressing to ignore.

On the night of October 26, 1943, the phone next to the bed of the German diplomatic attaché Ludwig Moyzisch began ringing. The thin, quiet, and currently exhausted Moyzisch rolled over and picked up the receiver. It was the wife of Albert Jenke, first secretary of the German embassy in Ankara, and his boss.

"Would you please come round to our flat at once?" Jenke's wife asked. She wouldn't reveal the reason.

Mrs. Jenke wasn't only the wife of Moyzisch's colleague; she was the sister of Joachim von Ribbentrop, Germany's foreign minister. Von Ribbentrop was important and his sister was highly strung; the combination could have caused issues for Moyzisch. He said he was coming, placed the phone in its cradle, and began to dress.

When he arrived at the Jenkes' home, he was shown into a darkened room where heavy curtains had been drawn over the windows. There, sitting in an armchair, was a balding man with arresting dark eyes. Moyzisch sank into an armchair opposite him. The guest, who didn't give his name, ignored him and went to the door. He paused, turned his head, and put his ear next to the lacquered wood. After a moment, he grasped the doorknob and yanked the door open and peered both ways down the hallway. Only after this melodramatic touch did he walk back into the room and sit down.

"I can give you extremely secret papers," he said. "The most secret that exist." They would be coming from the British embassy. Would that interest Moyzisch?

The German's business cards announced him as a diplomatic attaché at the German embassy, but that was only a cover. He was a spy; he directed the Nazi intelligence effort in Turkey. And that evening he was not overimpressed with the man fidgeting in the chair across from him or with his offer. Moyzisch guessed the man was a petty criminal looking for money. But his boss at the Sicherheitsdienst (SD), the Nazi intelligence agency, had been pressing him lately for "hot stuff." Perhaps this mystery man was in possession of some.

"Do you have the documents with you?" he asked.

The Turk scoffed. Was he a dunce who'd carry classified British documents through the streets? He'd been planning this for years, he said, and would supply the documents when the payment had been agreed to. He wanted twenty thousand pounds to begin.

The two worked out an arrangement. On October 30, the dark-haired man would phone Moyzisch's office at three p.m., calling himself Pierre. If Moyzisch was interested, the Turk would meet the attaché in the embassy garden near a caretaker's hut, and he would bring with him two rolls of film of top secret documents.

The man stood to leave. As he passed by Moyzisch, he grasped the German's arm at the elbow. "You'd like to know who I am. I'm the British ambassador's valet."

The man's name was Elyesa Bazna, and he was telling the truth. A failed singer, failed taxi driver, and failed husband, he'd worked for the American military attaché in Ankara, but soon became sexually fixated on the colonel's wife and resigned. He moved on to work for Albert Janke, the husband of the woman who'd made the phone call to Moyzisch. Bazna was ambitious, nervous, and not a very good person. He began photographing Janke's correspondence (he called it "poking my nose in") and showing the pictures to his wife in order to impress her. He wasn't thinking of selling the photos, not yet; he was simply an inveterate snoop. Janke fired him.

Bazna drifted aimlessly around Ankara for a while. He liked to hang out in the lounge of the Palace Hotel, sipping coffee and leafing through newspapers as if he were a dignitary or an agent without a portfolio, someone important. He had few prospects, except finding another foreigner to serve as a personal assistant, with all the humiliations attendant to the position. Something inside Bazna told him he was better than that. A thought popped into his jealous mind. *Why not set up as a spy?* The idea "fascinated" him and he could not escape it. He tried to distract himself by looking again at the newspaper in his lap. One of the first things he saw was an ad: "Driver Wanted for First Secretary of British Empire." Bazna, of course, played fast and loose with the truth, so this account of the opportunity following hard on the inspiration could be just a story. But whatever the chronology, he felt a door open.

He got the job. With his first paychecks, he bought a Leica, which he hid in a saucepan in the kitchen of the secretary's home. When the secretary and his wife were out at a party, he took the time to drink the man's brandy, go through his briefcase, and photograph some documents.

On the thirtieth, Moyzisch walked into the garden and headed toward the curator's hut. Bazna was waiting with two rolls of film for the attaché. Moyzisch printed out the photographs and brought them to Franz von Papen, the German ambassador to Turkey. Von Papen was gobsmacked: the documents promised they'd unearthed "a priceless source of information."

Bazna, now code-named Cicero, worked for the British ambassador, Sir Hughe Knatchbull-Hugessen. On his first day, the ambassador's butler had given Cicero a tour of the residence. Left in Knatchbull-Hugessen's bedroom, the valet could resist his impulses only for a moment; he soon went through the man's dresser, where he came across a bottle of sleeping pills. Later, he moved on to the man's cache of top secret cables.

The next batch of documents the attaché brought to von Papen were minutes from the Third Moscow Conference, where American,

British, and Soviet officials were meeting to hammer out their plans for the war's endgame. It was still going on as von Papen read the reports. Clearly, Cicero was in a position to give the Nazis top secret information nearly in real time. The Germans quickly paid their new operative thirty thousand pounds (more than $2 million today), which Cicero placed under the rug in his tiny room at the embassy. He enjoyed walking across the carpet, feeling his newfound wealth under the soles of his feet.

The news of this superspy electrified Berlin. Could Cicero be real? Or was he just a very good double agent? Moyzisch was summoned to Germany, where he was questioned closely; the film was taken to a laboratory for analysis, the documents examined by four experts. When no inconsistencies were found, a photography tech was sent to Ankara to process the film as quickly as possible.

Cicero, driven by motives the Germans couldn't quite make out, became consumed by his work. Photographing the documents became "like a drug he could not resist." When Knatchbull-Hugessen slept, Cicero crept into his bedroom and removed memos and letters from a black box sitting on the ambassador's night table; he was gambling that the pills the diplomat took every night would keep him under long enough for the theft to go unnoticed. He took the documents back to his room, snapped them with the Leica, then returned them. Hours later, when Knatchbull-Hugessen awoke, Cicero was there with a glass of fresh orange juice, which he left on the night table while he ran the man's bath. The diplomat suspected nothing.

Cicero was passing new rolls of film every few days: when one revealed that the Turkish president was meeting with Roosevelt and Churchill, Berlin buzzed. They hadn't known the Turkish leader had left the country. Cicero also revealed that the Allies had agreed that Germany's unconditional surrender was the only acceptable outcome of the war. When the Tehran Conference began with Joseph Stalin added to the lineup, Hitler and his lieutenants were reading the minutes just days after they were typed up.

The spy photographed top secret cables and telegrams between the embassy and London. He passed on accounts of meetings between Churchill, Stalin, and Roosevelt; bombing plans; and code words. The Germans used his intel in putting together Operation Long Jump, the planned assassination of the three leaders in Tehran, which was spoiled when Soviet agents uncovered the plot. But his most important information related to Operation Overlord, the code name for the invasion of Normandy.

In one of his nighttime prowls, Cicero snapped a photo of telegram no. 1751 from the British Foreign Office. It was marked "BIGOT," the highest security rating, and it contained the text of a message sent from the British Chiefs of Staff to General Dwight D. Eisenhower detailing the Allies' intent "to get Turkey into the war" and "maintain a threat until Overlord is launched." Even a junior analyst could have parsed the meaning: Overlord was not aimed at the Balkans, and the "threat" of an invasion there was stagecraft, cover for the real landing spot. That left France as the most likely destination.

The SD sent the document to Berlin, where Hitler studied it. It narrowed the timeline down. "I have mostly studied through these documents," he wrote. "There is absolutely no doubt that the attack in the west is coming in the spring." But *where* would it come?

The Allies first got word of a possible mole in December 1943. It came from an informant at the Hungarian legation in Stockholm. The Cairo Conference, where Churchill and Roosevelt had discussed the war with Japan with Chairman Chiang Kai-shek of China, had recently wrapped up. The informant told the Allies that the Germans knew everything that had happened during the talks. The intel reached Allen Dulles of the OSS; the leak seemed to be coming from Ankara, which meant that either the Turks or the Brits had a mole. From there it went to General Donovan to FDR and finally to Churchill, who ordered an investigation into the British embassy.

A security team hurried to Ankara, where they met with an annoyed Knatchbull-Hugessen, who resented the implication that his team was leaking secrets. The security agents invited Cicero in for tea, during which they asked him for sugar, speaking in German. Cicero adroitly answered that he didn't speak German, and the spy catchers dismissed him, thinking he was "too stupid to make a good spy." Meanwhile, Berlin was reading Cicero's "extremely valuable" intel and asking for more of it. Moyzisch forked over another ten thousand pounds.

The hunt for the mole put a crimp in Bazna's spying. He was already richer than the vast majority of people in Ankara, yet despite the investigation into Cicero's identity, he kept at it. "The thrill of playing with danger held me in its grip," he said. "I thought that things would go on like this forever."

In fact, he was already under suspicion. An unstable German secretary turned spy had latched onto him. Her name was Cornelia Kapp and she worked as Moyzisch's secretary. In a matter of a few months, the Greek Desk would become intimately acquainted with her.

CHAPTER 17

Platon

As Cicero passed intel to the Abwehr, a man named Nikolaos Platon on the island of Crete watched nervously over his museum, the Heraklion. At thirty-four, Platon was a trained classicist with a PhD from the École Pratique des Hautes Études in Paris; he'd served as the director of antiquities on the island for years and discovered the Minoan Palace of Zakros there. This "mild-mannered," "unassuming" scholar was currently at war with a German general.

When the German commander Julius Ringel arrived on the island, he installed himself in the relic-stuffed villa of the famous British archaeologist Sir Arthur Evans and began looting it. As his soldiers packed away Minoan statuettes and vases in straw-lined crates, Ringel ordered Platon to hand over the keys to his museum. The scholar refused. Instead, Platon began sleeping at the facility to prevent the Nazis from stealing its relics. The Germans threatened him but as of yet had decided not to press the matter.

Ringel did get into the nearby Stratigraphical Museum, saying he wanted to study the relics excavated from the palace of King Minos. Instead, he began removing them. His soldiers took sledgehammers to "perhaps the most important funerary monument belonging to the most brilliant peak of the Minoan civilization, the Royal Tomb." They destroyed the memorial, crushed the stone, then used it to build several houses for the Wehrmacht administration. "Undoubtedly," wrote Platon, "history will write down in black colors the destruction of this unique historical monument."

Ringel ordered an excavation of his own, a dig for Aryan relics. At the same time, Heinrich Himmler ordered excavations in ancient Sparta to look for Doric and pre-Hellenic relics with telltale Germanic features. The work was done without any scholarly rigor, the artifacts simply yanked out of the ground. Their location within the sediment and their relation to one another were all lost. "When you have power over life and death," one German officer admitted, "then it seems a simple matter to take a stone or make off with a statuette."

Furious, Platon stepped up his low-level war with Ringel. He sent the German a list of artifacts that had been reported missing. "Since, according to the countless archaeological laws, no object can be removed from museums and collections without official permission," he wrote the general, "we ask you, Mr. General, to give the necessary order to bring the mentioned objects in a short time to be re-exhibited in their place."

Ringel ignored the letter. Platon stormed into the palace and walked into the general's office. The German glanced at him, then looked away, not deigning to acknowledge his presence. Platon later heard that Ringel had chartered a military airplane to transport the first cache of his thefts to Germany.

The curator was persistent, even reckless, in his demands. "He wasn't a fearless man," said Platon's son, "but in this case, he conquered his fears absolutely. He was a man who gave everything to what he loved. . . . Saving antiquities was something he saw as a duty." Platon became so incorrigible that the Nazis finally threatened him with death if he didn't stop.

One morning, the archaeologist was handed a typewritten note. It came from the villa and was signed "those monitoring the general's movements." Platon guessed it was from one of the Greeks who worked as a servant there. It was a list of stolen goods:

1. A headless Hellenistic statue
2. A fragment of an urn with reliefs
3. A head of a male statue
4. A fragment of a stone slab with a relief depicting a man
5. One bronze sword
6. Three lamps
7. Various semifinished stones of the Minoan period
8. A vase made of steatite stone of Minoan art. South Villa storeroom.

Platon wrote the items down on a master list he was keeping of the relics leaving the country.

After months of mutual vitriol, a delegation of junior German officers came to see Platon. Ringel was being reassigned to a posting outside Greece. It was good news for Platon. However, the officers were searching for a going-away gift and had lighted on the idea of giving him "an important antiquity." From the Heraklion. Did he have any ideas?

Platon was astonished. "As a gift of gratitude from the city!" he wrote. The archaeologist said absolutely not. Ringel had stolen enough

Above: The fifth-century *Discobolus*, adored by Hitler
Public Domain

Below left: Jerome Sperling before the war
Courtesy of Ridley Sperling

Below right: Rodney Young as a young archaeologist
Author's collection

Above: Dorothy Cox, bottom right, and other archaeologists in Athens
Courtesy of the Trustees of the American School of Classical Studies at Athens

Below: Greek curators repairing an ancient bronze statue
Courtesy of National Archaeological Museum Archives

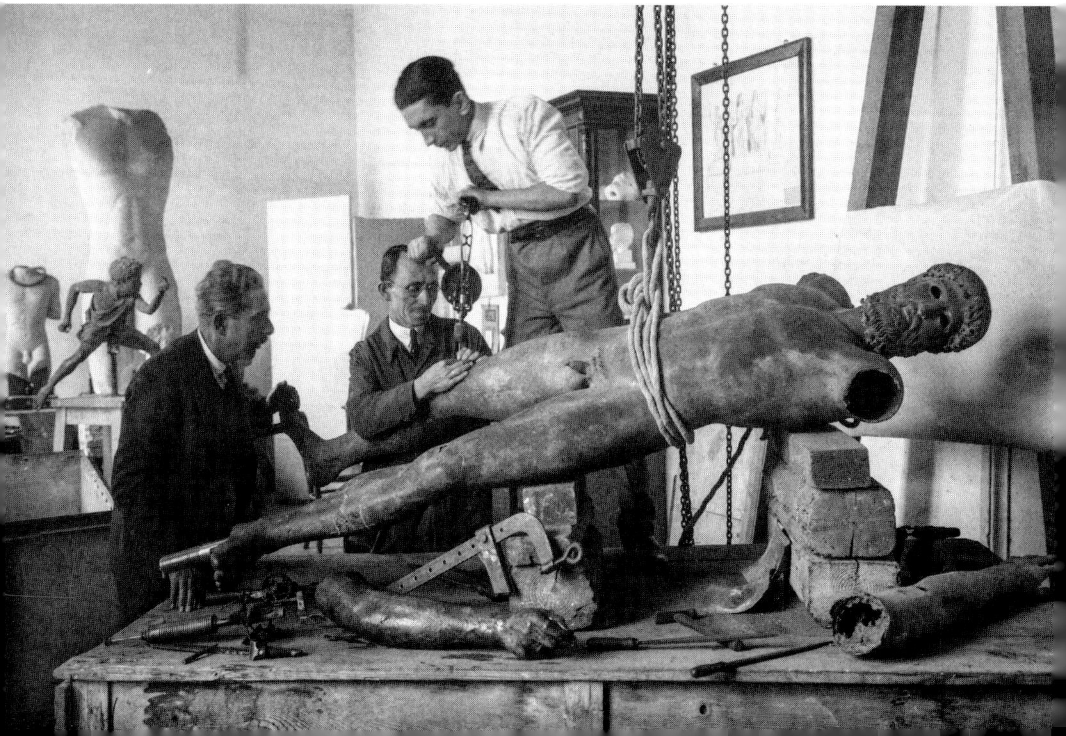

Above: Marble statues awaiting burial at the National Archaeological Museum
Courtesy of National Archaeological Museum Archives

Below: Boxing up large relics before the arrival of the Germans
Courtesy of National Archaeological Museum Archives

Above: A trench awaiting artifacts
Courtesy of National Archaeological Museum Archives

Right: Workers using a scaffold to lower a statue into the ground
Courtesy of National Archaeological Museum Archives

Below: The empty halls that greeted German officers when they visited the National Archaeological Museum
Courtesy of National Archaeological Museum Archives

Right:
The swastika being raised over the Acropolis
Courtesy of Bundesarchiv

Middle:
Greek American commandos training at Camp Carson, Colorado
Author's collection

Bottom left:
General William "Wild Bill" Donovan, head of the OSS
Public Domain

Bottom right:
Greek *andartes* and American commandos
Author's collection

John Giannaris (circled, center) with Greek and American fighters

Author's collection

Andrew Mousalimas

Courtesy of the Mousalimas Family

Above: Captain John Giannaris

Author's collection

Below: Helias Doundoulakis

Courtesy of the Doundoulakis Family

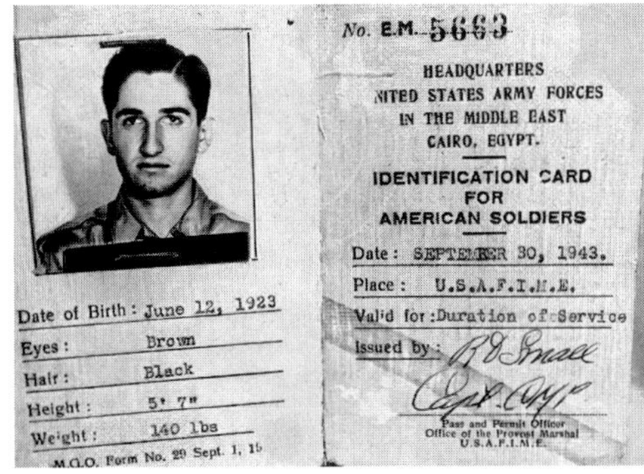

No. E.M. 5663

HEADQUARTERS
NITED STATES ARMY FORCES
IN THE MIDDLE EAST
CAIRO, EGYPT.

IDENTIFICATION CARD
FOR
AMERICAN SOLDIERS

Date: SEPTEMBER 30, 1943.
Place: U.S.A.F.I.M.E.
Valid for: Duration of Service
Issued by:

Pass and Permit Officer
Office of the Provost Marshal
U.S.A.F.I.M.E.

Date of Birth: June 12, 1923
Eyes: Brown
Hair: Black
Height: 5' 7"
Weight: 140 lbs

M.O.O. Form No. 29 Sept. 1, 1

Above: Roland Hampe after the war
Public Domain

Below: George and Helias Doundoulakis
The Doundoulakis Family

for a dozen generals; the damage he'd done to Cretan culture would be difficult to repair. The Germans left, fuming.

They didn't give up, sending soldiers to repeat their request. Platon must have begun to fear what the officers would do to him, or the Heraklion, if he didn't come up with something. Finally, he sent word to the palace that he agreed to hand over an icon to the general. He'd had an idea. He consulted with his craftsmen, who concurred. They would give the German fakes.

First, they selected a handful of small relics from the hidden collection—Platon never specified what they were, but most likely he chose small Minoan statuettes or icons. The artisans carried them down to the workshop in the basement equipped with chisels, lathes, and other tools of the trade. There they cleaned each relic thoroughly. They chose "parting lines," natural seams on the statues that divided them into two sections. Next, they molded clay beds to serve as bases for the statuettes; possibly they added blocks around the bases to support the molds.

The artisans applied a "release agent" to the statues, petroleum jelly, and coated the marble in the viscous balm to ensure that the statues, after being encased in plaster, would break cleanly from the molds. Then they mixed a batch of plaster and poured a layer over the statues' features, pushing it into the idols' crevices.

The layer was left to set. When it had dried, a second layer was poured, and a third. Perhaps the men added burlap or twine to the plaster to give it strength. Once all the layers had set, the artisans took knives and cut along the parting lines, then split the molds in two and opened them up. The artisans lifted the new icons out, cleaned the molds, then glued the two halves of the molds back together. More plaster was poured into the hollow structures and "negatives" of the molds were created. Once they dried, the casings were broken open and Platon and his men had clean white reproductions of the originals.

He presented the copies to the officers, who were beside themselves with anger. How could they give the relic-obsessed Ringel fakes? "They explained to me that they would come to the Museum 'to make a mess of it,'" Platon said. He held his ground, however, and eventually, the officers relented, took the reproductions, and presented them to Ringel. "According to reliable information," Platon said, "he showed them in his homeland as real antiquities."

Platon's inspiration found its imitators. A studio in the center of Athens became a factory for imitation relics to sell to Germans, many of whom were far less discerning than Ringel. Sculptors and technicians worked in secret to furnish the market with salable pieces, and much of their work remains secret. To produce the imitation relics, they first had to acquire marble. The most likely source was the Penteli quarries near Athens. Pentelic marble—famous for its beautiful fine grain, slight translucency, and warm white tone (sometimes with a faint golden hue)—was the workhorse of classical Greek sculpture. The Parthenon had been built with it, and the quarries were still active two millennia later. A sculptor who wanted a good-looking imitation could either find fragments from older projects or source a fresh block from the quarry and have it hauled to the studio.

There was a thriving black market in Athens for everything from bogus documents to fake IDs and adulterated olive oil. Relics joined the list. Sculptors who'd labored on restorations of old friezes and facades were around and out of work; some were half starving. Before the war, a neoclassical craze had swept through Athens; artisans were told to make new buildings in the city look old. Sculptors became experts in faux-Doric columns and noble-looking busts. Over the years, they'd mastered the ancient styles, even down to the wear patterns that centuries of use would leave on a piece of stone.

One of the favorites among the German soldiers were *portraits archaïques*, small oval or round likenesses of aristocrats or goddesses done in marble. Perhaps they reminded the soldiers of their loved ones back home, or perhaps the tiny pieces were simply cheap. Once the little portrait was carved, the sculptor could take pumice or sandpaper to wear down the high points on the stone, a nose or an ear, until it looked as though the piece had lain out in the wild for centuries, exposed to wind and rain. Applying vinegar with a rag would eat into the stone, pitting the surface and dulling the lambent glow of the Pentelic marble. But too much would cause the stone to fizz and "melt"; it took an old hand to get the decay right. Tea or tobacco juice gave the patina a yellow or brownish touch, and rust mixed with water, pounded into a paste, would streak the piece with the reddish-brown lines that exposure to iron gave real antiquities. Some sculptors held their work over flames, which covered it in soot; then they wiped most of it away, leaving smoky traces similar to the ones on the offering Rodney had found on Lycabettus hill. Another technique was to actually bury the items in the ground so the acids and fungi could work on them—though we don't know if the Athenian sculptors did this for their fakes. It was known that placing copies near manure piles or streams produced especially good results. For larger pieces, a sculptor might hack off an arm or a nose and even attempt an obvious repair, suggesting a beloved older piece that demanded a higher price. Copper sulfate gave marble a greenish tint, the result of oxidation. There were a thousand ways of aging a thing.

Once finished, the items were moved onto the street, where accomplices called over passing German soldiers to show them a special piece. German soldiers, eager for a keepsake or an investment, snapped them up. "They sold like hot cakes," said one female sculptor. "We made a lot of money." After the war, collectors would sometimes find that the pieces they'd bought at rock-bottom prices from German officers were, in fact, made circa 1943.

Some artisans surely used the proceeds to feed their families. One admitted she was "ashamed" of the work, as the Ancients were being prostituted for money. So she donated the proceeds to the resistance, which soothed her conscience. The drachmas the German soldiers paid went for guns and bullets.

CHAPTER 18

Cornelia

Cornelia Kapp was born in Berlin in 1919, but moved to Cleveland, Ohio, when she was six. Her diplomat father, an Abwehr agent, had taken an assignment there as consul general. By the late 1930s, he was collecting information on which Ohio factories were being retooled to make guns and tanks and what the mood toward Germany was. Ohioans said that Kapp "was the hardest man in Cleveland to see" and that he kept a life-size portrait of Hitler hanging in his office. What Mr. Kapp did or did not believe about Hitler would later become a topic of conversation within the Greek Desk, which settled on the idea that he "was driven temporarily insane by the conflict between his convictions and his sense of duty." Meanwhile, Cornelia was adapting well to Cleveland; her friends were American, as was her first boyfriend.

When war came, the Kapps were sent back to Germany, then on to Sofia, Bulgaria. Allied bombing raids sent Cornelia racing down into air raid shelters; when she reemerged, there were dead on the street. (Cicero, in his reports, had accurately predicted the bombing raid.) She grew anxious, so her father found her a place in Ankara at the German embassy, typing letters and opening mail for Moyzisch.

Like her father, Cornelia was intrigued by espionage and wanted to pursue it for the country where she'd felt most at home. She sought out a well-connected Jewish dentist and asked him to put her in touch with the Americans. What she wanted in return was a chance to return to the country and live her life there after the war.

Cornelia found Moyzisch to be fairly oblivious. He "fell for all my play-acting" and turned over the keys to his safe; she used them to read through his confidential telegrams and copied down lists of German agents in Turkey and other midlevel intel. As the weeks went by, Cornelia noticed that every Friday when a certain person phoned, the attaché would usher everyone out of the office and take the call himself. Clearly, something important was afoot. She gathered that whoever was calling Moyzisch was connected to the British embassy and had a code name: Cicero. After work, Cornelia staked out Moyzisch's rooms and once spotted a figure whose face she couldn't see slipping into the garden. By the time she ran out, he was gone.

But soon after, in March 1944, through a combination of observation and highly effective snooping, she narrowed the search to Bazna. He was Cicero. And he was passing intel about Operation Overlord to the Germans.

To get a fair estimate of Kapp's importance, one has to insert her work into the complex equation of Cicero as a spy. His authenticity was the subject of debate in Berlin. Moyzisch, von Papen, and others believed the agent's documents to be genuine. Von Papen called the intel "immensely valuable," because of the "the intimate knowledge it gave us of the enemy's operational plans." With Cicero ruling out an invasion through the Balkans from Allied bases in the Mediterranean, the supreme command might concentrate fully on France—if the Führer approved. "We were thus able to appreciate the intentions of our enemy in a way that could hardly have a parallel in military history."

But for intel to be effective, it has to be believed. Von Ribbentrop, the minister of foreign affairs, insisted the cables and letters were forgeries. The SD and their clients, including Hitler, wavered on Cicero. One reason was that he was supplying so much information. It awoke in German analysts a feeling of overkill: how could a Turkish valet have access to all this information? The obvious answer was that he was a double agent being run by MI6. If Cicero had been more discerning or simply less productive, he might have been taken more seriously.

Intriguingly, von Ribbentrop might have had other reasons for his position. The Cicero papers made it clear that Germany was losing the conflict. Even von Papen realized this. "It had become absolutely clear to me," he wrote in his autobiography, "as a result of reading all the Cicero telegrams, that I must do everything I could to hasten the end of the war." The relevant telegrams, however, weren't shown to Hitler. Von Ribbentrop might have cast aspersions on Cicero in an attempt to keep the Führer's thoughts away from the worsening military situation.

If Cornelia had been captured, that analysis would likely have changed. But in what direction? She would have been interrogated and tortured. If she had confessed, one thing would have been clear to the Germans: Cicero was not a double agent. If he had been, the Americans wouldn't have needed Kapp in the first place. Her search for Cicero's real identity proved the Allies didn't control the valet. It's possible the Germans would have suspected an even deeper plot: what better way to trick the enemy than to have another agent working for the Americans investigate Cicero? But that level of complexity seemed unlikely; the OSS was hardly as sophisticated as MI6, and even for the Brits, it would have been a reach.

It's difficult to say exactly how Berlin would have reacted to Cornelia's insights; there were simply too many variables, and Hitler's reasoning when it came to D-Day didn't always track the best intelligence available. But if Cornelia confessed and Cicero's work was taken as authentic, the implications could have been far-reaching. After the war, the British Foreign Office evaluated the risk this way: "It [Bazna's intelligence] provided the Germans with streams of information from the desk of the ambassador about British and Allied intentions in the Near and Middle East and for the conduct of the war generally, and might easily have compromised Operation Overlord."

In the spring of 1944, Cornelia was becoming increasingly unstable. She read letters from her brothers, who were fighting for Germany, and broke into howling sobs. Perhaps the stress of her espionage work was affecting her; if she were caught and sent back to Germany, she'd be taken to a concentration camp or executed. Perhaps she liked the attention—the embassy's press attaché called Cornelia "a specialist in nervous breakdowns." But the threat of being caught was a burden for a young woman already prone to being neurotic. And in fact, Cicero had begun to suspect her. One afternoon, in the lounge of the Ankara Palace Hotel, he spotted the secretary deep in conversation with a youngish man. In a fit of paranoia, he rushed home to his room at the British embassy, swept back the rug, and packed the cash into a suitcase. The Leica he threw into a nearby river.

Disturbed by his secretary's frequent outbursts, Moyzisch was looking for a way to get rid of Cornelia when she suggested an Easter trip to Budapest, where her parents were living. The attaché immediately agreed. On April 6, she would take the Istanbul train and then catch a flight to Budapest. He told her he'd meet her at the Ankara station to say goodbye. In fact, the Istanbul plan was a ruse concocted by the OSS and the Greek Desk to get Cornelia out of Turkey.

The oblivious Moyzisch drove to the station to make sure Cornelia left on the overnight train. He slipped the ticket clerk some cash to assure that she got a seat; then he waited by the locomotive, which chuffed out clouds of steam. As the departure time approached, he began to scan the platform more closely. Where was the girl? There was no sign of her distinctive blond bob among the porters' caps and the fedoras. He walked up the platform to the end, then back. He felt an unnameable dread rise up in his thoughts like air bubbles.

The conductor cried out a last call for passengers, then bound up the iron stairs into one of the cars. The train moved off slowly. Moyzisch turned and walked briskly to his car. He raced to Cornelia's apartment, where her roommate answered the bell and told him that the secretary was gone; she didn't know where. Moyzisch marched into the apartment, opened the door to Cornelia's bedroom, and found it empty except for a worn-out coat. Her clothes, her documents, all missing. He began to panic; no one visiting Budapest for a week took all their possessions with them. He hurried to see von Papen and told him that Cornelia was missing under suspicious circumstances. The ambassador was as furious as Moyzisch had ever seen him; the SD man had seemingly been tricked by a secretary. "In that case it meant ruin for me and possibly even death," he said. "A concentration camp, almost certainly."

Moyzisch cruised the streets of Ankara, looking for Cornelia. He rousted her acquaintances, revisited the railroad station, sat, and thought. He called the German consulate in Istanbul and told them to wait for the train; perhaps she'd boarded at another station. If she appeared, she was to be arrested immediately. He checked with a friend at the Turkish foreign ministry and asked him if a young German woman had been taken to a hospital or reported as a suicide. His friend said no.

The train arrived in Istanbul, and the blond wasn't on it. She had vanished. Back at his office, he ignored the calls from Cicero, who had heard rumors of Cornelia's disappearance and was dealing with his own escalating panic. Moyzisch composed "the most difficult signal of my life," informing Berlin of the disappearance and mentioning that she could now be under the care of the British. He notified his agents and subagents to keep watch on the ports, train stations, and airports and offered a substantial bounty for her capture. He issued a warrant for her arrest with the clichéd but quite rare postscript that he would take her "dead or alive."

CHAPTER 19

The Train to Istanbul

At that moment, Cornelia was in the hands of the OSS. She'd arrived at the apartment of her American contact; remarkably, it was the same young man who'd been her first boyfriend in Cleveland. The two had stayed in touch and ended up in Ankara by happenstance. When he opened the door, he found her near hysteria. "I've got to get out!" she cried. "You have to get me out!"

The man grabbed his coat. Fearing the Nazis would trace her to his flat, he hurried her out of the building, then shuffled her from one apartment to another over the course of a long night as he searched for a more permanent hiding place. Finally, he stowed her in the flat of two secretaries from the U.S. embassy. When the women's boyfriends visited, the secretaries hid Cornelia under the bed and told her not to say a word. The OSS told the women to make Cornelia over: if she was going to be extracted from the city, she had to look like a different person.

The secretaries bought some hair dye at a local drugstore, then found scissors. They sat Cornelia in a chair and clipped her hair short, then took her to the sink and applied the dark tint. One secretary couldn't get the dye off her hands and so had to call in sick at work the next day. They were terrified when the bell rang that morning; they stowed Cornelia under the bed again, only to find it was the secretary's boss at the door checking up on her, a bouquet of roses in his hand.

When it was time to move, the OSS contact arrived with a uniform; it was from a Wren, a British support worker. Once they dressed her, the man and the two secretaries took the risk of bringing Cornelia out on the street. The trio was walking briskly down an Ankara street when a pedestrian crossed their path. It was Cicero. He recognized the strange man he'd seen with Moyzisch's secretary in the Ankara Palace Hotel, but he was now with a brunette with short hair. Only when he studied the woman's gait as she walked away did he realize it was the same girl: Cornelia.

He found a phone and dialed Moyzisch. *I've found her,* he told the attaché, *and I want my reward.*

German agents were combing Ankara looking for Cornelia. The OSS had to get her to Cairo and quickly. But how? Nazi agents were stationed at the main transportation hubs in Ankara, looking not only for Cornelia but for any Allied officers who might have been helping her escape. The task of getting her out—and to the Greek Desk—fell to Lieutenant W. Ewart Seager, the assistant to the American military attaché. He devised an intricate, ticktock plan.

Seager went to the train station and stood on the platform waiting for the Taurus Express, which ran two lines, one north to Istanbul and one south toward Syria. Both trains came steaming into the station at the same moment. As soon as the doors on the southbound train opened, Seager walked aboard, turned and strode through the cars, turned again and exited a few doors down, then dashed across the platform and hopped on the northbound train. As German agents swept through the southbound train, then emerged onto the platform, the northbound conductor pushed a button to lock the doors and the train pulled away.

Meanwhile Cornelia, now dressed in stylish clothes and with a face covered in makeup, like a posh American girl on a Middle Eastern tour, was being hustled into a car by some boisterous workers from the U.S. embassy who'd scooped up the three women for an impromptu party that was really a cover to get her out of the city. In Cornelia's purse, she carried "Q" pills, cyanide, to be taken if she was arrested. Talking loudly as they exited the apartment, the men handed the three women into their sedan as if they were headed for a local tavern for a spree, then turned the car north. They'd been told to meet the northbound train at its first stop, in Ayash. There they'd hand Cornelia over to Seager, who was currently on the Istanbul train.

Before getting to Ayash, the lieutenant had thought carefully through the next steps. He found the conductor and struck up a conversation. He told the man he'd just gotten married and he and his bride were headed to Istanbul for their honeymoon, but complications had arisen. His bride and their wedding party had gotten to the station late and missed the train. They were hurrying to meet him at Ayash. Would the conductor give him a few minutes to get her and her luggage aboard? As he said this, Seager slipped the man a small stack of Turkish liras. The conductor expressed his readiness to assist the course of immortal love.

They pulled into the station. Seager dashed out as Cornelia emerged from the car. He snatched up her luggage, then escorted his bride to the compartment as the conductor looked on approvingly. Once they were aboard, the conductor locked the train doors. Seager got Cornelia into her berth, hoisted her luggage onto the overhead rack, then sat down and slipped her something: a loaded pistol, which she quickly hid in her fashionable jacket. He'd also thought to bring a bottle of Scotch; Cornelia, already prone to anxiety, was sure to be twitchy. She took a large shot, lay down on her berth, and announced she was going to be sick. As Seager waited in the corridor, the sounds of Cornelia retching clearly audible, the conductor came up to him with a sympathetic look. "Don't worry too much," he said. "They're often like that on the first night."

The car Seager and his "bride" were traveling in was decoupled from the Taurus Express and headed to Balikesir, where the pair detrained; Seager suspected Moyzisch would have agents watching the platform in the larger city. Seager had arranged to spend the night there. The next day, British military officers loaded them on a truck headed to Izmir, where the Greek Desk, in the person of the archaeologist Jack Caskey, took over. "Subject was in a seriously depressed nervous state," Caskey wrote, "knowing that her life was in danger from agents of the SD and officers of the German Embassy." Despite her high-strung condition, Caskey, who was known to be a bit of a rake, remarked on how beautiful the fugitive spy was.

Caskey thought MI6 could help get Cornelia out of Turkey. He arranged an interview with Rodney Young's nemesis, Rees. The aristocrat didn't disappoint. "That girl is German," he told Seager. "I'll have nothing to do with her. The only good German is a dead German." He refused to lend a hand. She was Caskey's problem now.

The archaeologist knew a good place to stash Cornelia: Dorothy's apartment. The harbor was aswim with rough-voiced sailors, prostitutes strolling along the piers, and peddlers and sketchy characters of every kind; the clean-cut groom and his pale, lovely bride would be among the more respectable people there. Cornelia, shaken by the meeting with Rees, was now so distraught that Caskey feared what she would do to herself if left unguarded. He posted a round-the-clock guard at her door while he plotted their escape.

A British acquaintance proposed the Aleppo train, on which

Cornelia could blend into the hordes of escapees and asylum seekers heading south. But Caskey mistrusted the trains; they'd gotten lucky with the Taurus Express and might not again. Instead, he would use the humble caïques that had been the workhorses of the Greek Desk's missions. Together with a British officer and a Turkish security agent, Caskey left Izmir at ten fifteen p.m. that night, picked up Cornelia and Seager, then headed to the OSS port of Boston in Chandarli, Turkey.

The place was bustling as they pulled in; men were shouting instructions in English, Greek, and Turkish, caïques were being loaded, supplies checked, sails mended. Caskey requisitioned a vessel called the *Mary B*; he saw to its provisioning and secured a Greek crew. On April 17, they glided out into the Gulf of Izmir. After hauling aboard food and gas at the next OSS station, Key West, they waited nervously for dawn to attempt the Samos Strait. At four a.m., the captain gave the signal, then puttered forward at six knots.

Behind them, back in Izmir, Caskey's agents reported unusual activity. A boat pulled into town and disembarked a number of Nazi operatives, including "one sinister Oppenheim character whom the telegrams describe as 'HUNCHBACK RPT HUNCHBACK.'" The consul general's Mercedes, down from Ankara, made an appearance. Vehicles associated with the German consulate drove past the entrances to Key West and Boston again and again. One stopped in front of the Key West gate; four agents emerged and began, of all things, picking daisies in a nearby field. Another operative strolled over to the guard and asked about the caïques bobbing on the tide just offshore. What the Germans were doing in the area was never confirmed, but it was likely they were there to see if they could catch Ms. Kapp at her last stop in Turkey. The next day, the local newspapers reported on the "feverish attempts" of the Germans to snatch the girl.

Cornelia felt better being out on the water and away from her pursuers. Despite a damaged propeller, the boat made respectable progress on the way toward Cyprus, a stopping point on the way to Cairo. Meanwhile, Moyzisch was ordered back to Berlin. His last night before departing, he stayed in a room at the Park Hotel in Istanbul. The phone rang. It was a British intelligence agent who'd somehow found out his room number. Returning to Germany was madness, the man told Moyzisch. Why was he going? It was quite possible he would end up in a concentration camp or dead. The agent suggested an alternate plan: if the attaché defected, the British would take care of him and his family for the rest of the war.

Moyzisch hung up. The phone rang soon after with the same voice on the other end of the line making the same offer. Moyzisch again put the receiver down. A few minutes later, more ringing. Finally, the depressed attaché took a knife and cut the phone line. "Was I perhaps beginning to doubt my own powers of resistance?" he later wondered. He left for Berlin the next day.

The escape made headlines across the world: "Daughter of German Ex-Consul Here Takes U.S. Refuge in Ankara," read an April 24 story in the *Cleveland Plain Dealer*. "While sources of information declined to discuss why Miss Kapp had been taken over by American authorities," the article said, "the assumption in Turkey was that she possessed information of considerable value." The *Toronto Daily Star* reported that she'd "deserted to the Allies" but gave no reason for her escape, while the *Manchester Evening News* in the UK did: "It is thought that romance may have had some connection with Fraulein Kapp's disappearance. It is known that she was in love with a deserter from the German Army." There was no German lover; whether this was simply bad journalism or a rumor put out by the Greek Desk is difficult to say. Caskey never reported feeding any story lines to the press, though von Papen did spread the word that

Cornelia was mentally unstable. In any case, Caskey had managed not only to get her out of Turkey cleanly, but to keep her connection to Cicero secret.

Word had reached Cyprus as well. When Cornelia's boat sailed into the port, her OSS contact had to scramble to stop it and redirect it to a harbor where she was not yet so well-known. The Greek Desk brought her safely to MI6, who whisked her away to Cairo by plane; there she was debriefed. Seager, who'd gotten her out of Ankara, wrote Caskey about "the mad, glad news" and complimented him on the precision of the operation, "at a time when we few Americans are reputed to be quite inept at skullduggery." Rodney sent his hearty congratulations as well.

It was a clean win for the Desk, a "bright spot of efficient smooth cooperation in a somber world of snafu." D-Day was six weeks away; a major threat to its success, the exposure of its true destination, had been neutralized.

CHAPTER 20

Salonika

Helias's partner Cosmas proved true to his word. His web of old friends began supplying the spies with reports on German troop movements, weapons and their locations, and cargo ships and troopships arriving in the port or sailing out. They also looked into rumors of American and British hostages being kept in the city. Helias even found an informant who worked as a janitor in Gestapo headquarters, though he was closely watched by his German guard. Their contacts made other contacts until Helias had a web of informants reporting to him daily.

Every morning, Helias would write out the transmission in simple words. Underneath the words, he would write out the lyrics to a song the OSS had told him to memorize. This was his cryptographic key. Once he had finished the ciphered text, he donned the headset, listened for the ghostly tap of the Cairo radio room, then tapped out his messages without spaces.

Helias was so busy that he ignored the training he'd received at the spy palace. His fake ID still contained the address that Dorothy had picked out of a phonebook back in Izmir. It was for a waterfront hotel, not a residence. Dorothy had specified that once an agent was in-country, he had to reapply for a new document: "The home address on the identity card must always agree with the place in which one is found." Helias, intent on growing his network, had let the matter slip.

A maximum of two messages could be sent on the wireless set on any given day. Any longer and one was "inviting the Gestapo for dinner," as field agents put it. Only in emergencies could a third message be sent and only after changing the frequency. This would cause any triangulation truck prowling nearby to have to scramble for the right spot on the electromagnetic spectrum, giving Helias perhaps a minute to get the final message out and then get off the air. Once he was done transmitting, he would take the radio from the table and hide it in a small hole under the floorboards covered by a piece of cloth.

After a couple of weeks of successful transmissions, Helias's fear level began to drop. The neighbors, even the German officers, had accepted him and his team as ambitious young Greek men making their fortune in the wholesale wood business. Helias dared a night out on the waterfront, where the men sat around a table at a seaside restaurant and, under the night sky, ordered a feast: shrimp, clams, fried potatoes, ouzo. The gold sovereigns he'd carried with him from Egypt were burning a hole in his nylon belt.

The men ate, laughed, and told stories about the close calls on the journey. It was a lovely night and they drank it in. Pedestrians strolled by, taking the evening air. A group of elderly Greeks came ambling by the restaurant; they glanced at the heaps of food at Helias's table and the grins on the men's faces. Incensed, they began to shout. "The day will come when you traitors will pay with your lives," one cried. "Eat now, you pigs! Soon you will be hanging from the trees."

Helias was startled; he said nothing. But after the group had passed, he realized the picture he and the others had presented: feasting like Ali Pasha, the hated Ottoman despot who'd earned the epithet "Semiz" (or "fat") with his rich banquets. Who else could they be but collaborators selling out the Greeks to the Gestapo? He chastised himself: how arrogant and blind could he have been? He was no longer in Cairo living at the home of the king's family. He'd received training on projecting the right image to the Germans, but little on fooling the Greeks, who might turn on him just as easily.

They wouldn't do this again, he said to Cosmas: no more expensive dinners, no more carousing. But Cosmas told him he was wrong. He wasn't thinking deeply about the social milieu. Any local who was making a lot of money in the black market would naturally flaunt it, splashing out cash so that others could seethe with jealousy. "We are behaving as all Greeks do," Cosmas said. To make money and live poorly would have been more suspicious, more un-Greek, than blowing it on a lavish meal.

The advice agreed with Helias, perhaps too much. "My friend's way of thinking bolstered my confidence to such a degree that I lost my fear." He took dance lessons three times a week, learning the rumba in the middle of a war. To keep in shape, he walked over to the nearby "Alexander the Great" pool and swam laps. He even slept with his beautiful landlord, the widow Sultanitsa. The "peasant boy from Archanes," as he described himself, began living like a Greek playboy with a shipping magnate father. "I just wanted to savor life," he said, "at any cost." There was another reason for his behavior, one he would admit to only after the war. He was convinced he was going to die in Greece.

One day at the pool after finishing his laps, Helias was lounging in a pool chair, feeling the oxygenated blood flow through him. He heard German voices. He opened his eyes and looked over. Two German officers had sat down next to him, ready for sunbathing. They'd noticed Helias's watch, the one the American soldier had given to him in Cairo, and they were talking about it.

Helias forced himself to say the first thing that came to mind. He turned toward the men, rotating his wrist so they could get a better look at the timepiece. "I received this watch from a German soldier," he said. He'd paid for it in fresh eggs and nuts. The guy must have taken it off an American officer or prisoner. Beautiful, wasn't it?

The words all just flowed out of him. His voice was strong and his hand was steady as the Germans stared at the watch. Helias chatted a bit more, then said goodbye and began walking home, "amazed at my impromptu fabrication."

Helias surprised Sultanitsa with bags of food from the market, parading down the street loaded with groceries. In a hungry city, the gesture did not go unnoticed, especially as his new girlfriend began telling her friends about the handsome, generous young American who'd apparently fallen madly in love with her. His neighbor across the street, the daughter of a professor, began turning up at the house; when he returned from the factory in the late afternoon, she would be there. Her father had apparently convinced her to make Helias's acquaintance. One night, Helias heard singing outside his window; he opened it and looked down. The girl was serenading him, like a lovestruck Juliet to her Romeo. Sultanitsa was furious, but Helias, still enmeshed in the dream of life that had begun at the palace, thought only of how sweet the woman's voice was.

Late one afternoon, while walking down Tsimiski Street after sending his three p.m. transmission, Helias passed a music store; in the window was a Hohner accordion. Hohners were German made with a distinctive reedy tone; the blues musician Lead Belly had made them famous in America. Growing up, Helias had always wanted to play the instrument, but his parents hadn't had the money to buy one. He walked into the store and asked how much it was.

"The accordion is not for sale," the salesman said. The Hohner was the only one in the store—in fact, the only one in Salonika. The salesman wouldn't even quote him a price.

"I have money," Helias replied. The salesman doubted that. Helias appealed to the manager, who told him to go home. Instead, he returned the next day with twenty gold sovereigns from his OSS stash and walked out the door with the Hohner. He began to accompany his neighbor in her nightly concerts, playing outside his house in the little lane, drawing even more attention to himself.

He did obey a few of the rules of his training. When Sultanitsa asked if she could work for him, he refused; he even refused to tell her where he went every morning. He didn't want to connect the two portions of his life, which was basic tradecraft. Intel was flowing in, and he was making his daily transmissions, but he was breaking one rule after another. He was spending money that couldn't be justified by his firewood business. He flashed gold sovereigns in public places. In the neighborhood, Helias became known as the "business-minded boy" who would make a fine husband. Young women from surrounding neighborhoods began gathering under the window to hear him play.

Cosmas was furious with him. Fearing sending the man into a fresh rage, Helias hid the fact that he hadn't updated his ID, something that could have gotten the entire team arrested. Getting a new one was tricky; making fake identification cards was punishable by death. One morning, Helias took out a pen and tried to change the address by hand but succeeded only in poking a hole in the paper.

Finally, he confessed to Cosmas, who was too horrified to be angry. He told Helias to lie low while he worked on getting him another card. Helias obeyed; he even gave up the nightly concerts with great regret.

While Helias was riding the trolley one day, the conductor announced that German soldiers were looking for partisans and that everyone aboard would be checked. “Have your IDs ready,” the man called from the front of the car. Helias felt successive waves of panic wash over him. Two German officers began working their way through the passengers; he watched them move down the aisle. Cursing himself for his flightiness, he took out his wallet and slipped the paper out. When the German officer handed back the card of the man in front of Helias and looked at him, he held out the ID, his thumb covering the hole. The officer glanced at it, then at Helias’s face, and slipped past.

When he returned to the factory and told the Greeks the story, they shook their heads in wonderment. One of them laughed. “Helias, for you, the war should never end.” But the trolley incident had sobered him; he’d been extraordinarily lucky. He curtailed his spending and attempted to appear less conspicuous.

Now, on returning to Sultanitsa’s place in the late afternoon, he would pause at the corner and dawdle as if he were enjoying a last bit of night air before going inside. Perhaps he lit a cigarette and savored the smoke. He studied the street. Were the housewives standing outside their doors gossiping with the neighbors as usual? Were kids playing? If so, he went on home. If not, he would go to a rooming house at the top of the hill, then send word to Cosmas that he needed to leave Salonika.

At the factory, he approached the old woman who lived in the gatehouse. He’d been giving her little gifts of olive oil and other household goods. Now he asked a favor. “It’s not easy to run a business in wartime,” he told her. His competitors wanted him to fail; they might send saboteurs to burn a pile of wood or make an accusation against him with the authorities. “Would you mind keeping an eye open for suspicious people or Germans who force their way . . . into our yard?”

The woman agreed. He told her that if she spotted anyone lurking nearby, she should open the shutters on the windows facing the street. That would be his signal to walk past the gate without entering.

One day, after finishing breakfast, Helias headed out to the factory. Threading his way through the low-slung neighborhood, he felt a creeping sense of unease. He thought back to his training. After turning a corner, he spotted an alleyway just ahead. He ducked into it and waited. A figure passed. It was Sultanitsa tracing his footsteps to the factory.

Helias slipped out of the alleyway and caught up with his girlfriend, turning her to face him. "If you ever do this again," he said, "I will move out of your home." He left her there and walked on.

However careful Helias was being now, he wasn't careful enough. Around this time, Rodney received worrying news from Salonika about a man connected to Helias's network. On April 25, a deciphered transmission crossed his desk: "Our agent Constantinos ALEXIADIS, resident of the village TRIAS . . . was arrested by members of the Gestapo. In spite of the pressure which the Germans exercised upon him he did not reveal anything, although he knew personally all of us and a number of some other sub-agents as well as the house where the W/T [wireless] set was installed." The man was "sent to Germany with a consignment of other prisoners."

The man had kept his secrets, but the Gestapo was clearly aware of Helias's network. "Our task is more difficult than we thought at first," Rodney warned his operatives. "It requires all the thought and discussion we can bring to bear."

CHAPTER 21

Viea

It had been three years since a boisterous Rodney Young raced an ambulance around the Epirus front with dash and brio. By mid-1944, he'd changed. The job had taken a toll on him, as it had on almost everyone on the Greek Desk. The archaeologists were unique among OSS operatives in that they all had a personal connection to their theater of action, to individual Greeks whom they loved and respected, and it showed. His fellow operatives were buckling under the workload. "WHAT A LIFE," one wrote him in February 1944. "If this goes on much longer, I am going absolutely and completely nuts."

Among Rodney's headaches were the agents. Some Greek operatives were timid; one radio operator had to be replaced because he was too scared to broadcast. An agent reported that his operator "suddenly asked urgently to have the radio. I asked him why he wanted the set; he answered that he wanted to use it to listen to the news." The operative had to explain that they were not there to hear the evening program on the BBC. The Greeks also imagined that the Americans, so powerful and so rich, could get them anything they dreamed of. One asked for a "female bicycle" to be sent via caïque. "I was afraid that if I accepted to send that she would be asking for a baby elephant next," Rodney grumbled.

Virginia Grace, the beautiful amphora expert whom Rodney might or might not have had a romance with, sent Rodney a letter asking for work advice. Clearly, she trusted him, but whatever had happened between them at the start of the war had soured her in the many months since they'd parted. "Don't feel called upon to be kind," she wrote, "as I would not believe it was you writing if you did. Love, Tig." Even Dorothy was sometimes intimidated. "Dear Rodney," she wrote him in a handwritten letter, "I am very nervous and unsure as your letters sound so angry with me, and I am afraid that whatever I write will be misunderstood." She was face-to-face with Greeks every day; Rodney was not. "You must realize the emotional pressure which these people exert is considerable."

Rodney felt Washington undervalued them all. As talented amateurs, they often weren't respected, even though Dorothy's intel was considered the gold standard for Greece. Perhaps their passion for saving the country was sometimes seen as verging on the melodramatic. "The trouble with you archaeologists," an intelligence officer wrote to a Greek Desk agent at one point, "is you are all prima donnas."

Rodney was increasingly short-tempered, sometimes with reason. When he got wind of criticism of the Greek Desk back home, he wrote his OSS superior that the agency had brought them to the battle late and hamstrung them when they got to the war theater. "Many of us here feel that we would like to be turned loose with a machine-gun in Washington," he wrote his boss, who himself was in Washington. In March, fed up with various machinations of his higher-ups, he sent in his resignation letter. In it, he wrote that he felt "personally responsible" for his operatives. Caskey, for example, "was working himself nearly to the point of exhaustion"; most of the agents were.

> *We in the office here are supposed to work an eight-hour day; we work a ten-hour day because that much time is needed to get the work done—so that the recruiting and training, equipping, sending off, communicating, and supplying of bases may be done. We could work eight hours, then say the hell with it, that's all we are paid for, and go sit in Shepheard's bar for the rest of the day.*

Rodney himself felt "twisted into the shape of a corkscrew" with stress. He was, in some ways, badly suited to administration. He longed to be out in the field, ideally in Greece, where he could release his suppressed rage on the enemy. He'd been far happier in his Hemingway days driving the ambulance and charming nurses.

Many of the other agents felt the same way, and sometimes they acted on their feelings. Rodney was forced to play the schoolmarm, continually reining his men in. At one point, he learned that one of his American lieutenants working on a mission code-named Pericles was thinking of abandoning his post in order to go into Greece and train radio operators, a riskier and much more fun assignment. "I think it might be well to point out to Dick," he wrote, "that he was sent to Smyrna because he was needed there and that if he wants to go off in the field having adventures and shooting Germans, he is not the only one who has those feelings, and that if everybody went off in that foolish way the Germans would very soon win because nobody was sufficiently responsible to stay at home and do the work that has to be done."

He was no better really. Early on, he tried to head to one of the OSS bases, then to the Greek island of Samos. The mission would have built morale, he said. Rodney was so looking forward to being out of the office and on the water, rubbing shoulders and drinking whiskey with the men. But when he told his superior in Washington, "his hair stood right up on end." The trip was denied: "too dangerous of getting intercepted and caught by the Germans on the way, and being made to tell all." When he pressed the matter, he was told there were certain actions by officers, such as taking the risk of being captured, that could result in court-martial.

Occasionally, the anger turned inward. "I must say I am good and sick of all these businesses," he wrote, "and wish I were dead. There seem to be very few people around here who think it is more important to get a job done than to fight each other."

General Donovan declined Rodney's resignation; he was too valuable to the war effort. The fraying archaeologist stayed on.

George Doundoulakis, known as X-53, was among the best agents Rodney had. He'd pulled together small teams of ten or twenty subagents to watch trains heading to Salonika and count ships in the harbor in Volos; operatives kept an eye on the shipping lanes near the island of Skiathos, contacting Rodney whenever a convoy of German ships was approaching. Rodney passed the reports to the Allied air command, which sent squadrons of planes and "completely cleared the Aegean of German shipping."

Doundoulakis quickly gained the full trust of the guerrillas and was even allowed to use the *andartes*' caïques. When one transmission was deciphered, Rodney found X-53's team was asking for explosives, guns, food, and clothes—as well as "a mimeograph machine, a field telephone, radios and two hundred gold sovereigns a month" to extend their network all the way to Salonika. The field telephone alone would have required at least five miles of wire. "They have been very busy and [are] suffering from megalomania," Rodney wrote. But they produced.

That summer, George sent a transmission: a troop train would be moving north on the Athens–Salonika line. John Giannaris and his men geared up, marched thirty miles in fourteen hours to get in position, and camped near the town of Ipati, known for its therapeutic hot springs. Giannaris timed the German patrols and, after darkness, placed plastic explosives on the tracks. His team and he would wait for the train and kill as many of the Germans on board as they could manage.

Giannaris laid his ear on the track and heard nothing. The moon shone down from a wind-picked sky; the wait went on for hours. Giannaris began to wonder if the intel was off. He could see blooms of orange flame far off in the valley; Greek towns set on fire by German patrols. He laid his ear on the track again. Now he heard the sound, a kind of low, fretful hum. He spotted the train moving across the valley lit up "like a Christmas tree."

But something was off; the Germans never traveled that way. Giannaris called to his men to pull the explosives off the tracks.

A civilian passenger train slipped by, with Greek faces staring out at the gray-on-black landscape from the brightly lit interior. Giannaris thought how close he'd been to killing them.

A few minutes later, another rhythmic hum sounded on the rail. The bazooka team retook their places and the demolitions men hustled toward the tracks. The darkened train clattered toward them. When it was close enough, Giannaris heard a loud *phoosh* and watched a burst of straight orange flame spear into the boiler. The thing exploded in a bloom of fire and spark. The train slowed to a walking crawl.

Several things happened at once. Engineers spilled out of the locomotive, shouting "*Paidia!*" ("We're Greeks!"), and ran for the embankment. Seven of the wooden cars toppled over; four of them sputtered with flames. German troops ducked out from the last car and turned toward the source of the bazooka shot. Tracers stitched across the blackness toward the Americans, who opened up with their Thompson submachine guns. After fifteen minutes, quiet returned.

The men headed into the hills. They tuned in to the radio the next day. "It was revealed that eighty Germans met death and innumerable injured," read the report. "Many died in the four cars burned to smithereens."

The locals weren't all angels; most villages had their informers and malcontents. But the commandos were moved by the risks the Greeks took for them. Villages would wait up all night for their arrival on a march; farmers and their sons watched the hills and rivers for German patrols. The guides were uniformly excellent, zigzagging around enemy camps so close that the Americans could hear Germans talking and the clink of cutlery or gun cleaning. Greeks would sometimes pop up in the middle of a live battlefield, carrying baskets of food or ammunition to the American line, or they joined in. In one attack on a fortified German position, men ran to the local church to ring the bell, calling locals to the fight. The commandos could hear faint cries of "Down with the Germans!" and "Long live freedom!" between the fusillades. In one small town, young, unarmed women and even children walked up to machine-gun posts, calling, "Kill us if you dare, but you'll never leave here alive!"

One woman the commandos rescued from a German raid gave birth to a boy that she asked Giannaris to baptize. She named the boy Eleftherios (freedom), and in the Greek tradition, all twenty-two of the Americans became the infant's godfathers and handed the boy from one to another while saying a quick blessing in Greek. When they finished their raids, the men were often exhausted from the trek and wanted to sleep. They found a gathering place on the way to Papas where a series of small grass huts had been built by the local shepherds. They used it as a resting place before making the long trek back.

After every operation, Giannaris would "just fall apart and sleep on the ground," along with the others. But curiously, when he woke up, he would find himself covered in a rough blanket. His boots had been removed and placed neatly next to him. His socks were hanging on a nearby bush, drying. The first time it happened, he called to his men, "Whose blanket is this?" but none of them knew. He folded the blanket neatly and left it on the ground.

One day, Giannaris spotted a girl, maybe seventeen, near the resting place. She was carrying a wooden cask. He asked for water. She lifted the cask to show it was empty. "Come to my house," she said. He followed her to her rough-timbered home; when they stepped inside, she gave him some water, then began preparing a meal, cutting noodles with scissors. Her name was Viea, and she was a shepherdess.

"Are you the American officer?" she said.

"Yes."

Giannaris said he would call his men so she could meet them.

"No! That won't be necessary," she said. "I've met the right one."

Viea told him that on his next mission, he should come to her house instead of sleeping in the field. She would have some food ready. Did he understand?

Yes, he said. He asked if she was the one who had taken his boots and socks off and provided the blanket.

She shot him a glance. "Why, is there something wrong with that?"

He couldn't think of anything wrong with that. Giannaris, perhaps thinking of Viea's beauty and what might happen when he returned, asked where her parents were. They were working the fields.

"Don't forget," she said to him as he left.

CHAPTER 22

The German Lieutenant

When D-Day finally arrived, the sprawling Balkan empire of the Greek Desk mostly read about it in newspapers or heard about it on radio transmissions. It provided a lift they badly needed.

In the weeks afterward, Helias's team lingered on street corners, watching groups of soldiers as they moved through Salonika; they counted units and memorized shoulder patches they hadn't seen before. Sitting at a café sipping his Turkish coffee, Helias spotted transport trucks on their way to the Thessaloniki train depot on Old Station Street near the port. He glanced at the trucks, quietly counting the men visible behind the flapping tarps. For now, it looked like small units were departing, ten or twelve men at a time, not more than a hundred or two. Troops were always flowing in and out of Thessaloniki as they were reassigned or replaced by other units, but these moves looked to be more permanent, as the Germans were taking their heavy guns with them. Helias was amused to see horses pulling howitzers through the city streets; mules, too, clopped by, heads pumping up and down, their backs stacked with bags and rifles.

But even as the troop trains and transport planes left Salonika, Helias noticed something odd: it felt as though the number of German troops in the city was actually *increasing*. How could that be? His brother, George, along with his network north of Salonika, was witnessing the same phenomenon farther south: more trains than ever trundling by, heavily loaded with soldiers. Early that fall, George wrote to Rodney: "My opinion on the situation is that the Germans are withdrawing from Greece the forces which they can afford to send to the other fronts."

Helias sent his informants out to confirm what was happening. They reported back within a few days: the city had become a disembarkation point for the Wehrmacht; troops were flowing in from Athens and eastern Thrace and the Peloponnese, even from foreign fronts in the East. There they gathered to await the final decision on leaving Greece and for trains to carry them away. The city was bulging with men in gray.

Tens of thousands of Axis troops remained in Greece by midsummer: the German 12th Army, SS troops, support units, the Gestapo, and others. The Germans wanted to get them out and moved to France and Germany in order to stop the Allied forces that had landed at Normandy from pushing east. The Greek Desk and its operatives were tasked with keeping the Germans in place for as long as possible and cutting their numbers down as they tried to leave. Every soldier who stayed in Greece was a trigger puller who wouldn't be killing Americans.

One morning on his walk to the factory, Helias spotted freshly plastered notices on the neighborhood walls. Any owners of private residences with two extra bedrooms and an extra bathroom, they said, were ordered to accept German officers as guests. Ordinary soldiers would bunk in factories or schools, pushing out the Greeks who worked there. Helias asked his network to give him an estimate of the number of soldiers in Salonika. A few days later, the answer came back: fifty thousand.

Cairo acknowledged Helias's accounts of troop movements, then sent a series of messages asking for him to pay close attention to "brigade or division-strength departures." If Helias saw major shifts, the Allies would send a bomber to stop them. Helias doubled his daily transmissions. *The Germans are preoccupied with the tangled logistics of departure,* he thought. *They won't have the time or motivation to hunt spies.*

Even relatives of Helias's team had to take in boarders. An informant named Yianni told Helias that his uncle's family was putting up a young German lieutenant. What was worse, his cousin Katerina had apparently fallen in love with the Nazi and even accompanied him to dances and dinners. The romance—Katerina swore it was love, not convenience—disturbed Yianni, who warned his cousin that the *andartes* would find her, shave her head, and march her through the streets for her sins. Katerina ignored him. Her lieutenant had promised to return to Greece after the war and marry her. She wouldn't give him up.

One evening in mid-September, Yianni dropped by his uncle's house to pass the time. Katerina was there, and she found a moment to speak to him. "Now, you don't have to worry about me anymore," she said. "The German is leaving this Thursday."

Yianni studied her face. "Is he the only one?"

"His entire company is leaving," Katerina said.

"Are you going to say goodbye to him?"

"No, I can't," Katerina said. The lieutenant had told her that the station would be too crowded and that it would be impossible to find him, even if the police somehow let her through. "Thousands" of Germans would be departing at three p.m. The officer had asked to see her the night previous to his departure instead, so that they could say a proper goodbye and he could bring her a last gift.

Yianni left the house and called Cosmas, who relayed the information to Helias.

The agents knew the Thessaloniki station well. It bordered the Baron Hirsch ghetto, where Salonikan Jews had been brought from their homes and penned up in terrible conditions. The city had been home to Jews since before Christ was born. Some biblical scholars have theorized that Paul's First Epistle to the Thessalonians (the residents of ancient Thessaloniki) referred to them: "For you, brethren, became imitators of the churches of God which are in Judea in Christ Jesus. For you also suffered the same things from your own countrymen, just as they did from the Judeans." What this population had suffered in ancient Judea did not compare to what the previous year had brought.

The nearness of the ghetto, a stone's throw from the terminal, was not accidental. Beginning on March 15, 1943, fifty-four thousand of the city's Jews were herded out of the ghetto and boarded onto train cars; they were told they were being relocated to work camps in the east. The tracks had led them instead to Auschwitz-Birkenau, where the majority were funneled into the showers hours after their arrival. Only about a thousand Salonikan Jews would remain in Greece after the war.

Helias coded a message and sent it the next day. "Thousands of Germans to leave at three o'clock in the afternoon at the main railroad station in Salonika." Then he waited.

Cairo came back to him: he should ask his source to verify that the trains were leaving on schedule. Helias acknowledged the transmission, then signed off and stowed the radio under the cloth cover inside its hiding place. He told Yianni to speak with his cousin after her meeting with the lieutenant on Wednesday night. Yianni couldn't give her any hint of the reason he was questioning her; the German could have no clue that Katerina was telling others about the departure. He should play the concerned relative.

The week went slowly. On Wednesday night, Yianni invented a reason to go to his uncle's house. Katerina's father let him in and the two made small talk. Yianni finally found a chance to speak to his cousin alone.

Had she met the lieutenant? She had. Was he still leaving at three p.m.? He was. She began to cry.

Yianni had to go, but he spoke to Katerina for a few minutes more. She told him the two had been unable to part without another meeting. Who had pushed for a last goodbye? Yianni never learned, or at least he never relayed the information to Helias, but the two lovers would come together once more at one p.m. the next day at a tavern behind Thessaloniki station. Yianni also got from his cousin an estimate of how many troops would be departing: three thousand. He made an excuse and left.

Helias coded another message, giving Cairo the estimated number of troops that would be at the station. He knew Salonika and he knew that the train station was sandwiched between the Frankish Quarter and its bustling markets and the Ladadika district, which was dotted with bars and brothels that serviced the sailors who rolled off ships in the nearby port. He relayed this to Cairo, stating the obvious: the Allies must do all they could to keep the bombs on the station itself. Cairo said they would contact him by noon.

The next day, Helias was at the little table early. He kept the headphones on, listening for the telltale beeps. Yianni, who was nervous and excited about the raid that had originated in a piece of family gossip, came by to wait with him.

Noon came and went without a message. They waited, pacing the long room and glancing out the windows at the lovely day, the hot blue sky.

There was nothing at twelve thirty. Helias began to grow agitated. Finally, he heard the operator in Cairo call. He wrote the message out as it came through. A squadron of American planes would be over Thessaloniki at three p.m. They should take care to stay away.

Helias finished writing out the message and showed it to Yianni. He hid the radio and left the factory. The exhilaration he'd expected, the lift in his spirits, never arrived. "I went home," he said, "feeling weak and sick to my stomach." When he reached the house, Sultanitsa asked him what was wrong. He looked pale. Was business OK?

"I'm just tired," he told her. He was going to lie down.

He was unable to rest. At two thirty p.m., he walked into the courtyard of the little house, looking for a way to climb to the roof. He went to a tree next to the wall that bordered the property. Sultanitsa spotted him and asked what he was doing. Helias was exposing himself to the curiosity of the neighbors; if they saw him on the roof just before the attack, they were sure to connect him to it. But Helias didn't care. He wanted to witness what was about to happen. He told his lover he was retrieving one of the children's balls that had gotten lodged on top of the house during a game.

He crawled up and stood gingerly on the curved clay tiles. After a few minutes, he heard a series of distant booms. They were the antiaircraft guns near the harbor. He turned, searching the fall sky. There was a string of silver shapes glimmering to the south.

Neighbors came out of their houses to find out what the booms were about. "What is happening?" one called to Helias.

"I think airplanes are coming," he said.

The shapes got closer, formed up in a straight line. There were twelve of them; Helias thought they were B-25s, medium bombers, their glass snouts winking in the sunlight. Trails of smoke streaked toward them, detonating in dark smudges as the flak rounds exploded. The wing of the first plane detached from the fuselage; it had been hit. As Helias shielded his eyes, he saw two white parachutes pop into view. The third plane dropped out of the line and disappeared in a burst of orange fire. There were four more parachutes visible.

The planes broke out of their formation and spread over the sky. The dark bombs separated from the wings and went swaying toward the ground. Helias saw the first burst of fire, followed by a column of heavy black smoke.

Then the sky was clear again. The planes were gone. The entire thing had taken less than a minute.

CHAPTER 23

The Bombers

Helias climbed down from the roof. He walked out of the courtyard and began running toward the harbor. Greeks were coming out of houses on the street ahead; soon hundreds were making their way with him toward Thessaloniki station. They could see more smoke in the sky now, the tendrils turning copper-colored as they mixed with the air.

He drew closer to the station, but the Greek police and German MPs had gotten their first, and they refused to let him pass. Instead, Helias stood alongside the locals. From their vantage point, all they could see was the copper-colored smoke and people rushing back and forth. It was an hour before a Greek man came walking away from the station. He crossed through the police line, and when he reached the ranks of Greeks, someone called to him and asked what he'd seen.

The trains had been destroyed, the man said. He said that the bodies of the soldiers were so entwined with the debris that it would take days to remove them all. "There must have been thousands killed," he said. Then he went on. "I heard that over one hundred homes were also destroyed or damaged."

A flatbed truck approached, with five men standing in the bed, parachute straps hanging down from their shoulders. The American pilots. As the truck revved by, the crowd was silent. Helias studied the somber faces of the airmen.

Something inside Helias caused him to call out to the pilots. One turned and looked toward him. Helias had imagined what Thessaloniki would show him: dead Germans in their twenties. But this was an American being dragged off to God knew where. *How could he have known,* Helias thought, *in his wildest imagination that it was I who had brought them to the spot where they had been captured.*

Helias felt nauseated. He turned away and began walking home, "guilt pervading every fiber of my being." His twenty-word telegram had led to the deaths of thousands of young Germans, an unknown number of Greeks, and perhaps the five Americans he'd just seen pass by. He'd engineered a feat of espionage, but it felt nothing like what he'd imagined it would.

When he was close to Sultanitsa's house, he met a neighbor standing in the street with others who were milling around and asking for information. The two of them had often talked about politics, about the war.

"Helias, do you see?" the man cried. "The Americans did not forget us, after all."

The man was excited; perhaps the end of the occupation was in view. In any case, the Nazis had gotten a taste of what they'd served the Greeks.

Helias said he wished it hadn't happened. He broke off and went to his room, where he sat dazed. He asked himself what he'd become, why he'd "departed from my true nature—a loving, compassionate individual, who so enjoyed and valued life." He said to himself that he'd been fleeing from the reality of the job since he'd arrived; convinced he was going to die, he'd had one last spree in the sun. But that wasn't the war; what he'd just seen was the war.

Guilt pressed down on him. He sat for a long time. Then his thoughts turned to American places like Canton, Ohio, his hometown, and the young men from there, men whom he would have been with in the trenches of inland France that afternoon had his grandmother not fallen ill, prompting his family's move back to Greece. Faceless Americans now at the front. "As I tried to calm my mind, I realized that if the Germans had been allowed to enter France or Italy, thousands of American lives would have been lost." He'd saved his countrymen from "chaos and destruction." Even if it wasn't possible to picture them, to see their faces as he saw the German faces, he'd served a cause. It would have to do.

The next morning, he walked to the local newsstand and bought a German-language newspaper. There was a story on how the "barbaric Americans" had bombed the city. The journalist wrote about Greek casualties but omitted any mention of how many Germans had been killed. He walked to the factory, unearthed the radio from beneath the floorboards, and wrote out a quick message to Cairo about the pilots. He learned that a total of six airmen had been captured, one a captain.

His team was already inside the long room, their voices booming off the walls. The Allies had finally punished the killers. Cosmas and Yianni were in a celebratory mood, pouring out glasses of ouzo. They looked at the brooding Helias and asked what was the matter.

"Don't you know?" he said. "My message cost three thousand people—soldiers, civilians—their lives. How can I be proud of that?"

Cosmas and the others were at first too shocked to respond. "Don't be foolish," one of them finally said. "It was your duty to send the message."

A few days later, Yianni went to his uncle's house. He suspected Katerina would be waiting for him. She was. "Now, you don't have to worry about me anymore, Yianni," she told him. Katerina had been waiting for a call from the lieutenant, but none had come.

"Did you know that my German lieutenant was an ancient-Greek scholar?" she asked bitterly. "[He] knew more about Greece than both of us." He knew the ancient language and would read the famous tragedies to her. He was different from the other Nazis. "He loved me and he loved Greece." Yianni couldn't say the truth: *it didn't matter what he did or how he felt.* With no word from the officer, his cousin later suffered a nervous breakdown.

Back in Izmir, Dorothy Cox got the news from Greek refugees. She was all in favor of killing as many Germans as possible but felt heartsick at the loss of Greek lives. She composed her first letter to her superior in Washington in six months. "I would like to write an official protest against the bombing," she wrote. "That is not possible, so I shall express an unofficial opinion." Why hadn't the bombers been more precise? Salonika was not "an important military objective."

The joyous response of Helias's neighbor was amplified in the things she heard from the refugees. "The Greeks well know and understand and even rejoice in the destruction of military objectives," she wrote, "even at the cost of many Greek lives." One reason she'd felt the need to write was that the Greeks she met *weren't* outraged. "The severest criticism is 'It's a pity,'" she wrote. Dorothy had been moved by this acceptance of things.

It was true that Salonika was not a priority as far as physical infrastructure went, but the German soldiers were an asset headed to France to fight the Allied invasion forces. Thessaloniki was a legitimate target. And the proximity of residential neighborhoods to the station—a hundred feet or so—made precise targeting impossible in an era before smart bombs. But in Dorothy's grief, she couldn't see that clearly. She'd helped Helias get into Salonika. She felt blood on her hands.

CHAPTER 24

The Shepherdesses

In September, Giannaris received a message from the OSS that was based on Helias's messages and others; it confirmed that the Germans were beginning their withdrawal from Greece. The Athens–Salonika railway would be one of the main routes of retreat. Could he blow the tracks and slow the tide? His brief was to keep as many of the fifteen thousand Nazi soldiers as possible in the area around the city of Lamia, about a hundred miles north of Athens, from joining the fight in Western Europe. Most of the soldiers were scheduled to leave by train. Giannaris was expected to rip up tracks, target choke points, blow bridges, and attack troop cars.

Giannaris also received word, either through Rodney's transmissions or his own informers in nearby villages, that the Germans had increased their vigilance on the train lines. Patrols were more frequent. The Germans were aware that Giannaris's band of men was active in the sector. Two *andartes* came to visit him. "The Germans are really out to get us this time," one told him. "And you, personally."

The other battalions scattered across the countryside were also planning destruction. "The damage they were to do to the Germans was phenomenal," wrote Anthony Cave Brown in his biography of General Bill Donovan. The OSS commander was so delighted by the raids that he had planned to fly into Greece to join one or two of them before his lieutenants restrained him. But he did read the commandos' after-action reports with glee; he forwarded the most thrilling ones on to FDR and often regaled guests at his Georgetown dinner parties with passages from them, including ones written by Giannaris. He intoned the words as if he were reading Homer aloud, all the while beaming with "the utmost pride."

Now Giannaris finalized the plan for his next mission. He sent three men out on recon and told the others to prepare for a major operation. As he waited for the scouts to return, one of his men, Technician First Grade Michaelis Tsirmulas, found him in his tent and told him about a disturbing vision he'd had in his sleep the night before. "I dreamed I was eaten by a snake," he said. In Greek lore, dreaming of a snake meant transformation or rebirth, but the soldier remained anxious. He left the tent and found another commando he was close to; he handed him seven hundred dollars that he'd saved. If he was killed, he wanted the money to go to his sisters back in America.

The recon team returned with a potential target: Lianokladi, site of a major rail junction. On alert for the new patrols, the commandos trekked out, avoiding the main roads. After four hours they reached the area; it was full dark with just the moon for illumination.

The black mouth of a tunnel leading through the base of the mountain ahead of them was a concern. The Germans might be gathered there, scanning the woods for activity. Giannaris could also see pillboxes hugging the rail line every fifty yards. He called for the unit to split into two groups, one on the right of the tunnel, the other to the left. They were walking downslope toward the base of the mountain when a line of orange flame shot from the slit of one of the pillboxes, and the air seemed to tear with the sound of a machine gun.

The men belly flopped to the ground; ahead of them, their lead scout fell awkwardly. It was Tsirmulas. Giannaris turned and whispered an order to retreat back to their rendezvous. The shadows of the men slipped back and hurried away from the train line while Giannaris eyed the unmoving Tsirmulas spread-eagled on the ground ahead of him. Still no movement.

Giannaris never considered leaving him. He pushed his carbine forward and began crawling toward the scout, then rose to a crouch and hustled forward. After two steps, he heard a roar and saw a white splash of light. Chunks of earth rose in the air and fell in slow motion. He'd stepped on a German Teller mine.

He fell heavily to the ground. He couldn't see his own wounds in the darkness, but he could feel strength leaking away. Giannaris resumed crawling toward his soldier. Flares sputtered to life above him, sending a phosphate white glare down on the prone figure. Giannaris reached Tsirmulas and pressed a finger to his jugular. The scout was dead.

Giannaris could feel a sticky warmth spreading across his legs and back. He turned and crawled on his hands and knees a hundred fifty yards until he spotted a large boulder. He wrenched his body behind it. The image of Tsirmulas's body stayed in his vision. He was enraged. He peeked around the corner of the rock and brought his gun up. As soon as he began firing, the brush near him erupted with tracers. Giannaris shrank back as tiny fragments from the face of the rock showered the ground around him.

His unit was headed away from him, thinking the captain was following behind. The Germans would surely find and kill him before the commandos realized their mistake. Giannaris waited for a lull in the firing, then started crawling. He could feel a hot pain from his backside; a piece of shrapnel had torn a three-inch wound next to his rectum. Other splinters, two hundred of them, had sliced into his back and legs; he had shrapnel in his scrotum, in his left arm, on the backs of his legs, between his toes.

He crawled all night, hearing nothing, moving slowly upward toward the top of the mountain, away from the train tracks and the German patrols. He tried not to cry out. When he reached the crest, the first rays of sunlight were streaming over a nearby ridgeline. He rested. He turned over and studied his body in the light; his knees were red with blood from crawling over rocks. He took his shirt off and tore a strip of cloth away, fashioning it into a tourniquet for his arm. As he pulled the knot tight with his teeth, he spotted movement below: gray uniforms, ten or twelve of them, moving among the green of the conifers. The Germans, having searched the valley all night, were now coming up toward him.

Giannaris reached for his carbine but found that his right hand was paralyzed. He felt a spasm of anxiety rise in his chest. He snatched the rifle up with his left hand, then laid it where he could reach it quickly.

The German soldiers were proceeding carefully three hundred yards below him. Five minutes later, it was two hundred. Giannaris watched them, remaining perfectly still. He was partially hidden behind a mound; the men hadn't been able to pick him out against the landscape in the brightening sun. A hundred fifty yards now. He unhooked four grenades from his pistol belt and laid them in the dirt. When the Germans were within five yards, Giannaris would pull the pin of one with his teeth.

He watched two of the soldiers pause. They looked around at the trees and swaying grass, then turned and began walking downhill. Another pair did the same. Finally, the rest circled back and tramped down the slope. Giannaris watched them go.

He began crawling down the back side of the mountain. He would throw the carbine out ahead of him, then drag himself to it. Throw and drag. The sun was baking hot already; the field ahead of him swayed in the heat shimmer. He paused and, to stave off infection, chewed some sulfa tablets (he had no water to wash them down). He estimated it was ten a.m.

He spotted something on the downslope ahead. It was a tiny grass hut; a sheepherder must have thrown it together to get out of the sun. He dragged himself inside. *Don't go to sleep,* he thought, *or you're dead.*

He felt as though he was going to hallucinate and drop off. He took a pin off his blouse—the crossed-rifles pin of the infantry—turned it over, and began pricking his skin. "Don't sleep, don't sleep, don't sleep." Blood seeped through his pants, along with excrement.

If he stayed there, he would sleep, and he would be found. He groaned, turned his body around, threw the carbine out the little entrance, and followed it. He couldn't see to the end of the downward slope. Every few minutes, he wrenched his head around and looked back up the mountain. No one.

It was the longest day of his life. After crawling for hours, he saw the ground ahead of him beginning to level off. He heard an odd noise like tinkling metal. It repeated, metal tinkling. It came to him that it was the sound of bells, goat bells, and perhaps he'd see the shepherd who'd built the little hut. He turned his head; there was the shepherd. Giannaris, his throat parched, called out. The man ran away.

Giannaris felt a wave of hopelessness. He threw the carbine, then dug his elbows into the soil and crawled after it. The ground was a bit more giving and moist. Was there water nearby? There had to be, he thought. He was moving on level ground now. Perhaps there was a stream ahead. Perhaps the man who ran away watered his goats there.

More tinkling metal. He raised his head up. He shouted again. There was no one there. He pulled his carbine to him, stuck the muzzle in the dirt, shoved the stock under his armpit, and raised himself up halfway. Now he saw them: two teenage girls watching their goats graze. He cried out again.

The look on their faces showed they were scared. "Don't be afraid," Giannaris called to them in their language. "I'm a Greek American. I am here to help your country. I'm wounded."

The girls ran up to him. Giannaris sank back to the ground, looking up at the sky and their faces peering down at him. "Oh, my God, he's wounded badly," he heard. They told him they would help. One of them went running to a grove of young trees nearby and tore off branches. The girls were carrying twine and a wool blanket, and with them the two constructed a makeshift stretcher. They dragged him onto the blanket and began pulling him.

Giannaris rocked back and forth over the slightly uneven ground. There was sky above and a while later not blue sky but something green. They were in another grass hut, and there was a man there. He said he was a doctor; perhaps he was staying there, or the girls had gone to find him.

The man spoke. "My boy, you're badly wounded," he said. What he needed was a hospital and a blood transfusion. The Greek doctor didn't have his medical bag with him, so he had no thread or needle for stitches. He found cloths and water, and he began to clean Giannaris's wounds. Giannaris's right arm remained paralyzed.

The captain told the doctor that his men would help him. He gave directions to their rendezvous point, and a messenger set off. When the commandos got word that he was alive, they organized some plasma and medical supplies, then sent two men back with the messenger. On their way, they passed by the resting place where they'd slept after missions. They saw Viea, the shepherdess who'd invited Giannaris to eat with her. She asked them where they were going.

"Our officer got hurt," they said.

"Where is he?" Viea said. When they told her, she ran off. She returned a moment later carrying a large watermelon on her shoulder. She nodded and began following the commandos, hiking two and a half hours on barely-there trails through the mountains away from the main roads.

Giannaris woke up to find Viea sitting next to him. "You eat something," she said. She took a knife and cut a sliver of watermelon and held it to his lips. When he'd eaten as much as he could, she found a cloth, soaked it in cold water, and held it to his forehead. She whispered comforting words to him as he dozed.

The doctor inserted a needle into his vein, but the plasma wouldn't flow. They waited for Nazi patrols to clear the area before they moved Giannaris. When it was time, his men lifted him onto a stretcher and carried him outside into the sunshine. He was paler and thinner now. He said goodbye to Viea. He jounced in the litter as they passed through a string of villages. Eventually they came to a small landing strip, where he waited for a plane. He'd been wounded eleven days before.

When the plane came, a sergeant sat beside the commando holding a hypodermic filled with heart stimulant, needle up. Giannaris's heart had stopped twice the night before and he'd been injected and revived each time. When they arrived, an ambulance whisked him away to the 11th British Hospital. Within the next two days, Giannaris received four blood transfusions and was given even odds to survive. An Army plane flew him to Kennedy General Hospital in Memphis, where five thousand "nerve cases" were recovering from the war. It would take him three years to regain the use of his paralyzed limbs.

He never saw Viea again.

CHAPTER 25

The Microbes

Archaeologists take artifacts from the soil and interpret them. They have little or no experience in putting artifacts back into the soil. Months after they'd buried the Ancients, the curators and archaeologists at the Ministry of Education came to a creeping realization: the relics might be decaying down there.

There were three main dangers: microorganisms, moisture, and chemical effects. The classicists knew that microbes could damage organic materials (the technical term is "biodeterioration"). The marble at the Acropolis had been plagued with these things for centuries; nineteenth-century painters used red oils to depict the Parthenon, which had had a pale crimson hue at the time. A long mid-century drought in Greece had caused certain fungi, bacteria, and lichens to grow on the stone; these organisms emitted red pigments, giving the columns a scarlet patina. Fifty years later, artists were using darker paints when they drew the monuments; wetter weather had invited in new bacteria, black and green molds that had turned the stone darker. In a thousand years, microorganisms can eat into marble to a depth of about two inches.

The archaeologists had done their best to avoid damaging the stone. They'd hidden "works made of sensitive matter" aboveground in caves whose entrances were then sealed up with concrete. But as time wore on, they wondered how the buried things were faring during Athens's wet winter. How dry was the sand they'd buried the relics in? Was the moisture eating through the tar paper and other materials that covered the relics? Were microbes changing the color of the bronze and the marble? Some of the artifacts had gone into the ground without any covering at all. More than one curator must have had nightmares about lifting the statues out of their burial pits after the Germans had gone and finding them irretrievably altered.

Hans von Schoenebeck of the Art Protection Service was concerned, too. A few pieces encased in wooden boxes were examined. The cotton the objects had been wrapped in had turned to mush; clearly, liquid had gotten into the boxes and onto the surface of the relics. At another hiding site, fabric sacks had deteriorated, spilling their sand onto the artifacts.

"In Athens the conditions are partly more difficult than in Thessaloniki," wrote one curator. Painted marble sculptures had been secreted on the Sacred Rock of the Acropolis in an ancient water tank that dated from the Bronze Age, when it had likely served the Mycenaean temple and palace. "If water has penetrated through underground channels," the classicist went on, "it must be considered certain that the coloring has disappeared."

The German asked that the "ancient Thessalonians" be unburied and stored in a warehouse. The director of antiquities refused. "I said that I prefer damage from lichens . . . than abduction or destruction." Von Schoenebeck persisted, but the Greeks were unmoved. Finally, the German admitted that there were no experts qualified to safely unearth the statues and let the matter drop.

The ministry wanted to do what it could without risking wholesale theft. They consulted a professor at the Polytechnic, "an expert on such things." He advised them to remove any sand that touched bronze vessels. The sand held rainwater "and transmits it to the ancient stones, which are then insulted and worn out." In Olympia, parts of the famous Temple of Zeus had been covered with wet river sand. When curators brushed the sand away, they found discolorations on the marble. Acting quickly, they were able to remove the stains from all the carvings except for the head of Apollo on the western pediment. To their credit, the Germans helped, providing bronze and other materials to refurbish fittings. The Parthenon was inspected and some of the iron links that held the marble together were replaced. The Greeks requisitioned a truck and drove to a cave where the bronze statue of Delphi had been hidden. It was removed from the damp cavern and driven to the National Museum in Athens.

By now innumerable relics packed away in the rucksacks of ordinary soldiers were flowing out of Greek ports in the first wave of German departures. Vases, marble statuettes, terra-cotta figurines. If a division sailed off, the number would increase ten- or a hundredfold. Stopping Nazi soldiers from making it to France or Belgium also meant keeping the relics in Greece.

Once the artifacts left, they could go anywhere: into private homes, bank vaults, garbage dumps, or the unmarked graves of their looters in France. The antiquities market in occupied Paris in 1944 was white-hot, with dealers buying objects from across the lands occupied by Germany. Sales in Switzerland and Germany were also "flourishing" as relics that had been stored in museums or private collections for decades came onto the market. The reasons were complex, but many German soldiers and officers, seeing dark clouds on the horizon, were selling their looted treasures for hard currency. Untraced and without written records, the relics would be difficult to recover.

Those that had been taken from new excavations, discovered while a trench was being dug or a fortification enlarged, had never gone through the documenting process. Their history was already lost. When German troops had been digging trenches near Salonika, they uncovered a stunning seven-foot statue of Herakleitos, "an art sculpture of exceptional merit," unlike any piece the archaeologists had seen before. The Nazis organized a handover to the Greek authorities, snapped pictures, then took the statue back and shipped it to Linz, Austria, where Hitler had grown up. It was displayed in a Vienna museum for two months, then became a showpiece in the Führer's Alps hideaway.

CHAPTER 26

The Triangulation Trucks

One of Helias's informants, though an unwitting one, was the janitor in the Gestapo building. His contact had kept his link to the Americans hidden for security reasons; the janitor had no idea who his intel was being passed to.

One day in September, when the janitor was emptying the wastebasket of a Gestapo lieutenant, the man asked him to sit. "Don't be afraid," the lieutenant said. "I want to speak with you candidly."

The Greek controlled the urge to run away and sat down. The Gestapo man asked if he was a member of any "patriotic organizations," which was a euphemism for the resistance. Waving away the janitor's denials, the lieutenant said they'd been following him and knew he was passing information of some kind. Was it to the Americans?

The lieutenant had a fairly clear idea of the war situation, and as someone who spoke a little Russian, he knew he would be relocated to the Eastern Front. He told the janitor that the office was aware there was a radio operating in Agia Triada, but they hadn't been able to locate it yet. That week, the Germans were planning to silence all comms, leaving the air clear for the triangulation trucks. Then they would visit Agia Triada.

The man proposed an arrangement. For tipping off the radio operators, he wanted to be taken prisoner by the Americans. Fighting the Russians would likely mean death. Having made his offer, the lieutenant sent the informant away.

The janitor hurried to his contact's home, furious. Only after being talked down by his friend did he reveal the offer. Helias found out about it while at the factory, where he was gathered in the long room with the rest of his team. "For the first time," he said, "we feared that our end was near." He'd known the Gestapo was looking for him, but in over a year, they hadn't been able to catch him; his luck had been good and he'd believed he was being protected by "an unknown force."

Cairo had recently—urgently—asked for the status of a ship in the Salonika harbor, an Italian minelayer. A few days before, Helias's informants had told him the ship was being provisioned, which indicated a departure within seventy-two hours. That morning, they'd sent word that the vessel would steam out of the port the next day. Helias's team urged him, in light of the janitor's revelations, to stay off the air. If the German was telling the truth, the triangulation trucks would be in the neighborhood with a clear spectrum to zero in on their radio. Why risk it?

Helias resisted. Cairo had radioed several times about the minelayer; clearly, it held some importance. He would limit his use of the radio as much as possible, but he had to answer Cairo's questions. Cosmas and the others took the news badly, but Helias felt he was close to the end of his mission and he wanted to complete it with integrity.

The next morning, Helias walked to the factory and set up the radio. At nine fifteen a.m., he sent a quick burst of code about the minelayer. As he was finishing the message, he heard sounds of a scuffle or some kind of disturbance in the courtyard. One of the guards ran in. "German trucks are surrounding the block," he said before turning and running out.

Helias was alone. He removed the headphones. He got up, took the .45 from the table, lifted two grenades out of the box, and walked through the door.

Once outside, he became aware of the stillness. There was no one in the courtyard. When he looked through the bars of the wrought iron gate, he saw the street was empty and silent. He turned back to the factory, ran into the radio room, and scooped the unit off the table. He yanked the carpet aside and pulled the plywood away, then shoved the equipment in, along with the .45 and the grenades.

He could hear shouts of *"Raus! Raus!"* He went to the window. A German soldier, wearing a crude metal plate over his chest, was pushing through the gate. Helias hopped up on the window ledge and jumped, banging the frame as he went. He landed in the neighbor's yard, the one belonging to the German officers, but saw no one. Trying to tamp down his anxiety, he composed himself before opening the gate and walking onto the street, vowing not to return until he was sure the Gestapo had passed over the place.

Helias thought back to the spy school at the palace, where the instructors had passed on a piece of intel from Dorothy: German triangulation teams, once they'd reduced the area of a suspicious signal to about the size of a city block, would remove their equipment from the trucks and hide it in local houses. The trucks would be sent away, and the radio team would wait. Once the Allied spies believed the danger was past, they would resume transmissions and the German technicians would be able to narrow the search for the radio.

Helias went to a café and ordered a coffee. Greeks walked by with a few German soldiers mixed in; it appeared to be a normal day in Salonika. There were delivery trucks and a few sedans, but none appeared twice. Then he heard a diesel engine rev to his right; a windowless German truck drove past, then turned at the corner. He stood up and walked home.

He and the team broke off from their normal routine. They stayed away from the factory. Cosmas contacted him and said the janitor had left the city with his family. Each day, there were fewer Germans on the streets, and those Helias saw had "their heads down, most likely contemplating the hard days ahead." One could sense the change in the Germans' mood; as the fall took hold, Athenians guessed at what would be the last day of the occupation.

Helias took a stroll most days and walked by the factory. Sometimes he would linger across the street for a cigarette. Perhaps he chatted with the old woman who lived by the gate, though he never reported doing so. He saw no one going in and out; the neighborhood was quiet. After two weeks, he opened the gate and walked in. His steps echoed faintly as he entered the radio room; it felt as if it had sat empty since the moment he left. He found the cloth cover undisturbed and the equipment intact. The Germans had passed by his station.

Helias resumed his transmissions once or twice a day, sending mostly reports of departing trains or truck convoys. But he could feel the lack of urgency in the questions from Cairo. The war was passing into a new phase.

At the end of October, Cosmas came to Helias with a report from several informants who lived near the port. The Germans were "placing dynamite along the harbor's entire length," including the storehouses where the Germans had kept wheat and corn for their troops. Cosmas sent a man to the archbishop of Salonika's office to ask him to intervene in the name of the starving thousands in the city.

The Wehrmacht refused to release the food. "Sadly, the German generals were impervious to reason," Helias said later. He learned when the detonations were planned to take place and walked to the harbor to watch. When he got there, he found that rumors had brought hundreds of locals, many of them "thin and pale from hunger," to the port. They had the slightly sweet odor that bodies give off when they are using their reserves of fat. The dynamite went off, sending fat black clouds into the air. The sound came a split second later.

When it was gone, an enormous flock of black birds and seagulls descended on the warehouses, pecking at the grain that had spilled from containers. German soldiers kept the crowd at bayonet length. "Thousands of starving Greeks in Salonika dreamt of bread that would never grace their tables," Helias thought. Whatever was left of the guilt he'd felt for the station bombing drained away. The locals stood shouting curses at the soldiers. "Leave, you animals!" one shouted. "Russia is waiting for you!"

The last regiments marched out of the city. As the final units passed out of the suburbs, church bells began to ring. Greeks rushed out into the streets. "We are free!" they cried. "God has saved us!" The singing began almost immediately: "Children of Greece, Children" and "Famous Macedonia," the army's marching song. Young men went along the walls, ripping down German posters. The Gestapo headquarters was ransacked.

Helias felt a burden slip away, one he hadn't realized he'd been carrying. "It would take months . . . for me to feel free and able to walk down a street without having to look over my shoulder."

When Helias was having breakfast one morning, the bell rang. Sultanitsa left the table and came back with an odd look on her face. "A car with an American flag is parked outside." The U.S. Army had arrived in the persons of a colonel and his two guards armed with automatic weapons. The man congratulated him on the mission, then said he was being moved to a hotel the OSS had rented on the waterfront in preparation for his leaving Greece. Helias was eager to talk; he and the colonel discussed his crazy year, the spy school, the hoped-for victory. Of the fifteen students Helias had trained with at the palace, the man told him, five had been captured and killed in-country. "I thanked God, who'd saved me countless times," Helias said.

The jeep had brought the neighbors out of their houses. They studied the soldiers' uniforms as Helias talked to the colonel. The girl who'd serenaded him months before was standing outside her house with her mother, whispering.

He went back in and told Sultanitsa that he was an American agent. "What?" she cried. He explained the mission and said he'd wanted to protect her from the Gestapo, so he had told her nothing. He gave her six gold sovereigns from his dwindling stash. After a few minutes, she accepted his explanation, then told her three children, who'd become fond of Helias, to say goodbye.

After he had said his farewells and gathered his things, Sultanitsa walked him out to the street. By now dozens of people were crowding outside the house, angling for a look at the secret agent who'd lived alongside them for months. "My Helias is an American soldier!" Sultanitsa called to them as he hauled his bag to the jeep. Helias walked over to the neighbors he knew best, including the girl who'd sang to him, and shook hands. They asked if he'd ever return, and he said yes, when the war was over. He'd worked as the only American spy in Salonika—in fact, the only American soldier—for nearly a year. He'd sent four hundred messages.

Before they drove to the hotel, the colonel asked to see the factory. Helias complied, and gave a tour, pulling the cover off the floor and hoisting the radio out. On the way back to the jeep, the old woman who lived in the gatehouse stopped him.

"Are the Americans buying your business?" she asked.

"Yes, something like that."

She said she approved, as the business did not seem to do so well.

PART III

CHAPTER 27

The Athens Plan

On Monday, May 10, 1943, a story appeared on page five of *The New York Times*, slotted beneath the story of the Dionne sisters, quintuplets who had been given the honor of naming five U.S. Navy ships. The headline of the less prominent article read, "Nazis Reported Planning to Destroy Greece If Driven Out in an Allied Balkan Invasion," and the piece detailed the Axis fear of a D-Day-type attack somewhere in the Balkans. German authorities were tightening their control through Central Europe and the Balkans; in Hungary, the *Times* reported, "dancing and public rejoicing" had recently been outlawed. But Greece, which was a possible landing site for the Allies, was being threatened by more than curfews and bans. "Nazi occupation authorities . . . warned," said the reporter, "that if they were obliged to abandon Greece they would leave the country in ruins."

There was a precedent: in April 1941, Hitler had reacted with fury when a coup d'état in Yugoslavia had removed the pro-Reich government. As the Wehrmacht crossed the border, Hitler ordered Operation Retribution. Hundreds of Luftwaffe fighters and bombers lifted off from German airfields and flew toward the capital city, Belgrade. The order was to raze the city with "merciless severity," Hermann Göring remembered the Führer saying. After destroying much of the Royal Yugoslav Army Air Force, the German planes dropped more than two hundred metric tons of bombs, incendiaries, and aerial mines on Belgrade. Thousands were killed and many of the capital's buildings, bridges, water plants, and electrical transformers were destroyed. The National Library of Serbia was targeted, and workers watched as its medieval manuscripts, some dating from the twelfth century, burned in the subsequent fire, along with ancient maps and archives from the Ottoman era.

"There must never again be a Yugoslavia," Hitler told his generals. That included its cultural infrastructure. Shortly after the bombing, the American ambassador to Greece, Lincoln MacVeagh, worried that Athens was next. "Planes this morning circled a lot overhead," he wrote in his journal, "and I wouldn't put it past the Boche to do a Belgrade here. The only hope is that Hitler is against it, on account of some fantastic liking for antiquity, which they say he affects. But that is a slim hope."

The bombs didn't come in 1941, and the Allies didn't invade in 1943. But in August 1944, Hitler cabled General Dietrich von Choltitz, the military governor of Paris:

> *Historically, the loss of Paris always meant the loss of France. The Führer repeats his order that Paris has to be defended. . . . The strongest measures to quell insurrection inside the city must be taken. . . . The bridges across the Seine are to be prepared for demolition. Paris must not fall into enemy hands except as a field of ruins.*

Von Choltitz was standing on a balcony in the Hotel Meurice on the Rue de Rivoli when an assistant handed him the message. He read it and passed it to his second-in-command, then gazed out on the Tuileries, which lay not far off across sunlit lawns. If he'd looked left, he would have seen the Louvre; if right, the Place de la Concorde. "The scene merely underlined the madness of the medieval command," he said.

His lieutenant handed back the message and von Choltitz put it in his pocket. Neither ever spoke of it again or put into motion any of its instructions. This would earn the general the postwar sobriquet of "the savior of Paris." But von Choltitz's refusal wasn't entirely, or perhaps even mostly, based on his reverence for French culture. The order had reached him as the Allies were moving quickly to encircle the capital; they'd already taken the important bridges. It was simply too late. "Four days ago, the factual order might have been considered," the general admitted. In his current position, he had no troops to defend against the tanks of the approaching U.S. Third Army under General George S. Patton, let alone to blow up the Louvre and destroy Paris. Had Hitler cabled him a week before, the calculus would have been very different.

There was no such problem in Greece. The Wehrmacht had tens of thousands of troops in the country and no enemy force marching on the capital. They could do whatever they wanted.

By late summer, Rodney was seeing disturbing transmissions from Dorothy's refugees and from his own agents inside the country: reports of sappers, explosives, and plans for widespread sabotage in Athens and elsewhere. He wrote to "George," one of his lead informants:

> *On intelligence, we are interested now in all sorts of economic information which will be needed for relief and rehabilitation when the Germans go: Public Works—Marathon Dam, Electric Power Station, phone company, Flour Mills (St. George), Piraeus harbor Works and so on. The Germans plan to blow them up.*

The American-built Marathon Dam was nearly a thousand feet across, and it held back, at peak capacity, 41 million cubic meters of water in hilly terrain twenty miles northeast of Athens. It was a link between old and new: clad in Pentelic marble (the same stone used to build the Parthenon) and named to commemorate the glorious Battle of Marathon during the first Persian invasion of the country, it was a mammoth engineering achievement that represented the emergence of Greece as a modern nation. The dam also supplied the capital with all of its drinking water.

By the fall of 1944, the intel was no longer just rumors. Sappers had been spotted at the base of the dam. Wire services reported that "76 tons of dynamite were laid in the reservoir," though where that highly specific number came from is anyone's guess. The *Los Angeles Times* reported on October 5 that the mining of the dam was rumored to be a negotiating tactic with the British. It wasn't; it was entirely serious.

The dam sat seven hundred thirty feet above sea level; the lowest point in Athens was about two hundred feet. Had the explosives gone off, millions of cubic meters of water—equivalent to a building the size of the Pentagon but fifteen stories high—would have been released from Lake Marathon. The water would have shot through the break in the dam and rushed down the dry beds of two rivers, the Charadros and Varnavas, that intersect at its base. The water would have ripped through houses, uprooted trees, and demolished buildings, then carried them along in a wall a hundred feet high or higher. As the stored water fell through the breach, its latent energy would have been released, accelerating the water to a hundred miles an hour, faster than a car trying to outrun it.

The flood would have sluiced along a natural drainage path southwest toward Athens, primarily along the Charadros River Valley. It would have destroyed farms, swept up farmers, and drowned families in their cottages before reaching the northern suburbs of Athens, where it would have slowed somewhat in the flatter plains outside the city. Momentum would have carried most of the water rushing toward the city center through low-lying areas like the ancient Cephissus River basin. Thousands would have died in the initial surge, and thousands more would have faced starvation or death from thirst in the weeks and months afterward. The Acropolis, sitting on its hill five hundred feet above sea level, would have been safe, but the waters would have wrecked excavations and flooded the caves and hiding places where the statues had been stowed, and driven into the Bank of Athens, which held archaeological records.

Rodney and the Greek Desk were aware of the threat, but they had no forces in Athens capable of stopping it. It would fall to a young enemy archaeologist and a loose assembly of native conspirators to do what they could to save the city.

As more Germans left Greece, a classicist named Roland Hampe continued to go to work every day in his office in the center of Athens. He was an archaeologist who would go on to become one of Germany's foremost experts on the origins of Greek art, placing it in the Mycenaean period and upending older theories about its Dark Ages genesis. But at the moment, he was stuck in Athens as an interpreter for the Wehrmacht.

Hampe had first come to Greece as a student on his summer break in 1932; he'd saved enough money to travel cheaply on a barge. Escaping the hot sun one afternoon, he had stepped into the National Archaeological Museum; he walked slowly through the halls until he was standing in front of a glass case that held a collection of splendid bronze brooches from the eighth century; they'd been discovered in Boeotia in central Greece. Hampe became somewhat obsessed with the pieces; later, he was able to take them out of the case and turn them over in his hands. After a long period of study, he discerned something in the jewelers' marks: images of what appeared to be scenes of gods, "barely recognizable and previously lost." Hampe, still a student, had discovered the first known reference to ancient Greek mythology.

That discovery should have launched a significant career. Hampe committed himself to classical studies and learned the language, then landed a plum job as an assistant at the University of Würzburg. It was a good start, but when Hitler came to power, Hampe's position weakened. He'd received a negative evaluation from the NS Dozentenbund, the Nazi teachers' union, as being insufficiently committed to the Führer's ideology; Hampe was a patriot but not a committed Nazi. After he finished his thesis on the Charioteer of Delphi, he managed despite his loss in standing to obtain a lectureship at the University of Kiel. But again he was blackballed, this time by the leader of the Nazi lecturers' association. As that nasty affair dragged on, Hampe received his call-up notice.

The scholar's fluency in Greek probably saved his life. Rather than being sent to the Eastern Front, he was assigned as an interpreter in Crete, which Helias had just left on his way to Cairo. In the summer of 1944, Hampe moved on to Athens; he was now an analyst as well, tasked with reading and evaluating the stream of illegal pamphlets and newspapers that emerged from the Greek underground. He studied leftist proclamations, press releases from the government in exile, tidbits from Allied announcements on the BBC, and after-battle reports from the *andartes*. They gave him a clear window into the thoughts of the enemy.

That spring, Stalin's armies had driven through central Poland and southeastern Europe, and Churchill was concerned that they would eventually reach the shores of the Adriatic. If they marched into Athens supported by those *andarte* groups that were on the left, Greece would be lost to British influence for at least a generation, perhaps much longer. "Improvise and dare," the British leader instructed his staff. "This is the time to play high." The country was not only crucial to controlling the Balkans; it was a gateway to Britain's immensely lucrative holdings in India and beyond as well as to the Black Sea and the Russian hinterlands, which held enormous reserves of mineral and agricultural wealth.

With Soviet armies advancing, Wehrmacht strategists began to worry that their Army Group E would be stranded, cut off from the rest of the continent and the battle against the Allies in France. Late that month, as Helias and the other Greek Desk operatives watched, the army began to move its battalions. And as with Paris, Hitler ordered that the capital be reduced to rubble. Dynamite, artillery rounds, and the fresh water behind the Marathon Dam would be the tools.

But even if the German generals on the ground ignored Hitler's order to raze the city, there was a second problem: Athens hadn't yet seen large, destructive battles. It had been saved from much of the ravages of conflict, but if the *andartes* and the Germans fought each other or the *andartes* battled the British or the competing factions of *andantes* themselves went to war, the city and its artifacts would suffer. Each side had its priorities: the Germans wanted to depart Greece with as much manpower and weaponry as they could; the *andartes* wanted to seize control before the British took over and installed King George II; the British wanted the opposite. Any large-scale battle between any two of the combatants could lead to "final, senseless destruction."

The Germans brought in units from distant regions and assigned them to protect the evacuation routes from attack. Meanwhile,

Luftwaffe transit planes evacuated troops from Crete and Rhodes and brought them to Athens. Roland Hampe watched them come. "Sea and air transports arrived daily from the islands of the Aegean Sea," he said. "At first, these transports were left unmolested by the British." That didn't last. On September 15, RAF fighters dove on the ranks of Ju-52 transport planes sitting on airfields around Athens, destroying half of them. British destroyers attacked ships ferrying men to the mainland. The Germans brought in more Ju-52s and flew them only at night, but the threat of a widespread battle notched up.

The Greek deputy prime minister flew to Belgrade to meet the Nazi "special plenipotentiary envoy," an Austrian named Hermann Neubacher. After hours of negotiations, Neubacher messaged the Nazi minister of foreign affairs, Joachim von Ribbentrop. He used business code to describe the negotiations:

> *In Greece, in connection with the general situation, there is evidently a competition between the two large firms, with the old firm [he meant Great Britain] wanting to benefit from our presumed abandonment of the market. . . . The business matter is extremely delicate. . . . Greek representatives of the company believe that such a discussion could prevent a special action [an uprising by the* andartes*] planned for the near future against the Greek market.*

Hitler was informed of the meeting and reacted badly, ordering that all contact with the enemy stop and demanding that the Greeks be annihilated, along with their capital. The timing was interesting; he'd recently learned that General von Choltitz in Paris had, after negotiations with the Allies and the French underground, declined to destroy that city. The linchpin of the French negotiations was the Resistance's agreeing not to launch an assault on the departing German battalions. A similar scenario existed in Athens; Hampe was trying to negotiate a Paris solution with the Wehrmacht. But Hitler was determined to avoid a second betrayal.

By the end of September, the message had gotten through to Neubacher. "To avoid misunderstandings," he wrote, "the aim of our disruptive policy in Greece is a purely negative one. . . . We are to intensify every conflict and create as many disputes and clashes as possible." Fighting in Athens between the British and the Russians would drain both sides of men and matériel. The German wanted to leave Athens scot-free, then watch the city burn behind him.

Roland Hampe was aware of this, and he disapproved. Even as a lowly interpreter, he decided to do what he could to stop the order from being carried out. He was, in some ways, the brother underneath the uniform that Greek archaeologists had dreamed of. At least in the beginning.

Hampe sent out feelers among his contacts. He talked to people. He found "confusion, conflicting efforts, rapidly changing constellations—in a word, chaos." German atrocities had embittered the *andartes*; they were eager to inflict pain on their tormentors and to install their leaders in power. The Germans had proved their indifference to Greek lives, and the British were terrified of a Soviet takeover. There must have been men in Athens who thought first of saving the city, but Hampe didn't find many. "In the midst of highly explosive materials," he wrote, "a match, even just a small spark, can trigger a catastrophe."

Hampe was not even an officer. That might have actually helped him. He found that "when it came to the issues at stake, both sides were more willing to listen to a man who did not deserve to be taken seriously in military terms." Talking to Hampe would endanger no one's career; he simply didn't rate. He had other things to offer, too: he was fluent in the language and knew the major players on both sides. Greek politics was dynamic and complex, and few Germans could penetrate the heavy fog. But through his job and his own quirks, Hampe delighted in the minutiae of the Greek political scene. He knew people he shouldn't have known.

He had a sense of himself as playing a part in history. "The setting is Athens," he opened his memoir of this time, "and it is about nothing less than the rescue of Athens at a time when the fate of this city . . . was threatened to the utmost." That matter was more serious to him than losing Belgrade; it simply was. Athens, Rome, and Paris were "not only capitals of modern states, but for the European consciousness they are foundations of Western attitudes and customs of symbolic importance that goes far beyond what can be rationally grasped." In this, he agreed with Rodney and Dorothy.

Hampe had another thing on his side: he was a classical archaeologist. In Greece, they were special. Junior archaeologists and employees of the Ministry of Education were seen as meddlesome bureaucrats and often despised; they claimed land for excavations that might have been used for grazing animals. But the more distinguished ones who worked with the foreign archaeological societies to unearth the Ancients enjoyed respect and prominence absent in England, say, or Germany. Servants of a concept called *leitourgia*, derived from the ancient Greek word for performing a public duty at one's own cost, they were "priests of a secular religion."

Classicists were celebrities often tapped to run for the senate or to lead political parties. Hampe not only spoke Greek; he could speak the language of stratigraphy and Bronze Age chisels with the people who mattered.

CHAPTER 28

The Young Plan

As Hampe contemplated how to keep Athens reasonably intact, Rodney was working along similar lines, though the two were unaware of each other. On Crete, Rodney's operatives were already experimenting with techniques to get the Germans out without destroying Greece's patrimony. The effort was headed up by the Greek Desk operative Morton Royse, a former Marine and bomber pilot. The intrepid Royse was trying to gauge the possibility of mass desertion or even mutiny, something Hampe never even considered.

Royse thought the prospects slim. Crete was a plush posting for a German soldier and "there was no Allied army in sight to give them an honorable excuse for surrender." But his Greek agents, who rubbed shoulders with German soldiers every day, noticed that some seemed less enthusiastic than others. Royse targeted them. His agents talked to the soldiers, trying to turn them into "inside men" who'd spread the Greek Desk's message: "The war was already lost; further resistance, demanded by party politicians for the sake of their own necks, was a matter of simple, suicidal mathematics for the whole

German nation." The soldier's duty in such a situation was to disobey his leader and look to "family, nation and the homeland."

Royse played on German fears, using rumors and village gossip. The Western Front was collapsing, the Wehrmacht was rushing to secure the homeland, and yet those soldiers were still patrolling olive groves and dusty villages. Didn't that seem unusual? With every day that passed, their chances of evacuation were growing slimmer. Royse's aim was to get 20 percent of a unit intrigued by the idea of surrender; it was tough going. Some of his best prospects were "lost in the shuffle," evacuated or relocated before any concrete plans for desertion could be made. Others actually left the ranks on their own and surrendered.

He scored some wins. Royse had one inside man within the Luftwaffe; after getting his instructions, the aviator talked to thirty enlisted men, "asking them to do all possible damage to fuses, wiring, etc., and try to get friends to do the same." Success metrics were impossible; the OSS couldn't very well go to German airfields and check an engine's spark plug connections, but "judging by the great number of unexploded bombs and a few intact buildings," the agents were having an impact.

Rodney was more ambitious. In what little spare time he had in Cairo, he composed a document that would become known as "the Young Plan." The archaeologist foresaw that Greece would become a pressure point in the postwar world, and he wanted American eyes and ears on the ground—to shape Greece's future without Greeks necessarily knowing about it. He'd created a spy outfit nearly from nothing. Now he wanted to project it into the future.

The Young Plan had three objectives: to create a permanent spy network on the ground; to gather intel on key economic and political matters, especially from those parts of Greece roiled by sectarian conflict and intrigue; and to supply said intel to the makers of American foreign policy in a secure manner. From the water supply to emerging epidemics to political gossip, he wanted the Americans to have a first-rate, firsthand source in place. His "customers" would be everyone from the American embassy to the Greek War Relief Association, but his aims were larger: his reports "will provide a basis for the formulation of U.S. Policy not only toward Greece and her neighboring Balkan states, but toward other larger powers which have interests in those states." The network would remain "as long as American interests demand."

They would do good, too. Operatives would find and eliminate the stay-behind spies and saboteurs the Germans would plant in Athens to sow chaos and cripple the Greek government. They'd see to the health of the Greeks. "Who is on local committees, whether they work well or badly in particular places and why, where there are doctors and nurses available, and if they are good or not; what diseases there are, typhus, typhoid, malaria, tuberculosis, venereal and any other; hospital facilities, and what medicines are available or needed." This was intel for winning the peace. When the operatives passed a field, they were to note the kinds of crops planted. Was good fertilizer being used? Did the farmer have work animals? Were sheep and goats visible and in what numbers? Boring stuff but essential if you wanted to save millions of Greeks and bring the country into the American sphere.

The archaeologist asked Washington for seventy men and women drawn from the Greek Desk and the wider OSS, plus three Greek radio operators and other local operatives. He would use the same "archaeological *ouija* board" that he'd used to recruit his spymasters and place them in the right places. As for himself, he'd go into

Athens at the earliest possible moment and begin setting up the organization. Once it was on its way, he hoped to hand the reins to one of his Greek Desk lieutenants and do what he really wanted to do: save Greek lives through humanitarian work and then return to his "natural" vocation, archaeology.

Archaeologists had been used in wartime before, but this was a radical expansion of the idea. Rodney suggested placing classicists in Greece who would train agents, run networks, and spy on the society that believed they were in Athens to unearth the Ancients. He even proposed that the American School could do double duty as an espionage front, a "permanent and plausible cover for American intelligence men." The plan spoke to a few things: Rodney's muscular approach to things in general, his fear that the British or the Russians would warp the country's trajectory toward democracy, and the realpolitik he'd learned on the job.

The trick was to get Washington interested in the scheme. Greece was seen as a sideshow in the unfolding contest between the East and the West. In late 1944, the State Department was cautious: officials told General Donovan that the OSS could keep people in Athens but only to observe and report. "No American agencies [will] become involved, directly or indirectly, with Greek domestic policies or factional disputes." Rodney saw that as surrendering before the first shot had been fired.

The British would be an obstacle to his plans. "I would be all for arming [the *andartes*] if only to spite the foolish British policy in the matter," he wrote. As a charter member of the American elite, he might have been expected to support a more conservative line, but his views had become thoroughly jaundiced. "In my own view, British policy is completely wrong." Washington was skeptical. It cut the proposed staff from seventy to fifty and renamed the project "Young Plan Jr."

In July 1944, Rodney had received jarring news. In the central Greek town of Karpenissi, where the leftist *andartes* had a base, mysterious parachutes had been descending from the sky. The OSS determined that they belonged to a Soviet military team. A "Colonel Popov" from the Soviet mission in Belgrade, along with three Yugoslav partisans, had arrived to meet with the leftist leaders.

The Cairo spy networks lit up. What was Stalin up to? His motives were unclear, but the State Department was suddenly paying close attention to events in Greece. Rodney hoped the bold Soviet move would spark the State Department to back his archaeologist-led spy network. And for a while, it did.

On August 31, one of Rodney's agents in Athens sent a message that the Germans were burning documents at their headquarters. The end of the occupation was approaching. Rodney was excited. "We here are sitting with our tongues out and panting from exhaustion," he wrote Caskey, "but with the feeling that we are on the last lap (thank God) and we had just better hang on grimly to the end. If it doesn't come soon, it will be the end of us—at least of me."

If Rodney was spending most of his time thinking of the geopolitical picture, Dorothy was thinking about starving Greeks. Sending letters composed with her impeccable courtesy, she pressed him, along with officials of the UN and Greek War Relief, to bring in food. What were the plans to stop the famine? It would do no good to arrange for Greek democracy if half of the Greeks were dead. "Each week I fully await news of the post liberation plans to feed the islands," she wrote Rodney on July 5. "No word yet from New York about how much money they wish to put in our hands. No word from [Greek War Relief's] Curtis about what he thinks, no word from Archer or others about what UNRRA thinks and no further word from you has come." It was her turn to be angry.

Dorothy, never strong, was now suffering from anemia and dizziness. She was also cranky; she treated the amphora expert Virginia Grace badly when the latter came to Izmir to help out. The job had wrecked her and she was too honest to hide it. She wrote to headquarters, evaluating herself as unsentimentally as she had evaluated the Greek refugees:

> *I am now an old lemon, squeezed perfectly dry and should be got rid of. My output from now on will be less and less and what there is of it will be more and more unreliable. In addition, my temper is foul and I am unfit to associate with civilized human beings. There is, I think, no danger of my collapsing on you and I do not ask to be removed, transferred or vacationed. I am just telling you I am a complete liability and you can do as you think best. . . .*
>
> *It will probably be wise to ship me home. In the meantime, I take pills. All of that seems to me beside the point which is that I'm no good to the business.*

There were moments when she couldn't collect her thoughts or remember the name of a key agent. Her once black hair had turned almost completely white and was beginning to fall out.

Depending on his mood, Rodney could be either brutal or solicitous. At one point, he wrote Caskey, "If there's anything left of her, perhaps it would be well to send her to a beach." But he bucked Dorothy up, too. "I am writing Hiram personally under separate cover," he wrote, "to tell her that she is a foolish old thing to run herself down on paper in a way that is so obviously contrary to the facts." His fellow archaeologists convinced him that "Hiram is really falling apart"; Rodney, though short of bodies, told her she should go home to recover. "She will never get fixed up in the Middle East, only in a green place like Connecticut where she can have peace and quiet. Let's see what a month of peace does for her—and a rest which I think she needs badly." He was the gruff father figure, but he did care.

Rodney had the luxury of being close to the action; his radio buzzed with reports of train cars destroyed and Nazis killed. There was a certain psychological relief in that. But Dorothy spent her days talking to Greeks, who were in bad shape. Two couriers came to visit her in Izmir, having made their way across the Aegean. Weeks earlier, they'd requested "a great many things" to fight the Germans, most likely guns and ammunition. Before they left Greece, Dorothy had written them that Rodney had sent "an encouraging answer" to their pleas. But that decision had later been reversed, and before Dorothy could get word to them, they'd shown up in her office.

After offering the two men tea, she broke the news that the OSS could give them nothing. Dorothy watched as their faces fell. One of them, "just returned from Evoia where things were still hot[,] . . . was ready to burst into tears." The other leapt to his feet and shouted that "if deserted by the Allies they would continue to fight." If no guns arrived, the *andartes* would haul down the mountains of Greece and throw them on the Germans, he raved in the little room.

Dorothy rarely expressed her personal feelings in her OSS correspondence. This time, she couldn't help herself. "It was awful," she wrote in a handwritten letter to Rodney. "I felt . . . that I was throwing my best friends to the wolves."

On October 7, Dorothy received a cable from the Greek War

Relief Association saying they needed medicine urgently. There was almost none on the Greek islands. Dorothy would usually request funds through the OSS bureaucracy, but the GWRA was begging. She took twenty-five hundred dollars (about forty-five thousand dollars today) from her own personal funds and cadged thirty-five hundred dollars from friends. Since the money was unauthorized, she doubted she would get reimbursed but was fatalistic about it. "I borrowed money where I could and got the things there," she said. She would never get the money back.

She was desperate to get into Greece. In a repeat of her attempt to get a job with an architectural firm in the 1920s, she looked at a particular male profession. "What hope of my being an officer in the Marine Corps?" she wrote another Greek Desk officer. "Army 2nd choice. I have an honorable discharge from the army (1919). . . . If I go into Greece, I would like to go as an American soldier." It's unclear if she ever formally applied for a transfer, but it was always unlikely the Marines would want a fifty-year-old woman at the end of her tether. Rodney wanted her to rest, but Dorothy refused. "I shall continue until ordered to quit," she wrote Rodney. He found her some nerve pills instead.

Rodney and the others knew, too, that the eyes of the archaeological world were upon them. Back in New York, the Archaeological Institute of America, which had a long history of protecting the world's historical artifacts, called off its yearly meeting. Instead, the head officers met at the Metropolitan Museum in New York to talk about "Europe's Monuments as Affected by the War." William Dinsmoor, chairman of the monuments commission, spoke. The hour was late and the fate of the antiquities was soon to be decided, he told the audience. It was every classicist's duty to force "the barbarian enemy from the sites and monuments which his presence has so long desecrated."

It was easy enough to say from the Upper East Side. The archaeologists never heard the speech, but the sentiment added to their anxiety levels. "What are my chances of getting out of here?" wrote an Izmir operative to Rodney. "I have lost most of the love I had for the Greeks and have almost lost the desire to go in. We have 45 men living here and no room for them. Flies are bad and so are mosquitoes. And so are sand flies. And so are Turks. And so are Greeks. And so are Americans. And so am I."

Caskey summed up the mood from Izmir. "Our good little organization seems to be cracking up."

CHAPTER 29

The Negotiations

To rescue Athens, Roland Hampe began with a report. In it, he emphasized that the Wehrmacht had to make contact with "important Greek personalities" in order to broker a ceasefire that would allow them to leave without significant fighting. Knowing the German repugnance for negotiating with the *andartes*, he didn't name any names, leaving the question of who was an important Greek personality open for the moment. The report "fell on worthy ground." He was invited to a meeting with General Hellmuth Felmy, the commander of the LXVIII Army Corps.

Hampe met the general; one of his first questions was about rumors of the Führer's orders to destroy the capital. Felmy dodged the question, which seemed to indicate the orders were real. But he told the classicist that he had loved Greece ever since he was a schoolboy and had "no inclination to destroy Athens." But how to save it?

The archaeologist suggested they try an open-city approach, that is, declare Athens a demilitarized zone that would not be defended from enemy advances. It had been used before in warfare to spare unnecessary bloodshed and protect a place's heritage. Felmy didn't reject the idea outright, but he said such a declaration would require that the *andartes* refrain from attacks. He asked Hampe to go to the Greeks and see if this was possible. The archaeologist would report directly back to Felmy.

Hampe probably wasn't aware, but Felmy bore a huge liability with the Greeks. He was ultimately responsible for the massacre at Kalavryta, the village where 438 Greeks (and one protesting Austrian officer) had been murdered with great savagery. Felmy hadn't been on the scene and he hadn't given the order to destroy the village, but he'd directed the soldiers to respond to an earlier ambush of German troops, knowing full well that doing so would likely involve brutal reprisals. The general later claimed that his men shot only those "suspected to be in connection with gangs" but his defense would be dismantled by postwar Hostages Trial judges, who convicted Felmy of war crimes. The Germans saw Felmy as "an old-school conservative professional soldier with a conscience and civil courage." The Greeks saw him as a killer.

To open talks with the other side, Hampe reached out to a man he'd met on Crete, Michalis Fumis. The Greek was a patriot, but Hampe trusted him. Later, he found out that Fumis's name was on a list of people to be taken as hostages if civil unrest—that is, guerrilla warfare on the part of the *andartes*—got out of hand. If the mission failed, Fumis would be taken hostage by the Germans. Hampe apparently never revealed this to his colleague.

Fumis began canvassing his contacts. Meanwhile, a crisis developed five miles from central Athens at the Haidari concentration camp. The prison held high-level Greek politicians and luminaries under the command of the notorious *Sturmbannführer* Paul Radomski, who enjoyed whipping or executing his subjects for the slightest infraction. That September, representatives of the Wehrmacht, the German embassy, and the SD met to discuss what to do with the inmates as the Germans withdrew. Officers from the SD issued a demand: they must be allowed to take all "politically important personalities" from their barracks and execute them.

This was unfortunate for more than the obvious reasons. The murders would eliminate some of the very men Hampe was hoping to negotiate with, including Themistoklis Sofoulis, the eighty-three-year-old leader of the Liberal Party who was imprisoned at Haidari. Handsome, honest, and courageous, Sofoulis was trusted by most factions in Greek life, except perhaps by the far left. Killing him would further embitter the *andartes* and make any hopes of an open-city agreement that much dimmer. Luckily for the archaeologist (and for Sofoulis), Felmy attended the meeting.

The general listened as the SD men delivered their ultimatum. He didn't respond right away but seemed to mull things over. When he spoke, he avoided rejecting the demand outright; in fact, he didn't address it at all. He merely suggested, as the representative of the Wehrmacht, that if the SD went ahead with the executions, they might find themselves managing their own retreat from Greece. Specifically, Felmy told the Nazi officers that, if Sofoulis and the others died, he would simply not be able to find the men to guard the withdrawal route or the train lines the SD would use to escape. They'd have to deal with the *andartes*, and the enraged, vengeful Athenians, on their own.

The SD reversed its position.

Soon afterward, Fumis made some calls and got a meeting with Sofoulis, who had just been released from the camp. Before seeing the distinguished politician, Hampe already had a leg up: Sofoulis was, rather predictably, a fellow archaeologist—in fact, a famous one. He'd been the first to excavate the ruins of the classical city-state of ancient Messene in the south of the country, the home of the Achaean Greeks, who'd fought valiantly against the Spartans.

Hampe walked into an apartment on Dimokritou Street and found the politician reading a German book, which Hampe found remarkable. He began by asking, rather awkwardly, how Sofoulis's experience at Haidari had gone. "I have seen a lot," the politician said. Hampe nodded, then laid out his case. Could Sofoulis speak to the right people and get the Greeks on board with a ceasefire? "I have just been released from the camp," Sofoulis said, "and I still don't have the threads back in my hands." But he would try.

The archaeologist had made contact with the Greek political world; now he tried the religious one in the person of Archbishop Damaskinos, a highly respected cleric who'd openly called for the concealment of Jews from the Gestapo. Damaskinos's unyielding opposition to the Germans, Hampe felt, would give him credibility with the partisans. He arranged an interview and arrived at the bishop's palace. He was early and sat in the cleric's waiting room as a stream of men entered and exited. His wait went on for hours.

A man who'd been in Greece only a short time might have gotten fed up and stormed away, but Hampe kept his composure. He knew from experience that "the convulsive concept of time in our world"—that is, the German world—didn't apply in the Mediterranean. Finally, the door opened and the cleric came out of his office to greet him; Hampe chatted for a moment, then made his pitch. Would the archbishop do his best to unite the Greek factions in a pledge not to attack the Germans until the withdrawal was complete? The archbishop said no, he couldn't go that far. Would he at least meet with Felmy? Hampe asked. The archbishop agreed.

The next day, the parties met, with Hampe serving as interpreter. The men spoke in long monologues, laying out their positions. Hampe struggled to keep up, experiencing "the most strenuous hour of my life" as he memorized the speeches, then translated them instantaneously in his head. He also tried here and there to shape the talks toward his ends. When the cleric mentioned the need to preserve the Marathon Dam, Hampe interjected in Greek.

"Archbishop, didn't you also want to mention the power station and the port facilities in Piraeus?"

To Felmy, it must have looked like the interpreter was asking for a clarification. The archbishop shot Hampe a "sly, understanding look."

"Of course," he said. "I just forgot." Hampe added the request to his translation.

By the end, they'd reached an understanding: the archbishop would talk to the partisans, and as a gesture of goodwill, Felmy would countermand the order to blow up the Marathon Dam. Two days later, sappers removed the dynamite from the concrete base.

Hampe was pleased. He kept up his rounds. A general and ex–prime minister, Theodoros Pangalos soon emerged on the archaeologist's radar. He led a group of six military men, conservatives who wanted to install a republican government before the Germans withdrew and the British arrived, blocking a Communist takeover. Pangalos lived in Aristotelous Street, his apartment building surrounded by "a force of burly men," his bodyguards, who were on alert for an attack not from the Germans but from the leftist *andartes*. Pangalos's reputation as a man who displayed "ruthless severity" toward all things Communist was well-known in Greece. Hampe slipped through the security cordon and gained an audience.

Pangalos was an amateur military historian fond of the sound of his own voice. The meeting began with his mini dissertation on the strategies of nineteenth-century battles, during which the general spoke and Hampe nodded along. Once the lecture was over, Pangalos told the German that, in order to install a new government, the current one would have to step down.

It was a problem. If Pangalos and his coterie assumed power, the *andartes* would erupt; a civil war would become much more likely. If pitched battles broke out in the city center, the Germans, who feared chaos, would intervene. Athens would become the stage for a three-cornered war that would "call into question everything we were hoping to achieve." *How will you do it?* Hampe asked nervously, that is, topple the government. "Leave that to me for now," Pangalos said. "I have some experience in coups."

Hampe was now deep in the weeds of Greek politics. He went to Sofoulis. *If the generals will name you as prime minister,* he asked, *with Pangalos as minister of defense, would you accept?* Sofoulis said no. Hampe had heard rumors that the British had offered him a viceroyalty in a new royalist government. Was there any truth to that? Sofoulis scoffed. "The German occupation will be followed by another occupation: the English." He'd turned them down, too.

If the Greek situation seemed to be devolving into a stereotypical Balkan quagmire, the German side was also, but not equally, divided. The split came in the thinking of the Wehrmacht versus the SD. The Nazi intelligence agency opposed the open-city idea, and so after a few weeks of negotiation, Hampe found himself maneuvering against his own side. He had to keep news of the talks from reaching the spies, and in order to do this, he needed to use the telephone; if he continued to visit leftists and Communists, the SD, which had informants everywhere, would eventually catch on. But the phone network in Athens had been shut down by the German authorities in part to stop the *andartes* from plotting, so the archaeologist spent long hours walking or driving to various apartments and cafés spread across the city to meet his coconspirators. These forays were made more uncomfortable by the fact that certain sectors were now controlled by the Communists, who'd forbidden German soldiers from entering.

Hampe was undeterred. His guile, his good Greek, and his bona fides with Greek notables got him through more than one roadblock. That strategy worked most of the time but not always. One afternoon, when he was meeting with Fumis in his apartment in the Rouf district, he heard a horn blaring. It stopped and then started up again. He walked to the window and looked down. It was his Italian driver on the street below leaning through the car window and pressing the horn; around him stood a number of armed men.

Hampe dashed down the stairs and onto the street. A crowd had gathered around his car, and a Communist patrol was questioning the driver. As Hampe ran up, the men pointed their bulky old-fashioned handguns at him.

The archaeologist slipped into the middle of the group. "Good evening," he said in Greek. "What wonderful pistols you have! Are you all so well equipped?" As he spoke, he nudged the driver in the ribs and sidled slowly toward the passenger door. After marveling over a couple of the guns, he gently opened the door and slid into the front seat. He gave a final wave and pulled the door closed, and the driver hit the gas pedal. As they sped off, one of the patrollers called to Hampe, "Don't show your face here again."

Soon after, the SD unintentionally solved his communications problem in the most gruesome way imaginable. On September 11, news reached Hampe that the spy agency had invited its Greek interpreters to Merlin Street and executed them. One of the translators jumped from a window to escape his masters and died in a nearby courtyard. Most likely, the SD felt the Greeks knew too much about what the agents had done in Greece and wanted them silenced before the withdrawal. Hampe was disgusted; he and his Athenian allies took to calling the intelligence agency by a code name: "the criminals."

Hampe sensed an opening. The SD officers he knew "were usually unable to remember Greek proper names for more than ten minutes." For years, they'd relied on their interpreters to keep track of which Adonises under surveillance were speaking to which Eliases and what they were saying. But the SD had wiped out their own interpreters, leaving a void in their local knowledge. Hampe called his contact in the SD, who was unaware that the archaeologist was plotting with the Greeks, and said he needed to be able to speak to certain prominent figures in order to fight the Communists. Could the man approve some calls to people Hampe needed to talk to? When the SD man asked for a list, Hampe wrote the names of a few well-known rightists at the top, then added the "personalities" he wanted to target for his conspiracy, including Sofoulis. The officer glanced over the list, which was quite literally Greek to him, and approved it.

CHAPTER 30

Going In

As September wore on, the Germans began their withdrawals in earnest. Rodney pressed his Crete operative Royse for fresh reports on "concentrated troop movements, air evacuation activities and German demolition plans." The Greek American commandos hit the trains again and again; joining forces with the *andartes*, they came down from the hills and confronted the Germans directly, strafing German barracks, running off with their horses, and dynamiting their storehouses.

After the Soviet team that had parachuted in finally departed, the State Department's attention was drawn away to hotter theaters. The staff for the Young Plan was cut again, this time to twenty-five. And it was given a deadline: January 1, 1945. If Rodney and his archaeologists could get into Athens as the Germans were leaving, they would have a few months to shape the country's politics and save as many souls as they could.

Rodney had been offered a new job with the United Nations Relief and Rehabilitation Administration. The outfit's brief was to feed the starving, house the displaced, and assist refugees as they rebuilt the countries the Nazis had ravaged. It would go on to help millions after the war. Rodney's position would be "important" and he would be on the ground, where he would move freely, solo, without a large staff.

On September 12, the archaeologist journeyed to Key West, the OSS base in Turkey, preparing to make the jump over the Aegean and into Greece. He had to time his arrival precisely: early enough to influence events but not early enough to get himself and his spies shot by the departing Germans. He made his way to Boston. Then on September 17, he motored away from the harbor in a caïque equipped with powerful engines and carrying a jeep to get him around Greece. The vessel hit bad, blustery weather.

Rodney reached Plomari on the island of Lesbos. He was the first Allied soldier to step onto Greek soil since the liberation had begun. The harbor was "black with people." When the caïque pulled ashore, the enormous crowd roared. Rodney was mobbed; his jeep was surrounded bumper to bumper by weeping, rapturous Greeks; people on balconies threw rice and flowers. In the town center, the mayor's wife sang "America" and dignitaries plied Rodney with big shots of ouzo. When told about a banquet planned in their honor, Rodney refused, as he was there to feed the Greeks, not be fed by them, which brought cheers from the crowd. (Later, their guard down, he and his companions "got some apples and walnuts stuffed into us.") Bottles of Scotch that had been hoarded until the Allies came appeared; villagers who had lived in Pittsburgh and New York were pushed to the front to chat. Letters to relatives in America were crammed into the men's hands and pockets. Hard drinking occurred. Wherever they drove, groups of barefoot boys accompanied them, screaming with excitement, while others hoisted a banner that read, "WELLCOME WORLTS SAVVERS."

The archaeologist spent nineteen days being feted, and apart from the initial jolt of happiness, he hated nearly every moment of it. "I have never felt so silly in my life," he wrote the others. He was being welcomed as a savior when, in his estimation, he hadn't done nearly enough for those people. No fan of public display of emotions, or any displays of emotion really, he was kissed by dozens and dozens of hysterical women (and men) who struggled to express their love and gratitude. And there was the problem of what came next. The Greeks thought FDR would save them in some unspecified but utterly miraculous way. Rodney suspected otherwise. He winced when one of his companions gave a speech that might or might not have implied "that a large American ship with everything necessary would be in the next day."

He got a feel for the political temperature. The leftists were hugely popular among the masses, which meant that the rich were terrified. There was a great deal of talk about Communism, "but nobody really knows what it means." He moved on to Athens, where people on the street looked surprisingly good: clean, well-dressed, no scabies. But his agents in the islands told him that many children were "alive and little more," their bodies wasted from years of near starvation. Despite the joy over the Americans' arrival and the relative calm, he felt a "bloodletting" coming.

There were hundreds of things to do and hundreds of Greeks clamoring for a moment. "[People] seem to think I am here to do the work of American Express, the Consulate, Athens College, the Archaeological School and MGM. . . . It's a hell of a life." His agents trickled into the capital for debriefs. He bought one breakfast—fried eggs, tomatoes, bread, and coffee—for 1.3 trillion drachmas. The presence of German stay-behind agents was front of mind; though blowing the Marathon Dam was probably beyond their capabilities, they could still spread havoc.

He met one of the operatives from Settler, the first mission to go into Greece. The man reported that he had prepared for the stay-behinds; months before, he'd begun training a twenty-year-old Greek man to be a double agent. The man became an informant for the Germans, passing harmless bits of intel and slowly building trust. The Germans warmed to him, and the Greek operative slowly weaned from them the phone numbers, addresses, and license plate numbers of the main sleeper agents, along with their cipher system, their call letters, and the frequencies for their contacts with Berlin. "I told him to keep the boy at it most discreetly," Rodney said, "and to give me all the dope." Rodney was chuffed to find that his Settler man was "damn good" at his job.

To decompress, he dove into the Aegean and lay floating on his back, staring at the cerulean sky. Surrounded by a few friends, he was at peace. "I feel ten years rejuvenated," he wrote. In the back of his mind was the fate of the antiquities. Had the National Museum been pillaged? Had the Agora survived intact? Had his dig on Lycabettus hill been bulldozed over (unlikely) or struck by a bomb (slightly more likely)? He was half tempted to get in his jeep and go to the excavations—he didn't specify which ones—but the jubilant crowds prevented him. The trip, "which I dread rather anyway, as it would mean more being kissed," would have to wait until the jubilation ebbed.

A month after Rodney went in, Sperling set off from Alexandria in a small caïque with a three-person Greek crew. In the hold sat a jeep fueled up and adorned with American flags. The boat motored northwest. Allied fighters had cleared most of the Axis shipping from the western Aegean, but the waters closer to Turkey still bristled with German vessels.

One night, Sperling was belowdecks dozing when a bright light suddenly shot through the hatch and illuminated the cabin. He sat up. It had to be a German patrol boat or perhaps a submarine. He listened. The crewmen standing above his head were talking to someone, a German officer. *If they board, they'll find me and the jeep,* Sperling thought. *I'll be killed or taken prisoner.*

The wooden deck above his head creaked. The crew was moving around. Suddenly, the light cut off and blackness returned. Sperling heard the hiss of a submarine submerging. The crew must have convinced the sub officer that they were fishermen positioning their nets for the grouper and mackerel that swam in the Aegean.

The boat skirted the shore of Mykonos and headed toward Tinos to take on supplies and gas. The captain put the boat just off a beach and one of the men swam ashore. After a brief wait, the man returned; the island was clear of German soldiers. The captain put the caïque on the beach, where rocks rasped against the hull, and Sperling and his men drove the jeep off. It was morning. Sperling rode in the passenger seat as they drove toward the main town. There they were startled to find what looked like a parade in progress; there were marching bands and traditional dancers. When the jeep was seen pulling off the boat, a local had run to the mayor, who took the news to mean Allied troops had landed on the island. Sperling's tunic was tugged and pulled as he made his way to the town center; people wanted to touch him, even for a brief second.

Sperling's team stayed the night, then reboarded the ship and headed toward the southern coast of Greece, landing a good distance from Athens. The American, a devoted anti-Communist, was thinking about the Soviets. "If [German bases] are overrun by the Russians," wrote one OSS operative, "our experience to date does not encourage the belief that we will be supported or even tolerated in efforts to organize secret intelligence networks in these areas." Instead of heading to Athens, he sped north toward the Albanian border, where any Russian incursion would have likely begun.

Greece looked stripped down. The green hills were nude, dun. Everything that could have been eaten had been pulled from the ground, and the people Sperling saw along the roads, mostly women and children, looked like wraiths and were often barefoot. He drove into a small town; as in Tinos, word quickly got around that the "liberators" had materialized. One of the people who rushed to see the American was a military officer wearing a cap with a bold red-and-yellow band around it and red collar tabs on his blouse. He was Russian.

The officer greeted him. "My superior is staying nearby," he called. "He'd like to see you."

Sperling was spooked with good reason. Greece was a no-man's-land of warring factions and invisible alliances, and he had no backup. He said nothing, gunned the jeep, turned it around, and headed toward Athens.

Finally, Dorothy arrived. She wanted only, as "a poor, frail woman with no political axe to grind," to feed and clothe people. She was now fully enraged by the British; like the Germans, they were playing favorites with relief supplies, hoping to establish "a political stranglehold on the Greek people." The *andartes* complained to her that London had promised "white elephants and rivers of milk," but had delivered nothing. The Americans were, sadly, almost no better. She'd hoped to dispense five hundred tons of badly needed wheat and rice and green vegetables, but her superiors cut that to fifty tons. She scraped and wheedled and pleaded to get as many boatloads of food as she could manage and headed off to the islands of Lesbos and Chios. There she found people dying from lack of medicine; the Germans had stripped many hospitals, even pulling sheets from the beds. "No surgical supplies, cotton, bandages, anesthetics, ether, catgut, rubber-gloves. There is not even one morphine injection." Around 400,000 Greeks had already died from starvation and related causes.

After much pleading, Dorothy got three hundred tons of food and clothes moving from the defunct OSS base known as Boston. She was able to see penicillin and sacks of rice put into people's hands and carried off to their simple homes. In the evenings after hours of work, she felt wasted by anemia. "I have not sufficient energy left to do even a passable job," she wrote a relief official. It wasn't true; she was rescuing thousands of Greeks from slow deaths.

Rodney sent two agents to check on the Acropolis. The marble of the Parthenon had bullet holes, some of the stone had turned dark from tracer bullets, and blocks of marble had been dragged around to serve as firing positions, but it was otherwise in good shape. The National Museum had suffered damage to the roof from mortars, and the exterior had been raked by gunfire, but little else. As for the statues and vases buried under the museum, they were all in place. The curators had remained silent, despite years of intimidation.

Rodney went to the Agora, the old marketplace where he himself had spent years excavating. In the Mycenaean *thollos* tombs, he found debris left behind by Greeks made homeless by the war. He was told a number of them had starved to death. The staff members came to greet him, some of them with bones visible through their flesh. Others stayed away; more than one had gone insane during the occupation. "A lot of mortars landed on the dig," Rodney said, but they'd done little damage. The excavation had fared better than the Greeks who watched over it.

Greek Deskers who'd been posted in other regions flowed into Athens. A few of them had news: they'd uncovered fresh caches of relics. The war hadn't stopped archaeological discoveries; both sides made them while building fortifications or simply exploring the countryside when not fighting the war. Charles Edson, a Greek Desk epigraphist who specialized in Macedonian inscriptions, told Rodney that he'd come across an intact Hellenistic tomb in Salonika during his espionage work. He was "lyrical" with happiness, as was Rodney. Other archaeologists reported promising finds, too, either ones they'd stumbled on or heard about from partisans who knew their allies were mad for relics. Tens of thousands of artifacts were missing, it was true, but hundreds of thousands more, including those recently unearthed, were safe, at least for now.

CHAPTER 31

The Open City

As Rodney inspected his old haunts, Roland Hampe got a call he had been dreading. It was from the Allied military commander in Greece, General Panagiotis Spiliotopoulos. The general wanted a meeting with Felmy. Up to that point, the archaeologist had been able to keep the Allies, especially the British, out of the main negotiations. But it was impossible to keep a secret in Athens for longer than a week or two.

Hampe was called to a meeting with two Greek representatives of the British-backed government in exile. This was a new level of audacity. He was going to meet with men representing the enemy, with whom Germany was still at war, and negotiate the future of a major European capital as a low-level Wehrmacht analyst. He greeted the two men and sat down, declining coffee before remarking that "officers of the German Wehrmacht had expressed their appreciation and genuine joy at the Greek achievements" at the Albanian front, which was most likely untrue, but which Hampe clearly hoped would set a warm mood. Then he launched into what was by now a well-rehearsed monologue repeated in meeting after meeting: the

German people were not enemies of the Greeks; they wanted to save the city, but they needed cooperation. Athens had survived so far, but a new battle would be a disaster. With the Allies poised to take the city, the capital had to be an open zone with no faction dominating.

After he finished, the officers looked at him. "You spoke of the imminent British landing in Greece," one finally said. "Are you saying that the English should not undertake any operations either?"

"Certainly," Hampe said. Especially the paratroopers, he emphasized. Flooding the skies with parachutes would cause the Germans to think an invasion to cut off their retreat from Greece was underway. In that case, they would "fight to the last bullet."

The Greeks shook their heads. The British would never agree. "Out of the question," one of them said.

Hampe remonstrated with the two men. The Greeks had to unite their factions and hold off the British for the sake of Athens and all it meant to people across the globe. "You cannot be indifferent to whether the Greek capital, the only thing Greece still has undamaged, is preserved or destroyed," Hampe said.

The Greeks were incensed. How dared a German preach to them about preserving Greek antiquities and Greek lives? It was absurd. "Do not," said one officer, "rely on the division of our people and do not think you will escape unscathed."

Hampe was, all things considered, a fairly good German, but he was blind to how awful he was being. Though he cared about the Greek people and their patrimony, even in his own retelling of the story he sometimes came across as offensive. He suffered from a mistakes-were-made tic that warped his view of what his side had done in the country. He told the Greeks that "the circumstances of the war had unfortunately led to the occupation of this country"; the passive phrasing must have rung like a cracked bell in the ears of the two officers. What the Greeks called "patriots" and "freedom fighters," he called "gangs" and "bandits." He insinuated that he cared more about Greece than his interlocutors did and that, if Athens were left a pile of rubble, it would be the natives who were to blame. At one point, he asked, "Gentlemen, do you really believe what you are saying?" and was astonished to find that the question "only increased the torrent of words from the other side." Hampe looked at the two men through the prism of timeworn Greek clichés—*Mediterranean types, so emotional!*—while believing he was the model of pure reason. He was, for a couple of hours, insufferable.

After hours of bitter diatribes, Hampe felt defeated. "No one understood me!" he said. He couldn't stand being in the room any longer. "Athens will be destroyed," he told the two men, and left.

Fall weather arrived in Athens. The occasional thunderstorm rolled in from the sea; the humidity dropped, freshening the air. Hampe ran from one meeting to another, evading roadblocks and talking his way past guerrilla patrols. It seemed to him that every time he met with one faction, he was told of another, some new splinter from the main group, that wanted to talk. Rumors abounded: one held that men from the Greek government in exile, with the Brits' support, were driving around the city in a Red Cross vehicle to persuade the *andartes* to join their side against the open-city plotters. The Gestapo, unaware of the negotiations, was hunting left-wing figures, the very people Hampe needed to talk to. Those men had a series of bolt-holes and apartments all over the city, and they often moved between them every couple of hours. Hampe tracked the men down.

The negotiations played out on handbills plastered on city walls, which were faster to the street than newspapers. "One only had to step out the front door to be informed of the news within a few minutes," Hampe said. One morning, he was walking down toward central Athens when he noticed a fresh one that had just gone up. He walked over to read it: the Communist *andartes*, it said, were issuing instructions to their troops to avoid attacks on the Wehrmacht. They would not prevent the Germans from leaving. Hampe glanced at the name at the bottom; it belonged to a prominent general. He felt his spirits lift.

The next morning, as he walked along the same street, he noticed another handbill pasted next to the first one. This one was from the central committee of the leftist EAM, and it bore a small cartoon: a Wehrmacht soldier crouched in a mousetrap. The message read: "No German soldier may leave Greece alive."

Which of the sentiments was true? He sent Fumis to find out. But Hampe knew that Fumis surely had his own sympathies, not necessarily aligned with his own, and it worried him. "It was difficult to check whether such intermediaries had actually carried out their mission," he wrote, "or whether they were deceiving us." Fumis came back with an answer: the first one was closer to the truth; the Communists had taken a "passive" policy toward German troops. Hampe hoped Fumis was telling the truth.

He felt relieved. But a few days later, he emerged from his small house on Lycabettus hill to find a *third* poster, a mimeographed copy of an actual telegram sent from Cairo, placed next to the two others. It ordered the leftist *andartes* to leave Athens. It was from the government in exile. Hampe, fed up, ignored it.

As the temperature dropped, "the situation in Athens was extremely threatening." Bursts of gunfire could be heard day and night as rival factions skirmished; the casualties were left laid out on the street. Bakeries and shops shuttered, depriving residents of bread and milk. Hampe's sources told him that the *andartes* had forty-four battalions, or about twenty-two thousand guerrillas, hidden in the city.

Later, they would detail the partisans' armory: forty-one thousand five hundred rifles, two thousand fifteen machine guns, and thirty-two artillery guns. "Everyone was aware that these were not all of the weapons available," Hampe remarked dryly.

Crossing a street in central Athens while out on one of his expeditions one afternoon, Hampe heard a rattle of gunshots behind him. He turned. A group of armed men was firing at something on the opposite side of the street. As soon as the shooting dropped away, a volley erupted from across the way. He'd stumbled into a gunfight between two unnamed Greek factions; he couldn't even tell who they were.

Hampe froze as the shots rattled around him. A voice called out, *"Germanos!"* One of the combatants had spotted his uniform. The Germans were not involved in this particular dispute. The gunfire stopped and Hampe hurried to the other side of the street. Once he was clear, the shooting resumed.

In early October, a far more serious affair consumed his time. On the road to Delphi, a partisan group had ambushed a squad of German sailors, killing several of them. The Kriegsmarine, the German navy, brought in antitank guns and began hunting the insurgents. The situation threatened to spiral. Finally, the Germans stormed the *andarte* stronghold and ended the battle, with numerous dead on both sides.

The "provocation" increased the pressure on Hampe. Why was he negotiating with men who were killing Germans in the street? Hampe met with the Communists to get answers, but "they swore sacred oaths" that none of their units were involved. On the way back to his home, he glanced out the window of his car as the Italian driver navigated the dark streets. In the headlights, he spotted new handbills plastered on roadside houses. When he stopped to read them, he saw they were from the faction he'd just left, and they were praising the ambush as a heroic victory. "I drove back to the corps in disbelief," he wrote, "and my report was received with disbelief."

A German general ordered the Pankrati district, a leftist stronghold, to be "razed to the ground." Hampe ran to see Felmy, who confirmed the report. The Germans planned to rain down shells on civilians and insurgents alike. Hampe objected. "General chaos would break out," he told the general. "Apart from the human side, the fate of the antiquities must also be considered." There was a famous site on the outer edge of Pankrati, the Temple of Olympian Zeus, begun under the rule of the Athenian tyrants and finished 638 years later under the Roman emperor Hadrian. It was a deeply significant monument. The Acropolis was only two miles away from the targeted neighborhood. If the battle spread, the monument could come under fire.

Felmy was unconvinced. How could he order the Wehrmacht to stand down when German soldiers were dead and the Communists were cheering? The ambush would be forgotten in a few months, Hampe said, growing heated. "But if we Germans bomb Athens, we will still be denounced as barbarians 300 years from now!"

Reluctantly, Felmy agreed to reverse the order. Messengers were sent to the troops who were already marching on Pankrati; they turned back to their barracks. Once the situation had cooled, Hampe sat down with Felmy and the two put together the text for a new poster, Felmy copying out the words in pencil on a scrap of paper.

> *The German Wehrmacht has done everything to avoid destruction in Athens; it intends to leave Athens without a fight. But if they are forced to defend themselves by attacks on the retreating troops, the responsibility for the blood that is shed and the destruction that is caused will fall solely on those who caused the unrest.*

Hampe took the note and went to a local Greek publisher he knew. They printed out the message as small leaflets—paper was scarce and there wasn't enough for a large-format poster. Then the archaeologist found a small German airplane to drop them over Athens. The leaflets fell from the sky on October 3.

The British requested a meeting with the Germans through the Swedish legation. Hampe was not invited. The Brits occupied one room in the Swedish headquarters, the Germans another. The president of the Swedish Red Cross ferried back and forth with offers and counteroffers.

Hampe was out in the cold for the moment, but his sources fed him the latest news. The British were making, in the archaeologist's view, "completely unrealistic" demands. For agreeing to Athens becoming an open city, they wanted General Felmy to hand over one hundred German soldiers as guarantees of good conduct. Felmy's representatives swatted the idea away. What then was the final British position?

The answer came back: "Unconditional surrender." They were back to square one. The talks failed.

Rodney and the other Greek Desk veterans heard the rumors, too. Gerald Else, who'd taken over from Rodney, told his compatriots he couldn't conceive of "any way of fucking up the fate of poor Greece that has not been tried in the past few weeks." He had the eerie sense that Greece was actually being led away from the heady days of the Albanian war and back into darkness. "We are passing out of the present," he said, "and into the past."

Felmy had had enough. He decided to declare Athens open without any input from the British. On October 10, he sat down and wrote the announcement on a half sheet of paper, then handed it to Hampe, who immediately left for Sofoulis's apartment. The streets were dark; there had been no electricity in the city for several days. Using the car's headlights, he and his driver navigated around potholes and barricades until they reached the ex–prime minister's apartment. Rushing upstairs, he handed the declaration to Sofoulis and gave him the precise date for the beginning of the German withdrawal: October 12. Not only that but Felmy was throwing in a sweetener: any excess food the Germans were leaving behind would be, unlike in Salonika, donated to the International Red Cross for feeding Greeks.

Hampe was delighted with Felmy's decision, but he soon ran into a problem. There were no journalists to hand the announcement to anymore. The Greek broadsheets had run out of paper or been sabotaged by their workers, who'd removed tiny components from the presses. Instead, Hampe attempted to get the word out through the underground newspapers, of which there were "countless" examples. Sofoulis's clique had contacts with many of them. The end was in sight.

The next day, the German archaeologist picked up a few illegal newspapers off the street and scanned the headlines. There was nothing about the agreement on the front pages. He turned them over. Nothing there, either. He was flabbergasted. The editors had seemingly imposed a blackout on the most important news in Greece. What was going on? Had the leftists rejected the offer?

He went to see Felmy, who expressed his annoyance. He'd made a grand gesture to save the city, one risky to his career and perhaps his life if the Wehrmacht were able to push back the Allies and Hitler stayed in power. And the Greeks were pretending it had never happened. Hampe went back to Sofoulis's apartment and gave him an ultimatum: "If the Greeks did not attach any importance to this declaration, the Germans will not adhere to it."

Sofoulis revealed the culprit behind the blackout: it wasn't the Communists; it was the Allied military commander. The declaration "wasn't in the Allied interest," he'd been told. The British wanted a fight. After a long back-and-forth, Hampe gained a concession from his fellow archaeologist. Sofoulis would call his friends within the liberal parties and get them to make the announcement in their party papers, which still had stock to print on.

General Felmy headed for Thebes to prepare for the full withdrawal, leaving Hampe in his small house on Lycabettus hill. He also left a twenty-five-man comms team higher up the slope to maintain a radio link between Athens and his headquarters. He was hoping the Brits would agree to the open city at the last moment. With the main players gathered in Athens, the endgame approached.

CHAPTER 32

The Kremlin

On October 9, three days before the scheduled withdrawal, Winston Churchill arrived in Moscow for what was codenamed the "Tolstoy Conference," along with the American ambassador to the Soviet Union, Averell Harriman. The portly British leader ambled through the gloomy corridors of the Kremlin, glancing at the portraits of Lenin and the Socialist Realist landscapes on his way to the magnificent Georgievsky Hall. He and Stalin sat down and promptly began drinking, Churchill sticking to a gassy Caucasian red wine while Stalin plied his retinue with vodka. Late that night, with Harriman out of the room, Churchill grabbed for a piece of scrap paper and began to write. "Romania," he scribbled, "90% Russian and 10% The Others." Yugoslavia was marked out as "50-50," and Hungary, Bulgaria, and Poland followed. The British prime minister was dividing Eastern Europe into zones of influence. When he came to Greece, Churchill tilted the percentages 90–10 in England's favor (he added "in accord with US"). He passed the paper to Stalin.

The Georgian looked it over, then picked up a heavy blue pencil and wrote a checkmark next to Churchill's neat writing. It was done. "Might it not be thought rather cynical if it seemed we had disposed of such issues, so fateful to millions of people, in such an offhand manner?" Churchill asked. "Let us burn the paper." Stalin said to save it. Churchill did, calling the note a "naughty document."

On the twelfth, a German honor guard marched to the Old Royal Palace in Syntagma Square and presented the keys of the city to the mayor of Athens. Together, the men then walked to the Tomb of the Unknown Soldier and laid a wreath. A member of the Greek Desk watched from the crowd; the Americans were, in many ways, relegated to the role of witness to history, even as they desperately tried to alter its path. "As soon as the Germans had left," the operative wrote, "[the Greeks] rushed forward and furiously tore the wreath to bits in order that the sacred memorial to the struggles of the Greek nation . . . should no longer be defiled."

Hampe had his own symbolic mission as the end of his stay approached. He made his way to the German Archaeological Institute's headquarters, a modest but handsome three-story building on Pheidias Street. There he relinquished the keys of the institute to the Greek Ministry of Education. Looting had already begun, as Greeks tore down the doors of the SS headquarters and other symbols of German power. Ever conscious of the archaeological side to things, Hampe wanted the institute's library, containing reams of excavation records and thousands of photographs, to be protected from the marauding crowds.

As he made his way back home in his car, he found the streets choked with Greeks mad with excitement; the car had to inch forward as the crowd streamed by, pounding on the roof and hood. "I have never seen people so beside themselves with joy and enthusiasm," he said. The car finally reached Lycabettus hill. Hampe spent the night in the house, waiting for word from the British, listening to detonations—were they fireworks or bombs?—rumbling in the dark city below. Looking out of the window, he saw small glimmers of light from homes lucky enough to have lamps and oil to fill them. He saw torches, Greeks marching, distant bonfires.

As the night progressed, the torches were snuffed out and unease set in. There was still no agreement on a ceasefire. Hampe's phone rang; it was one of his Greek contacts. "Do the Germans want to destroy Athens, too?" the man said. A rumor had gone round that sappers were going to set off charges on Lycabettus, sending tons of stone showering down on the city. Hampe assured the man that there were no plans to blow up the mountain. But other landmarks were still in danger if fighting erupted. Other calls from various sectors in the city followed. Hampe did his best to calm his friends and contacts.

Around ten p.m., another call came, this time from the comms team up the mountain. The Swede who'd conducted the talks between the British and the Germans had phoned; he'd kept the talks going even as the Germans left the city. "Why are we still negotiating about Piraeus?" he asked. "Piraeus has already been blown up." It was true; sappers had dynamited the port facilities five hours before. The detonations Hampe had heard weren't only fireworks; they'd come from the harbor. Felmy had ordered the harbor to be demolished. Why, Hampe didn't know.

It was time to go. Hampe walked to a nearby park and made his way to a stone tower that overlooked the city. He climbed up, joined by a grammar-school teacher, a Greek who'd come to look at Athens in its hour of emancipation. They watched the smoke rising from unseen fires, gray against lustrous black, and listened to a series of muffled explosions. The teacher, a committed leftist, talked about the British and how much he hated them. "That was the last thing I heard in Athens," Hampe said.

Once past the city limits, he fell in with an army column driving northward along a road with forest on both sides. The caravan came across "a strange sight":

> *Under the bright green of the pines, panje wagons stood and lay, broken wheels, red horse blankets that shone in the sun. Individual horses that had broken out of their harness stood patiently next to the wagons as if they were waiting to be re-harnessed. . . . As we came closer, however, we saw the bodies of the bearded riflemen in the thorn bushes on both sides of the road. They were all naked. Most of them had no gunshot wounds, but had been beaten to death with the butt of a gun or strangled. A paymaster was taking the dog tags from the dead.*

At least one group of *andartes* had ignored the decree to let the Germans leave unmolested, and had savagely punished the Nazi soldiers. As he drove by, Hampe thought that the scene could have come from another time, a battle scene from *War and Peace* perhaps.

The enraged German soldiers began to set fire to huts along the march route; the road ahead flickered with flame and shadow. Above Hampe, planes stalked the retreat—he recognized them as British—but didn't attack. The archaeologist passed cars with bullet holes sprayed along the sides, small licks of flame still visible inside. At one stop along the route, Hampe was finally able to raise Felmy on the radio. The general told him that he'd ordered Piraeus and the power station blown up because the British had, just before dusk, sent paratroopers dropping into Athens.

The port and the electrical transformers had suffered damage, but the rest of the city and its heirlooms were largely intact. Hampe was satisfied. "That Athens was declared an open city, although the British did not want it, and that the vital facilities of Athens, in particular the Marathon reservoir, were saved, although their destruction had been expressly ordered by the highest German authorities, must seem like a miracle."

CHAPTER 33

The Nocturnal Council

Rodney was making his way to Athens, his progress delayed by blown-out bridges (courtesy of the retreating soldiers) and roadblocks made of telephone poles and trees. On the morning of the twelfth, he was near enough to hear the explosions at Piraeus. He drove into Athens, left his car, and began walking through the streets as he had that memorable day four years before. He was the first American to arrive in the city after the German withdrawal.

Rodney went first to the American School, slapped back the gate latch, and walked through. There was no damage visible; the place was crawling with Swiss. The next morning, he began work. A Greek archaeological official presented him a list of buildings that could house the Greek Desk. Rodney chose the place Hampe had just left, the huge neoclassical structure of the German Archaeological Institute, savoring the idea of converting the Nazi espionage base to a headquarters for American agents. The official had no idea he'd just handed the building to a spymaster; he thought the American was going to focus on economics and relief. Rodney went up to the wide roof and began sending messages from the radio station installed in a shack there. The Greek Desk was now America's only communications link to Athens.

Its headquarters was packed with bodies. Men slept in shifts on cots set up in hallways, then woke up to call their sources and monitor the radio. In the evening, a "Nocturnal Council" met and pored over the reports. Some operatives hunted the sleeper agents using Settler's source; they found the stay-behinds were using their radios to inform Berlin about troop movements. Their operatives tracked the cell to its base and alerted the Greeks, who arrested the team.

Outside, Athens roiled with demonstrations of every kind. Graffiti denounced the British or the right or the left. Sperling, now based in Salonika, transmitted a report that police associated with the leftists were executing those seen as collaborating with the Germans. "Vociferous pro-Russian elements," led by men with megaphones and bells to summon the citizens to the streets, marched through the city; they demanded an end to the British alliance with the rightists. The German withdrawal had seemed like the saving of Athens, but the Americans worried that the civil war would kill more Greeks and destroy more antiquities.

FDR was concerned enough to cable Churchill. "In the present confused condition, the only hope I see for immediate favorable action is the presence of an aggressive and qualified officer," he wrote on October 22. "The only man I can think of now who might have a chance of success is Donovan." Having the general in control in Athens would alter the balance of power and give the Young Plan an enormous boost. Churchill responded the next day. "In spite of the vexatious broils . . . the situation in the Balkan peninsula is grievous for the enemy. . . . Our officers there . . . are very capable. . . . I have great admiration for Donovan, but I do not see any centre in the Balkans from which he could grip the situation." He rejected the offer.

The Desk agents were forced out into the open. Operatives were told not to go out into the streets unless they had a specific mission and a written note from Else. It was too dangerous for them to dress in civilian clothes; they might be mistaken for British agents and shot. One night, the support staff sat around sewing American flags onto their shirtsleeves and jackets. A twenty-four-hour watch—four agents carrying revolvers—now patrolled the building; the men were switched out every four days. Technicians engineered an intercom between the "war room" and the front entrance. A generator was installed so that the lights could run all night if blackouts struck the city. Else sourced flashlights, candles, and batteries in case of an emergency, and he sent workers up to the third-story roof to attach loudspeakers so that if combatants surrounded the building and the radio station couldn't be reached, they could still communicate with the outside world. Knowing his staff could be working in a suddenly anarchic capital, he was preparing for the possibility of a siege.

On December 3, Caskey got wind of a demonstration planned for that morning; he went out to keep an eye on events in order to apprise Washington. Streams of protesters were marching toward Syntagma Square, directly across from the Acropolis. To stop the crowd from filling the square, the Greek police, who were supported by the British, pushed barricades in front of protesters now singing and hoisting American and Greek flags. At about eleven ten a.m., Caskey heard a burst of gunfire. A man tossed a grenade toward the police; he was immediately shot down. When the crowd scattered, they left bodies lying on the asphalt.

"Men with American and British flags approached the police and dared them to fire," Caskey reported. He heard chanting: "Down with the killers!" and "Independence!" One group was calling the name of President Roosevelt over and over, like an invocation. "On

December 3rd," wrote one chronicler, "the world that the archaeologists had tried so hard to save was destroying itself."

The massacre unleashed the energies that had been building for months. An "orgy of assaults, vandalism, abductions, and executions spread throughout Athens." The British had a sniper's nest at the Acropolis; from it, they picked off leftists. "You would be walking in the city," said one Athenian, "and suddenly someone would fall next to you, all bloodied. . . . All you could do was run for cover." British planes roared overhead, dropping their bombs on the Communist strongholds. *Andarte* squads worked their way through the city, pulling suspected collaborators and rightists out of their homes and shooting them in the head. In the city squares, severed heads and dangling bodies hung from telephone poles.

The agent's reports of bloodshed and anarchy got the State Department's attention. On December 6, the Desk received a cable from General Donovan. "Nothing should be done that would in any way disrupt the operation," he wrote. Washington needed information on which way the battlefield was tilting and about political alliances and foreign interference. "Our various customers are practically screaming for intelligence," reported the OSS. The Greek Desk agents were working sixteen-hour days, then collapsing onto their cots.

The former archaeologist Themistoklis Sofoulis was still operating behind the scenes. On December 6, the leftist groups put him forward as the leader of a new government that would put an end to the skirmishes and assassinations. Georgios Papandreou, who'd led the government in exile and backed the return of King George II to the throne, refused to sign on. Churchill was in agreement; he wanted the left crushed. "Do not hesitate to act as if you were in a conquered city where a local rebellion is in progress," he wrote his commander in Athens. "We have to hold and dominate Athens. It would be a great thing for you to succeed in this without bloodshed if possible, but also with bloodshed if necessary."

Greece was emerging as an early front in the Cold War; the great powers maneuvered behind proxy leaders. The State Department was monitoring the Greek Desk's reports closely, but FDR never made his position entirely clear. During an interview with the BBC, the British prime minister told the nation that when it came to Greece, the two allies were "united in the present policy." Gerald Else was absolutely furious. He cabled Donovan and protested that attempt to dragoon America into the unfolding crisis as some kind of silent partner.

The State Department, peppered with reports from the Greek Desk, was coming around to the view that the British needed to be reined in at the very least. Any Greeks who tuned their radio dials to the Voice of America that month heard a statement from Secretary of State Edward Stettinius declaring that Americans had a natural sympathy for people who'd fought the Fascists, the Greeks among them. "American opinion was shocked by the spectacle of armed conflict between the British and Greeks," officials wrote in a letter to FDR, "and strongly reacted against British action." Ambassador Lincoln MacVeagh (almost predictably a former archaeologist who'd excavated under the Acropolis and donated artifacts to the National Archaeological Museum) was a vociferous anti-Communist, but he praised the spirit of the rebellion. Greece was "a fanatically freedom-loving country . . ." and Churchill was treating it "as if it were composed of natives under the British Raj."

Many Greeks, unaware of the machinations in Washington and London, were still crazy about Americans. One Greek Desk operative forgot to attach the Stars and Stripes to his car when he went driving through a rebel area. When he turned down a narrow street, bullets pinged off the chassis of his car. The agent jumped from the vehicle, calling out that he was an American. The shooting stopped and the snipers emerged from their hiding places carrying their own Old Glory to guard his way through their territory. It was a bitter experience for the Greek Deskers to know the truth and yet to be treated with something that approached reverence. They begged the State Department to at least ensure the delivery of grains and rice to the starving population, but they felt they were being stonewalled.

There were small acts of rebellion. The chief of U.S. naval operations, acting on his own volition, banned American vessels from carrying supplies to the British Army. A furious Churchill, smelling a whiff of rebellion, called FDR's personal aide, Harry Hopkins, and shouted down the phone that this was unacceptable. FDR proposed a milquetoast measure: that a special mission composed of representatives of the three great powers be sent to Athens to direct the reconstruction of the country. He specified it would be a "nonpolitical action," which made it almost meaningless in the current context. When Churchill asked to cut out the Russians, FDR let the proposal drop for fear of angering the Kremlin.

Rodney had disappeared from the Greek Desk correspondence. He didn't want to wait for the State Department. He commandeered relief trucks, loaded them with boxes of food and medicine, and drove them through Athens himself, bartering with rebel commanders whenever he encountered a roadblock. Dorothy was in the islands, doing the same thing. It was awful. "The lovely history-crowned barren islands of Greece are suffering worse in the famine report of Miss Dorothy Cox," wrote the Greek American *National Herald*. She told the newspapers that the "sailing clippers" bringing food to places like Samos and Chios came back with reports of "emaciated children hunting along wharfs for raw fish, begging for scraps with tin cans held in swollen hands." Dorothy's voice popped up in newspapers from Winston-Salem to Australia but was often buried on the back pages. She was a voice in the Greek wilderness.

Donovan went to bat for her by writing to the American ambassador in Turkey, though the text was likely composed by Rodney.

> *Miss Dorothy Cox of the Greek War Relief Association, in reference to whom you have been quoted as saying that she is "the best man we have in Turkey" . . . is discouraged (with good reason) by the prospect of the various official relief agencies being in a position to offer immediate relief to the Greek islands. . . . She is also most anxious that at least a part of the first relief sent in be American. She would like, therefore, to start accumulating an American supply of food, clothing and medicine. . . .*
>
> *I am sure you will do all you can to help Miss Cox in obtaining the facilities necessary for her project.*
>
> *Sincerely yours,*
> *Wm. J. Donovan*

Dorothy's eye was still keen and her sources unmatched. After a few weeks, she contributed "the best report on conditions in a large area of Greece that we have received from any source, American or British," according to one OSS officer. But fewer and fewer people cared.

The British and the government led by Georgios Papandreou did have support. When Churchill returned from the Yalta Conference, he made a surprise detour to Athens. He drove in a procession to Constitution Square, where forty thousand cheering and applauding Greeks waited for him; that night the Acropolis was bathed in floodlights in his honor. Churchill wrote his wife: "Athens was a most marvelous experience. I have never seen anything like the size of the crowd or so much enthusiasm." Over the next months and years, the British used their sixty thousand troops to crush the main revolt and disperse its leaders. "The lamp is shattered," wrote one colonel. "The light in the dust lies dead."

FDR died in April. The fighting would drag on, in reduced form, for four more years.

At one point early in the civil war, the fighting reached the Acropolis. The director of the archaeological service advised his workers to make every possible effort to guard and preserve the relics, which "are worth more than our lives." Curators tried to reach the site amid heavy gunfire but the English pushed them back, saying "everyone is being killed." At the end of the battle, dozens of dead and wounded lay around the Sacred Rock.

EPILOGUE

The Storm

On June 4, 1946, around noon, Athenians, curators, archaeologists, writers, and others stood around waiting in the north hall of the National Archaeological Museum. The hall had been cleared of furniture and the detritus of the occupation, and the concrete floor was bare. After a while, a group of workmen and volunteers entered with their tools. "In one of the old large halls," wrote the Greek poet and diplomat Giorgos Seferis, "familiar to us since our school days . . . the workers were digging with pickaxes and shovels. The floor, if one did not look at the ceiling, the windows and the walls with their inscriptions, could have been any other place of excavation." The concrete was broken up and wheeled away, and the workers began shoveling away the dirt packed below it. After a short time, the crowns of the Ancients' heads began to emerge. When the statues were clear of the dirt, diggers looped ropes around the relics' limbs and winched them slowly from the soil.

The Artemision Bronze, the statue of the bolt-throwing Zeus (or Poseidon), was brought up and its protective webbing unwrapped; it was then laid on top of a crate, where it looked "like an ordinary tired laborer." The poet spotted it and walked over. "I touched him on the chest, where the arm joins the shoulder, on the belly, on his hair," he wrote. "It seemed that I touched my own body." The statue was thoroughly cleaned and carried to its old place in the exhibition hall and set on its stone base.

Other relics lay prone on the ground after being unearthed; bas-reliefs were leaned against walls upside down. Seferis looked down into the pit:

> *Statues, still sunken in the earth, appeared naked from the waist up, planted at random. The arm of some colossal god, curved in toward his thigh, extended below the scaffolding, a naked woman who had turned her back to me was bonneted with a worker's gray basket that allowed only her smiling buttocks to show. It was a chorus of the resurrected, a second coming of bodies that gave you a crazy joy.*

Was Rodney present? We have no record of his whereabouts that afternoon, but he had been in Athens since at least May. A year before, he'd been on a ship headed for the island of Syros to stand in for a departing UNRRA director when the vessel had foundered and sunk. Rodney had managed to stay afloat for five hours until he was rescued. As he recovered, he received the news that Germany had surrendered and VE Day had been declared. Rodney witnessed Germany's invasion and its final defeat from a Greek hospital bed.

Now he was back at the Agora, the marketplace. The American School had finagled permission to dig there, despite a two-year embargo placed on all excavations by the Greek government. It's likely that he walked over to the museum that June morning to witness the unburying of the Ancients and to see up close once again the pieces that he and his fellow archaeologists—Greek, American, British, and one German—had fought for.

It would take another two years for the museum to be readied for a reopening. In 1948, archaeologists from the Americas, Europe, and the rest of the world boarded airplanes and ships to arrive in the Greek capital in time for the ceremony. Speeches were given, curators toasted. There was even a new acquisition on display: a "splendid" funerary statue of a young man, the *Aristodikos Kouros*, which had been discovered in Attica during the war. It was a transitional piece exhibiting the link between the late Archaic period and the Classical. With it came the expectation that Greek archaeology was again alive, that new beautiful finds would follow.

Parts of the patrimony remained scattered and hidden across Germany. In 1948, a Greek archaeologist named Spyridon Marinatos was ordered to the Axis countries to find as many of the stolen antiquities as he could. He went to Rome first and poked around the museums there with little luck, then moved on to Graz, Austria, where rumors had placed General Ringel. Marinatos knocked on the door of Ringel's house but found Russian officers living inside. The general, having abandoned his collection of stolen relics, including the fakes that Nikolaos Platon and his artisans had produced, was on the run.

The Greek archaeologist took a trolley to the weapons museum, the Landeszeughaus, and strolled the halls. He saw nothing familiar. He visited other collections before arriving at a university museum where he announced himself to an attendant. The woman "flushed with excitement" and led Marinatos to a large display case where fragments of 502 Minoan vases sat in a large display case. An inscription said that it was a temporary exhibition (*Leihgabe*) lent by an Austrian officer, Schörgendorfer, who had served as a *Referent für*

Kunstschutz in Crete and who had excavated there by order of General Ringel. Marinatos stared at the vases. He had never seen them before, nor had any Greek archaeologist.

Marinatos asked to see the director and then told him Greece wanted the relics back. The man replied regretfully that the collection was on loan from the Nazi officer. The archaeologist filed a request for repatriation, but after many delays, word came back that the officer had contradicted himself by claiming Platon had given him the artifacts; he wanted to keep them at the Graz museum. The Austrian government backed him. "It was stated to me that I cannot receive anything ancient," Marinatos wrote, "if its origin and the general circumstances of their arrival in Austria are not precisely ascertained."

He went to another museum, bought a ticket, walked through the halls, then told the usher he'd made the trip from Greece to find the "fugitives." The announcement caused consternation; Marinatos was brought into the director's office and he recognized the other man immediately: a German soldier who had served in the islands during the war. The man began apologizing for what had happened. *What about the stolen relics?* Marinatos said. "He told me that he was hastily summoned to the Ringel mansion to save 'some antiquities' during the time of the . . . tyranny." *Could he see them?* The man led the Greek to a display case. "I immediately recognized the small marble bull . . . [from] the courtyard of Ariadne's mansion." He hadn't known the bull had been stolen. It hadn't been on the list of Ringel's thefts.

On September 4, 1948, a large wooden box was unloaded from a ship at the port of Piraeus, which had been repaired after the German sappers had blown up its facilities. A few days later, the box arrived at the Heraklion Museum on Crete. Nikolaos Platon was there to greet it. Inside was the Ariadne bull plus many other artifacts that he unpacked and brought into the museum. Platon would spend the rest of his life caring for his Cretan relics and searching for the ones that had been stolen. Before he died, the scholar commemorated the life of a British archaeologist who had joined the *andartes* and been killed in action: "Beloved friend, Crete will guard your memory among her most sacred treasures," he wrote. "The soil which you excavated . . . and watered with a warrior's blood will forever enfold you with gratitude." The same could be said of Platon, who hadn't been wounded or killed but had risked both for the treasures.

Two years after Marinatos's trip, Greece held its first (mostly) free and fair elections far sooner than men like John Giannaris had imagined. By then, the United States had replaced England as the country's main external patron, providing hundreds of millions of dollars in aid and loans through the Marshall Plan and helping to stabilize the economy. Rodney's outfit, the UNRRA, shipped in 1.2 metric tons of wheat, legumes, and sugar, saving hundreds of thousands from starvation. The U.S. also covertly supported the postwar repression of the Communists, known as the "White Terror," in which thousands of men and women were arrested, tortured, and sometimes executed. The OSS's successor, the CIA, played a significant role in support of the campaign.

As the decades wore on, more relics came back to Athens. In 2013, the Greek Ministry of Culture announced the return to Greece of more than ten thousand relics from the Neolithic era, all taken during the Nazi theorist Alfred Rosenberg's illegal excavation in Thessaly during the war. Rosenberg's claims that the artifacts showed signs of Nordic influence had long ago been disproved; the Aryans had never built anything on the plains of Thessaly, let alone founded ancient Greece. Three years later, a receptionist at the Ministry of Culture in Athens was going through the mail when she opened a box postmarked Germany. Inside were seventy-three items: oil lamps, statuettes, vases, and coins dated from the Hellenistic to the Byzantine period. There was a letter, too. The writer said that he was the son of a war correspondent who worked for one of the newspapers published by the Wehrmacht. When the Germans invaded the island of Kos, first mentioned in *The Iliad*, soldiers entered the archaeological museum and looted it. Someone—presumably a soldier—took a large cache of objects and tossed them on the street outside. The writer's father had scooped them up and brought them home after the war.

Was he telling the truth? It was impossible to know, but the objects were gratefully received. Thousands of others were returned; thousands remain unaccounted for.

The Greek Deskers came back, too. John Giannaris brought his sons to see the Acropolis and the mass grave at Limni Xinias he'd passed by on his way into the mountains. He requested that, on his death, his body be returned to the *patris* and buried alongside the 103 Greeks interred there. Jerome Sperling divorced his American wife and married the Greek relief worker who'd found a big brother in Rodney Young at the Epirus front. And just before the 1950 elections, John Caskey returned to the American School as its president; he led the archaeological mecca for a decade.

In 1950, Rodney took on a new dig at Gordion on the Anatolian plateau in Turkey. He was after the lost civilization of the Phrygians, an ancient people who predated the classical Greeks by centuries. He chose a site seventy miles southwest of Ankara, where Cornelia Kapp had been spirited away six years earlier.

When he came to choose an architect for the excavation, he turned to Dorothy Cox. After being discharged from the OSS, Dorothy had gone back to a farm she'd bought in Wallingford, Connecticut, where she kept cows, goats, and rabbits. She'd worked at Yale, where she became the head of the numismatics department, then left New Haven for Santa Fe, where she lived with a female roommate. On her travels, she'd stopped at Princeton to review a paper on coins from the six-thousand-year-old city of Tarsus that she'd worked on before the war. "I thought I wouldn't even be able to recognize what I had once written," she wrote Rodney, "but in two shakes the whole thing came back and I felt as though I was continuing an argument left off the day before." She was still out the tens of thousands of dollars she'd sent to feed people on the island of Samos, but was past caring. "Don't let it really bother you," she told Rodney. "It's the sort of fool thing I'm always doing and I'll forget about it." Her mood had improved considerably; she'd gained ten pounds. She was back to thinking about old conquests and long-ago lives.

The funeral site Rodney and Dorothy finally unearthed in 1957 dated from the eighth and seventh centuries BC. Rodney made archaeological history by being the first to use an oil rig to drill down into the chamber of the Great Tumulus, where he uncovered a massive burial chamber, perhaps belonging to the father of King Midas, he of the golden touch. Climbing down into the chamber, he and his team discovered hordes of gold, silver, and electrum as well as wall paintings and frescoes not seen in nearly three thousand years.

Under the Americans' hands, the Phrygians came drifting slowly up from the darkness as if from the ocean depths: the craftsmen who'd built the tomb, one of the oldest standing wooden structures in the world; the king laid out on a bed of gold and purple textiles; clues to the mourners in the traces of the funeral feast's lamb stew. The Greeks had learned from the Phrygians. They adopted Cybele, the goddess of fertility and wild nature, into their pantheon, and the intricate rock-cut facades uncovered at Gordion found their imitators in Ionia and other places. "This rescuing of an important people of antiquity from oblivion," wrote one scholar, "has been among the most significant achievements of postwar archaeology." It made Rodney's name.

The archaeologist taught at Penn and lived on an estate near Philadelphia patrolled by Anatolian shepherds. He was killed in a car crash in 1974. "He was Rodney, *sui generis*," read one obituary, "and the world is a poorer and duller place without him." For years afterward, visitors to the university's archaeology department would find his office "sealed up like a shrine." He was one of the last of a particular breed.

In Gordion, where the excavation still went on, his successors gathered after a long day of digging to celebrate his birthday. They were drinking and telling stories when the thunderclouds that had slowly moved across from the far horizon toward the whitewashed dig house released their hailstones to drum on the roof above them. Through the windows, lightning flooded the seventh-century cityscape with flashes of phosphorescence. "Rodney Young is amongst us!" one of the archaeologists cried, laughing and raising his glass to the light.

ACKNOWLEDGMENTS

Many thanks to my editor, David Howe, for sharpening the narrative, and to my agent, Susan Canavan, for finding it a home. Kaitlin Kall designed the beautiful jacket. Dr. Maria Chidiroglou of the National Archaeological Museum in Athens was kind enough to hunt down photographs and read an early draft, while Dr. Katie Kelaidis at the National Hellenic Museum found seemingly unfindable photos. Thanks to James and Stephen Doundoulakis for fleshing out the life of their father and for contributing a close read of the text, and to James Mousalimas for talking about his dad's remarkable war. Ridley Sperling and David Sperling graciously sketched out their family history and provided photos. Thanks to Dr. Vassilios Petrakos, author of the authoritative history of Nazi thefts of Greek artifacts, and Dr. Georgia Flouda of the Heraklion Archaeological Museum for talking to me.

NOTES

PROLOGUE: The Sacred Rock

3 **"The bas-reliefs":** Interview with James Doundoulakis.

3 **"He really wanted us":** Interview with Ridley Sperling.

3 **"the best man":** Letter, January 8, 1944, National Archives and Record Administration (henceforth "NARA") 226, 190A, Box 22, Folder 55.

CHAPTER 1: The Sanctuary of Zeus

8 **"tramping the countryside":** "Rodney Stuart Young August 1, 1907–October 25, 1974," *American Journal of Archaeology* 79, no. 2 (April 1975).

8 **"organized tennis matches":** Susan Heuck Allen, *Classical Spies: American Archaeologists with the OSS in World War II Greece* (Ann Arbor: University of Michigan Press, 2013), 16.

9 **"I would rather have":** Jay Brooks, "Ballantine's Literary Ads: Ernest Hemingway," Brookston Beer Bulletin, July 21, 2016, https://brookstonbeerbulletin.com/ballantines-literary-ads-ernest-hemingway/.

9 **"The gardens and neo-classical design":** "The Warren Estate—Bernardsville," Mansion in May, https://www.mansioninmay.org/courses/the-warren-estate-bernardsville.

10 **"most companionable fellows":** *Princeton Alumni Weekly* 75 (1974).

10 **"Cary Grantish darling of New York":** Allen, *Classical Spies*, 8.

CHAPTER 2: The Italian Planes

12 **"a monumental cult image of the deity":** Colette Hemingway and Séan Hemingway, "Greek Gods and Religious Practices," The Met, October 1, 2003, https://www.metmuseum.org/essays/greek-gods-and-religious-practices.

13 **"He was absolutely gregarious":** Melissa Jacobs, "Trowel, Cloak and Dagger," *The Pennsylvania Gazette*, November 1, 2012, https://thepenngazette.com/trowel-cloak-and-dagger/.

14 **"An irrational euphoria took hold":** Allen, *Classical Spies*, 13.

14 ***"Attention, kiries ke kirii"*:** Sakis Papistas, "The War Tales of Paspati," *National Herald*, October 31–November 6, 2009, 11.

14 **"going wild, as if the news":** Papistas, "War," 11.

16 **"Greece is not fighting for victory":** "The 'NO!' Heard Round the World," The Greekish Life, accessed August 11, 2025, https://www.thegreekishlife.com/oxi-day.

16 **"[Greeks] were clear that these were works":** Chrysanthi Tsouli, "The Attitude of the Greeks Towards the Antiquities During the Last Twenty Years Before the Greek War of Independence and Throughout the Liberation Struggle: Testimonies of Travelers and Archival Sources," Antiquities and the Greek War of Independence, Exhibition Catalogue, National Archaeological Museum, Athens, February–July 2020, 72–85.

17 **"Archaeology was put aside":** Lucy Shoe Meritt, *History of the American School of Classical Studies at Athens, 1939–1980* (Princeton: American School of Classical Studies at Athens, 1984), 8.

CHAPTER 3: The Curators

18 **"The chilling message is presented":** Alastair Sooke, "The Discobolus: Greeks, Nazis and the Body Beautiful," BBC, March 24, 2015, https://www.bbc.com/culture/article/20150324-hitlers-idea-of-the-perfect-body.

20 **"We, with our spades":** Seweryn Szczepanski, "Archaeology in the Service of the Nazis: Himmler's Propaganda and the Excavations at the Hillfort Site in Stary Dzierzgoń (Alt Christburg)," *Lietuvos Archeologija* 35 (2009): 83–94.

21 **"that there was no way":** Kostas Paschalidis, "The Buried Statues of War," Places, March 30, 2013, https://placemanagementandbranding.wordpress.com/2013/03/30/guest-article-the-buried-statues-of-war/.

22 **"offer of the employees of National Aviation":** Vassilios Petrakos, *The Past in Shackles*, vol. 1 (Athens: Archaeological Society of Athens, 2021), 15.

23 **"cover the statues with sandbags":** Paschalidis, "Buried Statues."

24 **There were no backhoes or jackhammers:** This account of the relics' burial is based on Paschalidis, "Buried Statues," and Stephanie Makri, "How Greek Antiquities Slipped Through the Nazis," Greek Reporter, October 11, 2023, https://

greekreporter.com/2023/10/11/greek-antiquities-nazi/, and various memos and letters in Petrakos, *The Past*, vol. 1.

25 **"people in a demonstration":** Paschalidis, "Buried Statues."

25 **"Really early in the morning":** Hannah Steinkopf-Frank, "How to Bury an Entire Museum," Messy Nessy, September 24, 2021, https://www.messynessychic.com/2021/09/24/how-to-bury-an-entire-museum/.

26 **"The view of the museum":** Paschalidis, "Buried Statues."

CHAPTER 4: The Front

27 **"The ruins have a romantic":** George Mylanos, "Archaeology in Greece: An International Heritage," *The Atlantic*, June 1955, https://www.theatlantic.com/magazine/archive/1955/06/archaeology-in-greece-an-international-heritage/642140/.

27 **"One of the laborers stopped him":** Mylanos, "Archaeology."

29 **He telegraphed his father:** Laird Archer, *Balkan Journal: An Unofficial Observer in Greece* (New York: W. W. Norton & Company, 1944), 130.

29 **"a brazen decision for this coddled child":** Allen, *Classical Spies*, 29.

29 **"His imposing physical bulk":** Keith DeVries, ed., *From Athens to Gordion: The Papers of a Memorial Symposium for Rodney S. Young* (Philadelphia: University of Pennsylvania Museum of Archaeology and Anthropology, 1980), xvi.

30 **"as a precious witness":** Allen, *Classical Spies*, 39.

31 **"I have learned":** United Press, "New Yorker Drives Greek Ambulance," January 10, 1941.

31 **"Young thought he would never die":** Allen, *Classical Spies*, 46.

32 **"He was wonderful":** Allen, *Classical Spies*, 46.

32 **"threw a shower of steel fragments":** *Plainfield Courier-News*, August 25, 1941.

32 **"New American blood":** "Greeks Decorate Young; Wounded American Ambulance Driver Receives War Cross," *New York Times*, March 31, 1941, 7.

33 **His family dedicated:** Archer, *Balkan Journal*, 160.

33 **"we raise up the heroic":** Letter to the director of the American School of Classical Studies at Athens, March 31, 1941, from Petrakos, *The Past*, vol. 4, 198.

33 **"The capital is falling":** Philip Chrysopoulos, "April 27, 1941," Greek Reporter, April 27, 2025, https://greekreporter.com/2025/04/27/april-27-1941-nazis-storm-athens/.

33 **"shining in the sunlight":** Petrakos, *The Past*, vol. 1, 130.

34 **"We raised the German flag":** Petrakos, *The Past*, vol. 2, 149.

34 **"Now they understood well":** Petrakos, *The Past*, vol. 2, 149.

34 **"Corrupt," he said:** *Plainfield Courier-News*, August 25, 1941.

35 **"If Russia can hold out":** *Plainfield Courier-News*, August 25, 1941.

36 **"today every American":** Georgios J. Karamanos, ed., *Lest We Forget That Noble and Immortal Nation, Greece* (New York: Athenian Press, 1943), 69.

36 **"Greece will fight":** Karamanos. *Lest We Forget*, 25.

36 **The event raised a thousand:** *Hamilton Spectator*, April 25, 1941.

37 **"want to play the ostrich":** Allen, *Classical Spies*, 68.

37 **"He had inspected ordnance":** "Colonel Donovan's War," *Time*, March 31, 1941, https://time.com/archive/6764709/foreign-news-colonel-donovans-war/.

CHAPTER 5: The Museum

39 **On a sublime April day:** This account of the German visit to the museum is drawn from Steinkopf-Frank, "How to Bury"; Paschalidis, "Buried Statues"; and Chryssoula Katsarou, "New Exhibit at National Archaeological Museum in Greece Details How Antiquities Were Hidden from the Nazis," Windy City Greek, November 27, 2017, https://windycitygreekarchive.wordpress.com/2017/11/27/national-archaeological-museum-hiding-antiquities/.

40 **"from all directions":** William St. Clair, *Who Saved the Parthenon? A New History of the Acropolis Before, During and After the Greek Revolution* (Cambridge, UK: Open Book, 2022), 594.

41 **"If that can happen":** Florence Fisher Perry, "I Dare Say," *Pittsburgh Post*, November 21, 1941, 2.

42 **"The huge number":** Petrakos, *The Past*, vol. 1, 201.

CHAPTER 6: The Greek Desk

43 **"We need people like you":** Richard Dunlop, *Donovan: America's Master Spy* (Chicago: Rand McNally, 1982), 364.

44 **"I did not think":** Elias Vlanton, "The O.S.S. and Greek-Americans," *Journal of the Greek-American Diaspora* 9 (Spring 1982): 31.

45 **"Dad always said":** This and the rest of the information on Dorothy's upbringing is from an unpublished Cox family history. Courtesy of the Cox family.

46 **"Miss Dorothy Cox, just in":** Ruth Agnes Abeling, "Terre Haute Will Soon Boast a Girl Architect," *Terre Haute Star*, August 29, 1917.

48 **"as a substitute housekeeper":** Unpublished Cox family history.

48 **"Living was rough":** Unpublished Cox family history.

49 **"It had occurred to me":** Letter, July 16, 1942, NARA 226, 190A, Box 22, Folder 55.

50 **"Thanks for your letter":** Letter, n.d., NARA 226, 190A, Box 22, Folder 55.

52 **"I have not been worried":** Letter, July 1, 1942, NARA 226, 190A, Box 22, Folder 55.

52 **"Membership in . . . an expedition":** Letter, February 14, 1941, NARA 51-20512.

CHAPTER 7: The Farm

56 **"Dorothy can be recommended":** Memo, Dr. Kenneth H. Baker to Col. U. L. Amoss, September 23, 1942, NARA 226, UD 92A, 190, 38, 18, Shelf 4, Box 20, Folder 301.

56 **"It is difficult to predict":** Memo, Dr. Kenneth H. Baker to Col. U. L. Amoss, August 13, 1942, NARA 226, UD 92A, 190, 38, 18, Shelf 2, Box 13, Folder 8303.

57 **"You know," Sperling replied:** Memo, Baker to Amoss, August 13, 1942.

CHAPTER 8: The Sanctuary of Artemis

58 **"I was able to see for a moment":** Report by A. D. Keramopoulos, April 9, 1943, in Petrakos, *The Past*, vol. 3, 44.

59 **"the utmost care":** "Commons Plea for Xmas Truce," *Evening Express*, December 21, 1944, 1.

60 **"Underground shelters, munitions stores":** Petrakos, *The Past*, vol. 3, 74.

60 **"German troops are suspected":** Paschalidis, "Buried Statues."

60 **"We are called Huns":** Petrakos, *The Past*, vol. 1, 134.

61 **"scattered and destroyed":** Petrakos, *The Past*, vol. 3, 160.

61 **"The inhabitants of the city":** Petrakos, *The Past*, vol. 3, 228.

61 **"are not intended":** Petrakos, *The Past*, vol. 4, 18.

62 **"spirit of the eternal civilization":** Petrakos, *The Past*, vol. 1, 259.

62 **"Whoever destroys the artistic decoration":** Petrakos, *The Past*, vol. 1, 212.

63 **"The main result":** Petrakos, *The Past*, vol. 1, 341.

64 **"Today Mr. K. Kourouniotis told me":** Petrakos, *The Past*, vol. 2, 118.

65 **"German archaeologists treated the Greek archaeologists":** Petrakos, *The Past*, vol. 4, 401.

CHAPTER 9: The Apartment in Izmir

66 **"informers have infested":** Memo, Field Station Files—Athens, undated, NARA NND 877190, Box 5.

67 **"There was at hand":** COI/OSS Central Files, NARA 226, 92A, 94, Shelf 1, Box 20, Folder 301.

67 **"three special qualities":** COI/OSS Central Files, NARA 226, 92A, 94, Shelf 1, Box 20, Folder 301.

68 **"I find reliability":** Letter to Rodney and Sterling, June 17, 1943, COI/OSS Central Files, NARA 226, 92A, 94, Shelf 1, Box 20, Folder 301.

69 **"He seems to have covered":** Letter to Sterling, July 1, 1943, NARA NND 963044, Box 20.

69 **"My house is sort of a boarding house":** Letter to Mr. Wallace, August 16, 1944, COI/OSS Central Files, NARA 226, 92A, 94, Shelf 1, Box 20, Folder 301.

69 **"are combed every day":** This and subsequent extracts from the report are at NARA NND 877190, Box 5.

71 **"I am worried":** Letter to Sterling, March 30, 1943, COI/OSS Central Files, NARA 226, 92A, 94, Shelf 1, Box 20, Folder 301.

CHAPTER 10: The Caïques

73 **"officers were warned":** Artemis Cooper, *Cairo in the War 1939–45* (London: John Murray, 2013), 123.

74 **"of the Sears Roebuck variety":** NARA 226, 190, 9, 24, Shelf 3, Box 1, Folder Athens-7.

75 **"Pete, on a rumor":** Letter, January 7, 1944, NARA 226, 190, 9, 24, Shelf 3, Box 1, Folder Athens-10.

76 **"Look, we are running a five-ring circus":** Letter, July 20, 1943, NARA 226, 190, 9, 24, Shelf 3, Box 1, Folder Athens-7.

76 **"Damn it all":** Letter 25, 1944, NARA 226, 190, 9, 24, Shelf 3, Box 1, Folder Athens-10.

77 **"racing yachts in the bay":** Allen, *Classical Spies*, 109.

77 **"I would not take these rages":** Letter to Jack Caskey, January 20, 1944, NARA 226, 190A, Box 22, Folder 55.

77 **"We have requests from Greece":** Letter to Lt. Commander E. E. Pratt, USNR, March 28, 1944, NDD 877190, Box 5.

78 **Alpha: *I saw this:*** Letter to George, March 6, 1944, NARA 226, 190, 9, 24, Shelf 3, Box 1, Folder Athens-10.

79 **"a Syrian imitation":** NARA 226, 190, 9, 24, Shelf 3, Box 1, Folder Athens-12.

79 **"The Turks urged":** NARA 226, 190, 9, 24, Shelf 3, Box 1, Folder Athens-12.

80 **"prowling about Elis":** NARA 226, 190, 9, 24, Shelf 3, Box 1, Folder Athens-12.

80 **"We had in Washington":** Letter, February 8, 1944, NARA 226, 190, 9, 24, Shelf 3, Box 1, Folder Athens-10.

81 **"In all other ways":** COI/OSS Central Files, NARA 226, 92A, NN3-226-94-001, Box 13, Folder 8303.

82 **"They DID NOT come up,"** Letter, August 26, 1943, NARA 226, HC1-51866548, OSS History Office, Box 41, Folders 200A–204.

CHAPTER 11: Helias

85 **Helias Doundoulakis stepped into a white caïque:** This chapter is drawn from interviews with James Doundoulakis and from Helias Doundoulakis and Gabriella Gafni, *Trained to Be an OSS Spy* (Bloomington, IN: Xlibris, 2014), 139–69.

CHAPTER 12: The Commandos

96 **Andrew Mousalimas stood:** Unless otherwise noted, the information on Andrew Mousalimas is drawn from his memoir, *Greek/American Operational Group Office of Strategic Services (OSS) Memoirs of World War 2* (privately printed), and interviews with James Mousalimas.

98 **"You are an undesirable citizen":** James Scofield, "Forgotten History: The Klan vs. Americans of Hellenic Heritage in an Era of Hate," *Congressional Record* 154 (November 6, 1997), https://ahepa.org/wp-content/uploads/attachments/4b15ec_ce19d3d3285c4f22bcd45fea56a9c338.pdf.

98 **John "Yannis" Giannaris, whose parents had emigrated:** Unless otherwise noted, the information on John Giannaris is drawn from his memoir, *Yannis* (Tarrytown, NY: Pilgrimage Publishers, 1988), chapters 1–4.

100 **"We had often been told":** Dunlop, *Donovan*, 365.

105 **"suffered from a malignant plague":** Kyriakos Nalmpantis, "Time on the Mountain: The Office of Strategic Services in Axis-Occupied Greece, 1943–1944" (PhD diss., Kent State University, 2010), 147.

CHAPTER 13: Bodies

107 **"Trouble past, I hope":** Letter, August 29, 1943, NARA 226, 190, 9, 24, Shelf 3, Box 2, Folder Athens-15.

108 **"About 23 years old":** NARA 226, 190, 9, 24, Shelf 4, Box 9, Folder 77.

108 **"Already one third":** NARA 226, 190, 9, 24, Shelf 4, Box 9, Folder 77.

109 **"Many of the police":** Final report, Crete operations, M. W. Royse, Records of the OSS, OSS History Office, NARA 226, E-99, NM54, Box 52, Folder 215B.

110 **"A round-about bribe was our assurance":** Final report, Crete operations, M. W. Royse.

110 **"At the time finding houses":** NARA 877190, Folder 1549-Caserta.

110 **Helias found a temporary place:** Doundoulakis, *Trained*, pp. 177–97.

113 **"A high-ranking officer":** Operational Report, July 12, 1944, NARA 877190, Folder 1549-Caserta.

113 **"Bridge situated at the railway station":** NARA 226, 190, 9, 24, Shelf 4, Box 9, Folder 77.

114 **Voutyros: *70 year old woman denuded:*** Final report, Crete operations, M. W. Royse.

115 **"The flames, the smoke":** Report of George Skouras, NARA 226, 210, 484, 2.

115 **"Every terror act sent fresh recruits":** Final report, Crete operations, M. W. Royse.

116 **"The Greeks brought in":** Letter, July 6, 1943, NARA 226, 92A, 190, 38, 18, Shelf 4, Box 20, Folder 301.

116 **"He talks about cooperation":** NARA 226, 190, 9, 24, Shelf 3, Box 2, Folder Athens-15.

117 **"I didn't feel it was up to me":** NARA 226, 190, 9, 24, Shelf 3, Box 2, Folder Athens-18.

117 **"Royalist pests go on here":** NARA 226, 190, 9, 24, Shelf 3, Box 2, Folder Athens-18.

CHAPTER 14: The Memos War

120 **"Mr. President, I accept the honor":** Petrakos, *The Past*, vol. 4, 200.
121 **"In a time of war":** Dr. Maria Lagogianni-Georgakarakos, "Memories 1940–44," National Archaeological Museum, https://www.namuseum.gr/en/to-moyseio/istoria-toy-moyseioy/the-rescue-of-the-statues/.
121 **"We have the honor":** Petrakos, *The Past*, vol. 1, 263.
122 **"we intend to build a special museum building":** Petrakos, *The Past*, vol. 1, 263.
122 **"The Office of the Prime Minister":** Petrakos, *The Past*, vol. 1, 284.
123 **"I replied to him":** Petrakos, *The Past*, vol. 3, 122.
123 **"Retrieving part of the hidden antiquities":** Petrakos, *The Past*, vol. 1, 177.
126 **"ancient inscriptions, many of which":** Petrakos, *The Past*, vol. 2, 33.
126 **"There was a lot of noise":** Petrakos, *The Past*, vol. 4, 45.
127 **"raised an objection":** Petrakos, *The Past*, vol. 4, 45.
127 **"where, lying dormant":** Petrakos, *The Past*, vol. 3, 18.
128 **"enemy propaganda":** Petrakos, *The Past*, vol. 3, 6.
128 **"Many times, my head was found":** Petrakos, *The Past*, vol. 2, 332.

CHAPTER 15: Giannaris

130 **John Giannaris's landing craft:** Details on the commandos' missions are drawn from Giannaris, *Yannis*, chapters 4–9.
132 **"On his insistence":** NARA, 226, E99, Box 57, Folder 8.
133 **"GERMAN OFFICERS! For you and your soldiers":** Mousalimas, *Greek/American Operational Group Office*.

CHAPTER 16: Operation Honeymoon

140 **"Subject desires above all":** Letter to chief of Secret Intelligence from Dow, January 13, 1944, NARA 974345, Folder 10558, 10560–10565.
140 **"Phalanx has informed us":** Letter to Caskey, June 8, 1944, NARA 226, 190, 9, 24, Shelf 3, Box 2, Folder Athens-10.
140 **"These torpedoes, to be launched":** NARA 877190, Box 97, Folder 108-Caserta.
141 **"The weight of the bomb":** Memo, Skouros to Lt. Commander McBaine, March 4, 1944, NARA 877190, Box 192, Folder 1549.
141 **"On the night of October 26, 1943":** Details about Cicero are drawn from Mark Simmons, *Agent Cicero: Hitler's Most Successful Spy* (Stroud, UK: Spellmount, 2014) and from various Greek Desk reports, NARA 226, 190, 9, 24, Shelf 4, Box 1, Folder 4.

CHAPTER 17: Platon

148 **"mild-mannered," "unassuming":** Bill Giannopoulos, "Nicolaos Platon," Greek City Times, January 8, 2022, https://greekcitytimes.com/2022/01/08/nicolas-platon-8-january-1909-28-march-1992-was-a-renowned-greek-archaeologist/.

149 **"perhaps the most important":** Tsouli, "Attitude of the Greeks," 72–85.

149 **Furious, Platon stepped up:** The account of Platon's struggle is drawn from Petrakos, *The Past,* vol. 4, 103–50.

149 **"He wasn't a fearless man":** Yiannis Papadopoulos, "Return of Stolen Antiquities Puts a WWII Hero in the Spotlight," Kathimerini, January 12, 2018, https://www.ekathimerini.com/culture/224787/return-of-stolen-antiquities-puts-a-wwii-hero-in-the-spotlight/.

153 **One of the favorites:** Pipelia Eleni, "The Looted Antiquities in Greece During World War II: Case Studies of Return and Restitutions," European Shoah Legacy Institute, Athens, June 2014, 1–8.

154 **"They sold like hot cakes":** Eleni, "Looted."

CHAPTER 18: Cornelia

155 **Cornelia Kapp was born:** Unless otherwise noted, the account of Cornelia's work and escape is drawn from Simmons, *Agent Cicero,* 87–110.

158 **"It [Bazna's intelligence] provided the Germans:** National Archives, UK, Cicero 19A file, KV 6/8 (3).

CHAPTER 19: The Train to Istanbul

161 **At that moment:** Unless otherwise noted, this chapter is drawn from Simmons, *Agent Cicero,* 110–67; Jack Caskey's report "Escape of American Agent from Turkey," April 19, 1944, Previously Withdrawn Materials, NARA NND 974345, Box 262; the Greek Desk's response to Caskey's report; and NARA NND 974345, Box 262.

CHAPTER 20: Salonika

168 **Helias's partner Cosmas proved true to his word:** This chapter is drawn from interviews with James Doundoulakis and from Doundoulakis and Gafni, *Trained,* pp. 157–255.

174 **"Our agent Constantinos":** NARA NND 877190, 226, UD 190, Box 192, Folder 1549.

CHAPTER 21: Viea

175 **"WHAT A LIFE":** Letter, Pete Daniel to Rodney, February 21, 1944, NARA 226, 190A, Box 22, Folder 55.

175 **"suddenly asked urgently":** Report on operator X-6, April 5, 1944, NARA NND 877190, 226, UD 190, Box 192, Folder 1549.

176 **"I was afraid":** NARA 226, 190, 9, 24, Shelf 3, Box 2, Folder Athens-10.

176 **"Don't feel called upon":** Handwritten letter, April 5, 1944, NARA 226, 190A, Box 22, Folder 55.

176 **"I am very nervous":** Handwritten letter, June 13, 1944, NARA 226, 190, 9, 24, Shelf 3, Box 2, Folder Athens-17.

176 **"The trouble with you archaeologists":** Handwritten letter, April 5, 1944.

177 **"We in the office":** Allen, *Classical Spies*, 178.

177 **"I think it might be well":** Letter to Jack Caskey, May 11, 1944, NARA 226, 190A, Box 22, Folder 55.

177 **"his hair stood right up on end":** Letter, October 26, 1943, NARA 226, 190, 9, 24, Shelf 3, Box 2, Folder Athens-10.

178 **"I must say I am good and sick":** Letter, December 19, 1943, NARA 226, 190, 9, 24, Shelf 3, Box 2, Folder Athens-10.

178 **"a mimeograph machine":** Letter, June 8, 1944, NARA 226, 190, 9, 24, Shelf 3, Box 2, Folder Athens-10.

178 **That summer, George sent a transmission:** Unless otherwise noted, the information on Giannaris's missions is drawn from Giannaris, *Yannis*, chapters 15–19.

180 **"Kill us if you dare":** *Thrakiki Foni* (The Voice of Thrace), February 18, 1944, information bulletin nos. 43–44, NARA 877190, Box 5.

CHAPTER 22: The German Lieutenant

182 **In the weeks afterward:** This chapter is drawn from interviews with James Doundoulakis and from Doundoulakis and Gafni, *Trained*, pp. 225–55.

CHAPTER 23: The Bombers

189 **Helias climbed down:** This chapter is drawn from interviews with James Doundoulakis and from Doundoulakis and Gafni, *Trained*, pp. 255–75.

192 **"I would like to write an official protest":** NARA 226, 190, 9, 24, Shelf 3, Box 2, Folder Athens-17.

CHAPTER 24: The Shepherdesses

193 **In September, Giannaris received a message:** Unless otherwise noted, this chapter is drawn from Giannaris, *Yannis*, chapters 19–23.

194 **"The damage they were to do to the Germans was phenomenal":** Anthony Cave Brown, *The Last Hero: Wild Bill Donovan* (New York: Times Books, 1982), 431.

CHAPTER 25: The Microbes

201 **"In Athens the conditions":** Petrakos, *The Past*, vol. 2, 27.

201 **"I said that I prefer damage":** Petrakos, *The Past*, vol. 2, 25.

202 **"and transmits it to the ancient stones":** Petrakos, *The Past*, vol. 2, 31.

202 **Sales in Switzerland:** Milton Esterow, "New Research Tracks Ancient Artifacts Looted by the Nazis," *New York Times*, January 18, 2022.

CHAPTER 26: The Triangulation Trucks

204 **One of Helias's informants:** This chapter is drawn from interviews with James Doundoulakis and from Doundoulakis and Gafni, *Trained*, pp. 207–35.

CHAPTER 27: The Athens Plan

214 **"There must never again":** Alfred J. Rieber, *Storms over the Balkans During the Second World War* (Oxford, UK: Oxford University Press, 2022), 177.

214 **"Planes this morning":** John O. Iatrides, *Ambassador MacVeagh Reports: Greece, 1933–1947* (Princeton: Princeton Legacy Library, 1980), 340.

214 **"Historically, the loss of Paris":** Jean Edward Smith, "On Hitler's Last Desperate Plan to Destroy Paris," Literary Hub, July 30, 2019, https://lithub.com/on-hitlers-last-desperate-plan-to-destroy-paris/.

215 **"The scene merely underlined the madness":** Smith, "On Hitler's."

215 **"On intelligence, we are interested now":** Letter to George, March 6, 1944.

216 **"76 tons of dynamite were laid":** "Fleeing Nazis Damage Port of Piraeus" *McAlester News-Capital* (Oklahoma), October 18, 1944.

216 **The *Los Angeles Times* reported:** "Bottled-up Germans Afraid to Surrender to Greek Army," *Los Angeles Times*, October 5, 1944.

218 **"barely recognizable and previously lost" [translated by author]:** Roland Hampe, *Die Rettung Athens im Oktober 1944* (Wiesbaden: Franz Steiner, 1955), 9.

219 **"Improvise and dare":** John Keegan, ed., *Churchill's Generals* (New York: Grove Weidenfeld, 1991), 176.

CHAPTER 28: The Young Plan

223 **"there was no Allied army":** Final report, Crete operations, M. W. Royse. Unless otherwise noted, information on Royse's mission is drawn from this source.

225 **"will provide a basis":** Young's plan is described in Despina Lalaki, "Soldiers of Science—Agents of Culture: American Archaeologists in the Service of the Office of Strategic Services (OSS)," *Hesperia* 82 (Spring 2013): 179–202.

225 **"archaeological *ouija* board":** Letter, March 1, 1944, NARA 226, 190, 9, 24, Shelf 3, Box 2, Folder Athens-10.

226 **"I would be all for arming":** Letter, May 11, 1944, NARA NND 877190, Box 192.

227 **"We here are sitting":** Letter, August 8, 1944, NARA 226, 190, 9, 24, Shelf 3, Box 2, Folder Athens-10.

227 **"Each week I fully await news":** Letter, July 5, 1944, NARA 226, 190, 9, 24, Shelf 3, Box 2, Folder Athens-10.

228 **"I am now an old lemon":** COI/OSS Central Files, NARA 226, 92A, 94, Shelf 1, Box 20, Folder 301.

228 **"If there's anything left":** Letter, August 25, 1944.

230 **"What hope of my being an officer":** NARA 226, 190, 9, 24, Shelf 3, Box 2, Folder Athens-7.

230 **"the barbarian enemy":** Allen, *Classical Spies*, 257.

231 **"Our good little organization":** Memo marked "Copy for Young Only," March 22, 1944, NARA NND 009006, 226/A1-216/9.

CHAPTER 29: The Negotiations

232 **To rescue Athens:** Descriptions of Hampe and his efforts are drawn from Hampe, *Die Rettung Athens.*

CHAPTER 30: Going In

241 **"black with people":** Handwritten "Letter to Colleagues," NARA 226, 190, 9, 24, Shelf 4, Box 9, Folder 79. The subsequent information on this journey is taken from the same source.

243 **A month after Rodney went in:** Interview with Jerome Sperling's son, David.

244 **"If [German bases] are overrun":** Information on this period is from NARA 226, OSS History Office, 226, 190, 6, 10, Shelf 5, Box 35, Folders 3, 4, 6.

245 **"a poor, frail woman":** Allen, *Classical Spies*, 218.

245 **"white elephants and rivers of milk":** Letter, National Guerrilla Band of Evros District to Mr. Gerogiades, July 7, 1943, NARA 877190, Box 1.

246 **"No surgical supplies":** NARA 226, 190, 9, 24, Shelf 3, Box 2, Folder Athens-5.

246 **"I have not sufficient energy":** NARA 226, 190, 9, 24, Shelf 3, Box 2, Folder Athens-7.

247 **"A lot of mortars":** Handwritten "Letter to Colleagues."

CHAPTER 31: The Open City

248 **As Rodney inspected:** Unless otherwise noted, descriptions of Hampe and his actions are drawn from Hampe, *Die Rettung Athens.*

CHAPTER 32: The Kremlin

258 **"Might it not be thought":** "Churchill, Stalin Division-of-Europe Document Disclosed," UPI, January 12, 1992, https://www.upi.com/Archives/1992/01/12/Churchill-Stalin-division-of-Europe-document-disclosed/1395695192400/.

258 **"As soon as the Germans":** Allen, *Classical Spies*, 223.

CHAPTER 33: The Nocturnal Council

263 **"In the present confused condition":** Tamás Meszerics, "Undermine, or Bring Them Over: SOE and OSS Plans for Hungary in 1943," *Journal of Contemporary History* 43, no. 2 (April 2008): 195.

263 **"In spite of the vexatious broils":** Warren F. Kimball, ed., *Churchill and Roosevelt: The Complete Correspondence*, vol. 2, *Alliance Forged, November 1942–February 1944* (Princeton: Princeton University Press, 2015), 554.

264 **"Men with American and British flags":** Allen, *Classical Spies*, 242.

265 **"Nothing should be done":** NARA 226, 99, Box 35, Folder 6.

265 **"Our various customers":** NARA 226, OSS History Office, 226, 190, 6, 10, Shelf 5, Box 35, Folders 3, 4, 6.

265 **"Do not hesitate":** John O. Iatrides and Elias Vlanton, "Unearthed Documents About the First Act of the Greek Civil War," Kathimerini, January 17, 2024, https://www.ekathimerini.com/in-depth/1229348/unearthed-documents-about-the-first-act-of-the-greek-civil-war/.

266 **"a fanatically freedom-loving country":** Iatrides, *Ambassador MacVeagh*, 660.

268 **"Miss Dorothy Cox of the Greek War Relief":** NARA 226, 190A, Box 22, Folder 55.

268 **"Athens was a most marvelous experience":** John O. Iatrides and Nicholas X. Rizopoulos, "The International Dimension of the Greek Civil War," *World Policy Journal* 17, no. 1 (Spring 2000): 95.

269 **"are worth more than our lives":** Petrakos, *The Past*, vol. 4, 290.

EPILOGUE: The Storm

270 **"In one of the old large halls":** Giorgos Seferis, *A Poet's Journal: Days of 1945–1951* (Belknap Press, 1974), 39–40.

272 **a Greek archaeologist named Spyridon Marinatos:** Marinatos's trip is recounted in Petrakos, *The Past*, vol. 4, 14.

274 **"Beloved friend, Crete will guard your memory":** Peter Stormonth Darling et al., *The Trusty Servant* ("Pendlebury Supplement: The Uncrowned King of Crete"), November 2014, 11, http://www.helleneschooltravel.com/pdfs/Pendlebury%20supplement%20TS118_layout%206.pdf.

276 **"I thought I wouldn't even be able":** Letter, January 22, 1945, NARA 226, 92A, 190, 38, 18, Shelf 4, Box 20, Folder 30.

277 **"He was Rodney, *sui generis*":** "Rodney Stuart Young," *American Journal of Archaeology* 79, no. 2 (April 1975).

277 **"Rodney Young is amongst us!":** Richard Hodges, *Travels with an Archaeologist: Finding a Sense of Place* (New York: Bloomsbury, 2017), 149.

INDEX

Index

Index

Index

Index

Index

ABOUT THE AUTHOR

STEPHAN TALTY is the *New York Times* best-selling author of *The Black Hand*, *The Good Assassin*, *Agent Garbo*, *A Captain's Duty*, and, most recently, *Koresh*. His books have been made into two films, the Oscar-winning *Captain Phillips* and *Only the Brave*. He's written for publications including *The New York Times Magazine*, *GQ*, and *Playboy*.